BASIC GREEK
IN 30 MINUTES A DAY

BASIC GREEK
IN 30 MINUTES A DAY

*NEW TESTAMENT GREEK WORKBOOK
FOR LAYMEN*

JAMES FOUND

WITH BRUCE OLSON, MDIV, EDITOR

BETHANYHOUSE
a division of Baker Publishing Group
Minneapolis, Minnesota

© 1983 by James Found
2012 Edition

Published by Bethany House Publishers
11400 Hampshire Avenue South
Bloomington, Minnesota 55438
www.bethanyhouse.com

Bethany House Publishers is a division of
Baker Publishing Group, Grand Rapids, Michigan

Printed in the United States of America

Library of Congress Cataloging-in-Publication Data

Found, James.
    Basic Greek in 30 minutes a day : a self-study introduction to New Testament Greek /
James Found, with Bruce Olson
        pages cm.
    Includes bibliographical references and index.
    ISBN 978-0-7642-0985-7 (paperback : alkaline paper)
    1. Greek language, Biblical—Self-instruction. I. Olson, Bruce. II. Title.
PA817.F68 2012 2011
487'.4—dc23   2012000965

Note: The pronunciation system used in this book is not the same as modern Greek pronunciation; it is only one of several different systems that are in use for pronouncing ancient Greek.

The internet addresses, email addresses, and phone numbers in this book are accurate at the time of publication. They are provided as a resource. Baker Publishing Group does not endorse them or vouch for their content or permanence.

Cover design by Eric Walljasper

15   16   17   18   7   6   5   4   3

Contents

New Testament Greek Workbook for Laymen

Why the Subtitle?

New Testament Greek—Every Greek word used in this book is found in the Greek New Testament. You will not have to learn any words that you will not need for studying Scripture.

Workbook—The author is convinced that "learning by doing" will lead to the greatest understanding and retention for the student. On almost every page of this book you will find yourself filling in blanks, matching words, and even using guesswork as tools for successful learning.

For Laymen—The author is also convinced that there are a great many practical concepts about the Christian faith that can be learned even with the easy introduction to Greek found in this workbook. This book will not make you into a Greek "scholar," but you will reap the benefits of understanding the Bible better from learning the basic Greek presented here.

What Are These Benefits?

After completing this workbook, you will:

1. Be able to pronounce Greek words fluently and feel "at home" with the alphabet.
2. Know the meanings of hundreds of New Testament words.
3. Understand the background of dozens of religious terms through seeing the Greek components that form them.

4. See relationships between Bible words that are not easily apparent in English translation.
5. Be able to use Greek dictionaries and other valuable reference books.
6. Understand the general outlines of Greek grammar.

Could You Give Me Some Examples?

1. Did you know that the word "bishop" developed over centuries by gradually changing the pronunciation of the word from which we get "episcopal"? And that this word "episcopal" is made up of two parts: *epi*, which means "over" in Greek, and *scope*, which means "look"? And that the original Greek form of this word was used to designate the person appointed to "over-look" or "watch-over" the Christians in a given place?
2. Did you know that the English words "holy," "sanctify," and "saints" are all translations of various forms of a single Greek word-family?

What Is Unique about the Approach of This Workbook?

1. The student reads entire words right from the start, using Greek letters that resemble the English letters. This builds confidence and fluency, and removes the fear of mastering the Greek alphabet.
2. Scripture quotations are used very early in the book.
3. The student's vocabulary is built up quickly and easily through much use of Greek words that resemble English words of similar meaning ("cognates").
4. Technical terms are avoided as much as possible.

Who Should Use This Workbook?

This workbook is meant especially for the person who does not have the time to take two years of college-level Greek. It is also valuable for the person who would like to take college-level Greek, but is unsure about whether he would be able to understand it—this book should give him the confidence to proceed into a standard academic course. Finally, the author believes this book could be used as the first few weeks of a full-fledged college Greek course. After completing this book, the student will be at a high level of confidence and motivation which will carry him through the drudgery of learning rules and memorizing grammatical endings.

What Are the Author's Qualifications?

The author taught in the public schools, in the field of music, for eighteen years; he is now a Director of Christian Education. "Languages" and "language-learning theories" were major hobby interests which led him to study the basics of many modern languages. When a fresh commitment to Christ led to many opportunities to lead Bible studies, he began to study Greek on his own (using the textbook, *New Testament Greek for Beginners*, by J. Gresham Machen). Even before finishing that book, he was already sharing many of the materials and approaches found in this workbook with youth Bible studies, with small groups of adults, and with the eighth graders in a Christian school. The excitement and appreciation of those who used these materials are what have caused him to believe they could be of value to a wider audience.

An explanation of the approach used in this book is included on page 302, for the benefit of the Greek specialist.

Part I

READING AND THE ALPHABET

After completing Part I, you will be able to:

1. Pronounce all the Greek letters.

2. Read Greek words quickly and fluently.

3. Know over 200 Greek words.

4. Use the words you have learned in context in Bible passages.

Lesson One

Reading English Words in Greek

The words on this page are English words, but they are written in Greek letters. As you begin to read, simply imagine that you are reading "fancy" English lettering. Answers for exercises are given in the answer pages at the end of the book (304).

Instructions: Read all three words in each box, then circle the word that corresponds to the picture. Check your answers with the answer page in the back of the book.

Words	Picture	Note
βεδ (circled) δοττεδ βετ		Note that there is a small tail at the bottom of the letter "β" (b), and note the curved form of the letter "δ" (d).
δαδ βατ (circled) ταβ		The letter "a" is written like a circle crossing itself: (α).
κατ (circled) κιτ κοτ		Note that the letter "i" is not dotted, and is curved: (ι).
κιδ βιτ καβ (circled)		Some of the words on these pages are spelled "wrong," and must be sounded out to get the meaning. There is no "c" in the Greek alphabet, so we must spell "cab" as "kab."
βοςς κοςτ δοτ (circled)		Note uneven shape of s (ς). Notice the way you say the letter "o" in the first two of these words. That's the way you'll always say it later on when pronouncing Greek words.

12

Exercise Two

More English Words in Greek Letters

This page introduces four Greek letters that do not look like English letters.
There is a pronunciation guide at the bottom of the page.

Circle the word that corresponds to the picture.

πετ
ποτ
⊂τοπ⊃

ρωπ
ρωδ
⊂ρωβ⊃

πιτ
⊂τιπ⊃
διπ

κριβ
δριπ
⊂δαρτ⊃

ποπ
πωπ
⊂βωτ⊃

καρτ
κορκ
⊂παρροτ⊃

τωδ
κωδ
⊂κωτ⊃

πιν
⊂καν⊃
παν

ρατ
⊂ραββιτ⊃
βρεδ

⊂βων⊃
κωτ
κων

Pronunciation Guide

π = p   ρ = r
ω = long "o"   ν = n

Note the two kinds of "o": o as in "log," ω as in "pope."

Exercise Three

Additional Greek Letters

Refer to the pronunciation guide at the bottom of the page.

Circle the word that corresponds to the picture.

Pronunciation Guide

λ = l (L)   γ = g (always "hard")

σ = s   μ = m

Note: The sound for "s" is written ς at the end of a word, but is written σ anywhere else.

Exercise Four

Names from the Bible

These are spelled as they appear in the Greek New Testament.

Match the Greek to the English equivalent.

I.   **c** βαραββας   a. Anna

      e Αραβια   b. Cana   I've omitted some capital letters

      f ρεβεκα   c. Barabbas   and accents at this stage for

      a Αννα   d. Nain   simplicity. All we're after is

      b Κανα   e. Arabia   recognition.

      d Ναιν   f. Rebecca

II.   **h** Αβελ   g. Barnabas

      j Αδαμ   h. Abel

      l Ααρων   i. Samaria   Ααρων would be pronounced

      g βαρναβας   j. Adam   Ah-roan.

      k δαν   k. Dan

      i σαμαρια   l. Aaron

These have different "endings" in Greek and English:

III.   **d** Ιταλια   a. Mark

      a Μαρκος   b. Messiah   All the a's in Greek words should

      c Μαρια   c. Mary   sound like the a in father; so pro-

      e σατανας   d. Italy   nounce σατανας sah-tah-nahss

      b Μεσσιας   e. Satan

These are pronounced differently in Greek and English:

IV.   **i** σιμων   f. Isaac

      j σολομων   g. Abraham   Greek doesn't have a letter for the

      g Αβρααμ   h. Peter   "h" sound. Pronounce each "a"

      h πετρος   i. Simon   in Αβρααμ separately: Ah-bra-

      f Ισαακ   j. Solomon   ahm. Ισαακ would be: Izz-ah-ahk.

      k Ανδρεας   k. Andrew

For your quick reference, all the Greek letters are listed on page 72.

δαδ   ελλα   κοδια

α β κ δ ε γ ι κ λ μ ν ο π ρ σ τ

βωκ

Lesson Two

Some Pointers on Pronunciation

Circle correct answer.

Since all "a's" are pronounced like the "a" in "father":

    1. Αβελ would be: a. Ah-bell   b. Abe-ell.

All e's are like the "e" in "pet":

    2. πετρος would be: a. pe-tross   b. Pee-truss

All i's are often pronounced like the "i" in "machine": (Sometimes i's are pronounced as in pin)

    3. Ιταλια would be: a. Ea-ta-lee-ah   b. Eye-tal-ee-ah

All o's are pronounced like the "o" in "log":

    4. σολομων would be: a. sha-lah-mun   b. saw-law-moan

All w's are pronounced like the "o" in bone:

    5. σιμων would be: a. sigh-mun   b. see-moan

Diphthongs

Two vowels together, pronounced as one sound.

    αυ sounds like "ow," as in cow
    αι sounds like "ey"
    οι sounds like "oi," as in foil
    ου sounds like "oo," as in boot

English words used as examples:

1. Three strikes and you're αυτ.
2. In Holland, water is held in by a δαικ.
3. Let's flip a κοιν.
4. You eat soup with a σπουν.

I. Matching sounds, using English words.
   Match the letter of the picture or English word to the corresponding word spelled with Greek letters.

<u>b</u> 1. αιλ   a.   b. aisle   d.
<u>c</u> 2. οιλ
<u>a</u> 3. αυλ   c. petroleum
<u>d</u> 4. μουν

II. Some Grseek Names with Diphthongs.
   Match the English name and the Greek pronunciation with the equivalent Greek name in the left column.

<u>h</u> <u>k</u>   5. λουκας   e. Claudia   k. lew-kahss
<u>e</u> <u>l</u>   6. κλαυδια   f. Galilee   l. klow-dee-ah
<u>i</u> <u>o</u>   7. σαδδουκαιος   g. Paul   m. pow-loss
<u>g</u> <u>m</u>   8. παυλος   h. Luke   n. gah-lee-lie-ah
<u>f</u> <u>n</u>   9. γαλιλαια   i. Sadducee   o. sah-dew-kye-yoss
<u>j</u> <u>p</u>   10. καισαρος   j. Caesar   p. kye-sar-oss

Exercise Three

I. Cognates (Words with similar spellings that mean about the same in Greek and English).
   Match the Greek words and their definitions.

<u>c</u> 1. αρωμα   a. my "self"; this is the Greek word for "I";
<u>b</u> 2. μαννα   related to our word "egotist."
<u>d</u> 3. μετροπολις   b. bread from heaven
<u>a</u> 4. εγω   c. something sweet-smelling
                   d. very large urban area. (πολις is Greek for "city.")

II. Cognates with slight spelling changes. Match the English words with their Greek equivalents.

g 5. βαπτισμα   e. leper
f 6. αγωνια   f. agony
h 7. λαμπας   g. baptism
i 8. λεων   h. lamp
j 9. σκορπιος   i. lion
e 10. λεπρος   j. scorpion
k 11. γενεαλογια   k. genealogy

Exercise Four

Pronunciation Check

Select the correct pronunciation for each Greek word

b 1. Μεσσιας   a. Mess-sigh-us   b. Mess-see-us
a 2. σατανας   a. Sah-tah-nus   b. Say-tah-nus
a 3. σιμων   a. See-moan   b. Sigh-moan
b 4. πετρος   a. Pee-tross   b. Pe-tross
a 5. Ισαακ   a. Iz-ah-ock   b. Eye-zack
b 6. παυλος   a. Paw-luss   b. Pow-loss
b 7. γαλιλαια   a. Gah-li-lay-uh   b. Gah-lee-lye-ah
a 8. λουκας   a. Lew-cuss   b. Low-cuss

Six Greek Words

These are all real Greek words.
Copy the Greek word on the long blank after the English word.

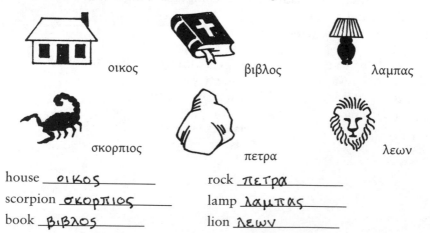

οικος   βιβλος   λαμπας

σκορπιος   πετρα   λεων

house   **οικος**   rock   **πετρα**
scorpion   **σκορπιος**   lamp   **λαμπας**
book   **βιβλος**   lion   **λεων**

Pronunciation Check of the New Words

b 9. πετρα   a. te-trah   b. pe-trah
b 10. βιβλος   a. bye-bloss   b. bi-bloss
a 11. σκορπιος   a. score-pee-oss   b. oh-core-pie-oss
a 12. λαμπας   a. lahm-pahss   b. lamb-pace
a 13. οικος   a. oy-cuss   b. oo-cuss
b 14. λεων   a. Le-on   b. leh-own

Exercise Five

Phrases

The English word "in" is a preposition. The Greek word for "in" is εν.
Guess at the meaning of the following phrases, and write a or b in the blank.

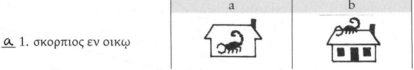

a 1. σκορπιος εν οικω

The word after a preposition, such as οικω, will end differently than it does at other times. You must be able to recognize the meaning of a word no matter how it ends. (The actual endings will be the subject of Part II of this book). The little mark under the last letter of the word οικω, above, is a small letter "ι." Do not pronounce it. Pronounce the ω as if there were no small ι there (oy-coe).

b 2. λαμπας εν σκορπιω

b 3. βιβλος εν οικω

a 4. οικος εν βιβλω

a 5. πετρα εν βιβλω

The Greek word for "on" is επι.

	a	b

_b_ 6. λεων επι βιβλω

_a_ 7. σκορπιος επι πετρα

_b_ 8. οικος εν πετρα

_a_ 9. λαμπας εν οικω

_b_ 10. λαμπας επι οικω

Start Your Dictionary

Set aside one page in a notebook for each letter in the Greek alphabet. There are 24 letters all together; you'll find the entire alphabet listed on page 72. You do *not* need to put names or obvious cognates in your dictionary, but start by putting in the words you learned on the previous page. Then add every new word in this book as you come to it. You will need to refer to your dictionary constantly in order to proceed through this book!

Lesson Three

Accent

Greek New Testaments published today are written in small letters with accent marks included in the proper places. This workbook will usually omit the accent marks. When you take an academic course in Greek, you will find that the accent is very important. In order to give you a little exposure to accents, they will be used in this workbook on pages such as this one that present quotations from the Scripture.

The Greek accent is written in three ways, but all sound the same—a stress, just like English. The three ways are: ´ ` and ˆ.

Scripture Quotes

Be sure to pronounce the Greek word, even if you know what the answer should be. Fill your English answer in the blank, and check your answers with your Bible. Your challenge is to recognize the Greek word even though its ending may be different than the way it was presented on a previous page.

1. Therefore everyone who hears My words and does them is like a wise man who built his __house__ __on__ the __rock__ (Matt. 7:24).
   οἰκίαν   ἐπὶ   πέτραν

2. Thou art __Peter__, and __on__ this __rock__ I will build my church (Matt. 16:18).
   Πέτρος   ἐπὶ   πέτρᾳ

3. For David himself says __in__ the __book__ of Psalms . . . (Luke 20:42).
   ἐν   βίβλῳ

4. A great star fell from heaven, burning as if it were a __lamp__ (Rev. 8:10).
   λαμπὰς

5. If he asks for an egg, will he give him a __scorpion__? (Luke 11:12).
   σκορπίον

Exercise One

More Cognates from the New Testament

Select the correct definition for each Greek word. (Add these words to your dictionary.)

<u>c</u> 1. διαβολος
<u>e</u> 2. δογμα
<u>b</u> 3. στιγμα
<u>f</u> 4. μεμβρανα
<u>a</u> 5. βαρβαρος
<u>d</u> 6. σκανδαλον

a. foreigner, barbarian
b. brand-mark, stigma
c. looks like "diabolic"; it's the Greek word for "devil."
d. looks like "scandal"; used in scripture to mean "offense" or stumbling block.
e. a rule; dogma
f. animal skin: membrane

One more Scripture quote:

6. Your adversary, the <u>Devil</u>, walks around like a roaring <u>lion</u>, seek-
   διάβολος   λέων
   ing to devour (1 Pet. 5:8).

More Examples from Scripture

Pronounce each Greek word and write its English equivalent on the line above it. Check your answers from your Bible.

1. (There is) one Lord, one faith, one <u>baptism</u> (Eph. 4:5).
   βάπτισμα

The word for "and" in Greek is καὶ, pronounced "kye."

2. (Jesus said:) "<u>I</u> <u>and</u> the father are one" (John 10:30).
   Ἐγὼ   καὶ

3. (In garden of Gethsamane:) <u>And</u> being in great <u>agony</u>, he prayed
   (Luke 22:44).   Καὶ   ἀγωνία

4. Jesus went into Bethany, to the <u>house</u> of <u>Simon</u> the
   <u>leper</u> (Matt. 26:6).   οἰκίᾳ   Σίμωνος
   λεπροῦ

5. <u>Andrew</u>, the brother of <u>Simon</u> <u>Peter</u>, was one of the two
   Ἀνδρέας   Σίμωνος   Πέτρου
   who heard this from John and followed him; so he first found his

   own brother <u>Simon</u> <u>and</u> said to him, "We have found the
   Σίμωνα   καὶ
   <u>Messiah</u> (John 1:40–41).
   Μεσσίαν

Exercise Two

Some More Cognates

Match the definitions from the right column with the corresponding Greek word in the left column. Add these words to your dictionary.

<u>c</u> 1. λινον   a. insignia, inscription, title
<u>d</u> 2. διαλεκτος   b. housetop; we use it to refer to a housetop that
<u>b</u> 3. δωμα   is round
<u>e</u> 4. σιων   c. linen
<u>f</u> 5. κιναμωνον   d. dialect: a variety of speech
<u>a</u> 6. τιτλος   e. Zion; one name for Jerusalem
                          f. cinnamon (a certain spice)

Exercise Three

Continuing with the Alphabet

These are English words spelled with Greek letters.
Write these words in English.

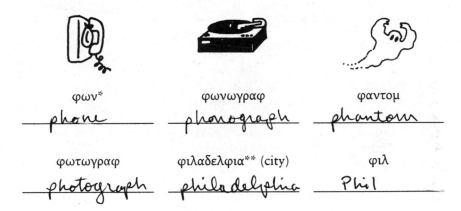

φων*

<u>phone</u>

φωνωγραφ

<u>phonograph</u>

φαντομ

<u>phantom</u>

φωτωγραφ

<u>photograph</u>

φιλαδελφια** (city)

<u>philadelphia</u>

φιλ

<u>Phil</u>

*φ = ph
** from φιλια (love) plus αδελφος (brother). Add these two words to your dictionary.

Exercise Four

Follow the same directions as for Exercise Three.

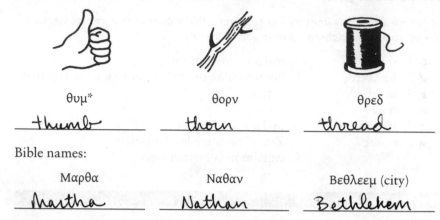

θυμ*   θορν   θρεδ

thumb   *thorn*   *thread*

Bible names:

Μαρθα   Ναθαν   Βεθλεεμ (city)

Martha   *Nathan*   *Bethlehem*

*θ = th

Exercise Five

Matching. Real Greek Names

Match the English words with their Greek equivalents. (Add these words to your dictionary.)

_c_ 1. γολγοθα   a. Ruth
_a_ 2. ρουθ   b. Pharisee
_g_ 3. φαραω   c. Golgotha
_e_ 4. Ματθαιος   d. Methuselah
_f_ 5. φιλιππος   e. Matthew
_h_ 6. στεφανος   f. Philip
_d_ 7. Μαθουσαλα   g. Pharaoh
_b_ 8. φαρισαιος   h. Stephen

New Words

Match these Greek words with their definitions. (Add these words to your dictionary.)

c 9. θεος
d 10. φωσφορος
b 11. παρθενος
a 12. καθολικος
e 13. οφθαλμος

a. Means universal, worldwide; a church body uses this word in its name, but it is also used in the Nicene Creed to indicate the all-encompassing nature of the body of Christ.

b. Virgin. A temple in Athens was named using the word (The Parthenon).

c. God. We get our word "theology" by combining this word with λογος (word, study of).

d. Phosphorus (φως = light, φορος = bearing).

e. Eye. Basis for English word for eye-doctor.

Exercise Six

New Greek Words to Guess

Match the English words and definitions with their Greek equivalents. (Add these words to your dictionary.)

c 1. λιθος
b 2. λογος
a 3. ανθρωπος
e 4. ορφανος
f 5. καρδια
d 6. θρονος

a. Man. We get the word anthropology from this word.

b. Word. The word "logic" is related, and so is the "-logy" which we put on the end of scientific terms.

c. Stone. Lithography was a printing process that involved etching onto a piece of limestone.

d. Chair for a king: throne.

e. Person without parents: orphan.

f. Heart. Compare our medical word "cardiac."

Exercise Seven

Using the New Greek Words

Match the picture with the Greek phrase which describes it.

	a	b

_b_ 1. ανθρωπος εν οικω

_b_ 2. καρδια εν ανθρωπω

_a_ 3. λιθος εν καρδια

_a_ 4. λογος επι βιβλω

_a_ 5. λογος επι λιθω

_a_ 6. θρονος εν οικω

_b_ 7. λιθος επι θρονω

_a_ 8. καρδια εν ορφανω

_a_ 9. ορφανος επι θρονω

Answer yes or no.

___No___ 10. ανθρωπος και ορφανος εν οικῳ

___No___ 11. πετρα και λιθος επι οικῳ

Exercise Eight

Pronunciation Check

Match these Greek words with their respective pronunciations.

a	1. βιβλῳ	a. Bib-low	b. Bib-loo
b	2. φιλιππος	a. thill-lip-oss	b. fill-lip-oss
a	3. ρουθ	a. Rooth	b. Pooth
b	4. Ματθαιος	a. Mott-thigh-oss	b. Matt-they-oss
a	5. φαρισαιος	a. far-iss-eye-oss	b. Fair-iss-ay-oss
b	6. ανθρωπος	a. on-thrah-poss	b. on-throw-poss
b	7. πετρα	a. Pee-traw	b. Pe-trah
a	8. οικων	a. oy-cone	b. oy-coon
b	9. ανθρωπῳ	a. on-throw-poo	b. on-throw-poe
a	10. λιθου	a. li-thoo	b. li-thowe
b	11. βιβλος	a. Bye-bloss	b. Bi-bloss

Meaning Check

Match these Greek words with their corresponding pictures.

___f___ 12. βιβλος
___a___ 13. οικος
___g___ 14. λαμπας
___d___ 15. πετρα
___h___ 16. ανθρωπος
___b___ 17. καρδια
___e___ 18. λιθος
___c___ 19. λογος
___k___ 20. θρονος
___i___ 21. ορφανος
___j___ 22. σκορπιος

Pronounce each Greek word, and then write its English equivalent on the line above.

What __man__ among you, when his son asks him for a loaf, will he give
ἄνθρωπος

him a __stone__? (Matt. 7:9).
λίθον

__In__ the beginning was the __Word__, __and__ the __word__ was with __God__.
ἐν   λόγος   καὶ   λόγος   θεόν

__and__ the __Word__ was __God__ (John 1:1).
καὶ   λόγος   θεός

Lesson Four

Try to identify the Greek word no matter what ending is put on it. Write in the English equivalent above each Greek word. Check your answers from your Bible.

1. Resist the __devil__ __and__ he will flee from you (James 4:7).
   διαβόλῳ   καὶ

2. But that which comes out of the mouth proceeds from the __heart__,
   and that "defiles" the __man__ (Matt. 15:18).   καρδίας
   ἄνθρωπον

Some of the names in the following passages may "throw" you:

3. Leaving the next day, (Paul) came to __Caesarea__, __and__ entered
   Καισάρειαν   καὶ
   into the __house__ of __Philip__ (Acts 21:8).
   οἶκον   Φιλίππου

The blanks with an "s" supplied, mean the word is "plural."

4. __Paul__, knowing that some of them were __Sadducee__ s __and__
   Παῦλος   Σαδδουκαίων   καὶ
   the others __Pharisee__ s, cried in the council: "Men, brothers, __I__
   Φαρισαίων   ἐγὼ
   am a __Pharisee__, a son of __Pharisee__ s"(Acts 23:6).
   Φαρισαῖος   Φαρισαίων

Though many of the following words are "cognates," the words customarily used to translate them may surprise you.

Check your Bible after writing in your guess.

5. (Christ, the cornerstone, is also a) __stone__ of stumbling __and__ a
   λίθος   καὶ
   __rock__ of __offense__ (1 Pet. 2:8).
   πέτρα   σκανδάλου

6. It happened __in__ those days that there went out a __decree__ from
   ἐν   δόγμα
   __Caesar__ __Augustus__ that the entire domain be enrolled (Luke 2:1).
   Καίσαρος   Αὐγούστου

7. (Paul writing:) When you come, bring the cloak I left in Troas with
   __Carpus__ , __and__ the __book__ s, especially the __parchment__ s
   κάρπω   καὶ   βιβλία   μεμβράνας
   (2 Tim. 4:13).
8. For __I__ bear the __wounds__ of Jesus __in__ my body (Gal. 6:17).
   ἐγὼ   στίγματα   ἐν
9. When the Sabbath had ended (the women) brought __oil__ s that
   they might come and anoint him (Mark 16:1).   ἀρώματα

Exercise One

Some Compound Words

Some of these were put together by the Greeks themselves; others by English
speakers using Greek words as roots.

*From the word list at right, select the two words that you think were used to form the
English words, and then write these Greek words in the two long blanks.*

*Select the meaning from below the word list that best fits each word, and write the
corresponding letter in the blank. Be sure to add all Greek words on this page to
your dictionary.*

e 1. microscope	μικρος + σκοπος		μετρον (measure)
g 2. micrometer	μικρος + μετρον		θεος (God)
f 3. sophomore	σοφος + μωρος		κοσμος (world, universe)
a 4. Timothy	τιμιος + θεος		μικρος (small)
i 5. microcosm	μικρος + κοσμος		μακρος (large)
c 6. theosophy	θεος + σοφος		σοφος (wise)
b 7. macroscopic	μακρος + σκοπος		μωρος (foolish, "moron")
h 8. cosmology	κοσμος + λογος		τιμιος (honored, precious)
d 9. macrocosm	μακρος + κοσμος		λογος (word, "study of")
			σκοπος (watcher)

a. This name means "honored of God."   b. Large enough to see with the naked
eye.   c. A religious system that claims to have direct knowledge of God, without Bible or Jesus.   d. The entire universe.   e. Something to look at tiny things
with.   f. A student who knows little, but regards himself as very smart.   g. Used
to measure small things.   h. Study of the universe.   i. "The universe in a drop
of water."

g 10. energy __εν__ + __εργον__   μονος (only)

d 11. monolith __μονος__ + __λιθος__   φιλος (friend)

j 12. monologue __μονος__ + __λογος__   εν (in)

βιος (life)

h 13. philosophy __φιλος__ + __σοφια__   λογος (word, "study of")

a 14. philanthropy __φιλος__ + __ανθρωπος__   εργον (work)

c 15. photograph __φωτος__ + __γραφω__   ανθρωπος (man)

e 16. anthropology __ανθρωπος__+ __λογος__   σοφια (wisdom)

γραφω (write)

i 17. biology __βιος__ + __λογος__   λιθος (stone)

b 18. megalith __μεγα__ + __λιθος__   μεγα (large)

f 19. lithograph __λιθος__ + __γραφω__   φωτος (light)

a. Showing your love of mankind through your generosity.   b. A huge rock.   c. Marks made on paper through exposure to the light.   d. A stone structure standing alone.   e. Study of man.   f. A printing process which involves etching upon stone.   g. The ability to put work in a task.   h. Love of wisdom.   i. Study of life.   j. A conversation by one person.

The following compounds are found in the New Testament.

Match to the number of the English word above and from the previous page.

4 A. τιμοθεος   **13** B. φιλοσοφια   **10** C. ενεργεια   **14** D. φιλανθρωπια

Scripture Examples

Disregard any unfamiliar endings and simply write in the meaning of the main part of the Greek word. Check your answers with your Bible.

But __God__ has chosen the __things__ (things) of the __world__ in order to
θεὸς   μωρὰ   κόσμου
confound the __wise__ (1 Cor. 1:27).
σοφούς

All that is __in__ the __world__ —the lust of the flesh and the lust of the
ἐν   κόσμῳ

__eye__ s and the pride of __life__ —is not of the Father but of the __world__
ὀφθαλμῶν   βίου   κόσμου
(1 John 2:16).

While you have __light__, believe in the __light__, that ye may be sons of __light__
(John 12:36).   φῶς   φῶς   φωτὸς

Greater love than this has no one: that anyone should lay down his life for his _friend_ s; you are my _friend_ s, if you do the things I command you
      φίλων   φίλοι
(John 15:13–14).

The following have word order different from English:

If anyone build on the foundation with gold, silver, _stone_ s _precious_ s, wood, hay, stubble . . . (1 Cor. 3:12).
                                                λίθους   τιμίους

Who can forgive sins but _only_ _god_ ? (Luke 5:21).
                          μόνος) θεός

Lesson Five

More Alphabet

*Say the number "8." Spell in English: __eight__. The diphthong "ei" sounds like "ay."
It also does in Greek. The words in the left column are English words spelled with
Greek letters. Match with the corresponding word in the right column.*

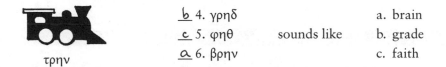

τρειν

__b__ 1. βρειν

__c__ 2. γρειδ   sounds like

__a__ 3. φειθ

a. faith

b. brain

c. grade

*The Greek letter η also sounds like "ay"; so "8" = ειτ = ητ. Same directions as pre-
vious section.*

τρην

__b__ 4. γρηδ

__c__ 5. φηθ   sounds like

__a__ 6. βρην

a. brain

b. grade

c. faith

*Identify these Bible names. The words in the middle column are simply to help you
read the Greek words in the left column. Match the Greek words with their English
equivalents from the right column.*

__c__ 7. δανιηλ   dah-nee-ale

__a__ 8. Ισραηλ   Iss-rah-ale

__b__ 9. γαβριηλ   Gah-bree-ale

a. Israel

b. Gabriel

c. Daniel

Note: When names with "η" are written in English letters, the letter "e" is used.

Cognates

Match these Greek cognates with their meaning from the right column. (Add these words to your dictionary.)

_d_ 10. εικων

_g_ 11. αμην

_h_ 12. αλληλουια

_e_ 13. ανατολη

_a_ 14. αλληλορεω

_f_ 15. σεισμος

_c_ 16. πατηρ

_j_ 17. προφητης

_m_ 18. αηρ

_h_ 19. βιβλος

_o_ 20. σωτηρ

_k_ 21. παραβολη

_n_ 22. θεραπεια

_l_ 23. ορφανος

_i_ 24. καμηλος

a. allegory

b. alleluia

c. father (compare our word "paternity")

d. icon. These images are valued in the Eastern Orthodox Church.

e. This word means "east"; a region of the ancient world was named Anatolia.

f. Means "earthquake." Compare our word "seismograph."

g. This word means: "It is true!" Used to end a prayer.

h. Looks like "Bible," but means "book" in general in Greek.

i. camel

j. prophet

k. parable

l. orphan

m. air

n. therapy

o. savior. Theologians use the word "soteriology"—the study of salvation.

Exercise Two

Pronunciation Check

Match each Greek word with its correct pronunciation.

_a_ 1. γαβριηλ   a. Gah-bree-ail   b. Gay-bree-ell

_b_ 2. αμην   a. aim-men   b. ah-mane

_b_ 3. δανιηλ   a. Dah-nee-ell   b. Dah-nee-ale

_a_ 4. πατηρ   a. pah-tare   b. potter

_a_ 5. προφητης   a. praw-fay-tace   b. prophetess

_b_ 6. ισραηλ   a. Is-rye-all   b. Iz-rah-ale

_b_ 7. ενεργεια   a. en-er-jee-ah   b. en-air-gay-uh

_b_ 8. σεισμος   a. size-mos   b. saze-moss

Scriptures with η-Words

Pronounce the Greek word, write its English equivalent above it and check your answers with your Bible.

And the twenty-four elders and four creatures fell and worshipped **God**
καὶ   θεῷ

who was seated **on** the **throne**, saying, **Amen**, **Alleluia** (Rev. 19:4).
              ἐπὶ   θρόνῳ   Ἀμὴν   Ἀλληλουϊά

(The two dots above the ι in Alleluia tell you to pronounce both the ι and the
α, rather than running them together into a diphthong.)

                                                east
When Jesus was born, wise men from the **anatolia** came to Jerusalem, say-
                                        ἀνατολῶν

ing, ". . . we have seen His star in the **east anatolia** and have come to worship
                                        ἀνατολῇ
Him" (Matt. 2:1–2).

An older name for the country we now call Turkey: Anatolia.

How much more will your **father** **in** heaven give good gifts to those
                         πατὴρ   ἐν
asking Him? (Matt. 7:11b).

Blind guides! Straining at a gnat, and swallowing a **camel** (Matt. 23:24).
                                                    κάμηλον

Amen amen I say to you: If anyone keeps my **word** he shall not see death
Ἀμὴν ἀμὴν   λόγον
(John 8:51).

Scriptures Showing Various Endings

Pronounce the Greek word, write its English equivalent above it and check your answers with your Bible.

1. For **God** so loved the **world** that he gave his only Son . . . (John
      θεός   κόσμον
   3:16).

When some words end with -ου, this may indicate "possession"—so use the
word "of" when translating. βιβλου = of book.

2. **And** the peace **of God**, which passes all understanding, will keep
   καὶ   θεοῦ
   your **heart** s and minds **in** Christ Jesus (Phil. 4:7).
        καρδίας   ἐν

If there already is a preposition, don't add the word "of":

3. Grace to you and peace __from__ _God_ our _Father_ (Eph. 1:2).
                            ἀπὸ   θεοῦ   πατρὸς

(The word πατρος is the word πατηρ [father], contracted to πατρ, with an ending added.)

Some words must end with ῳ when written after the word εν:

4. _And_ to show . . . the mystery hidden __in__   _God_ who created every-
   καὶ   ἐν   θεῷ

   thing, to make known . . . the wonderfully-varied _wisdom_ _of_ _God_
   (Eph. 3:9–10).   σοφία   θεοῦ

5. He was _in_ the _world_, _and_ the _world_ was made by him, _and_ the
   ἐν   κόσμῳ   καὶ   κόσμος   καὶ

   world did _not_ know him (John 1:10).
   κόσμος   οὐκ

Or the word may end that way without any word εν being there:

6. _Abraham_ believed _God_ and it was reckoned to him as righ-
   Ἀβραάμ   θεῷ

   teousness (Rom. 4:3).

In the next example, there is an -ου indicating possession; I had to write in the word "the," since you don't know that word yet.

7. Beware lest anyone capture you through _philosophy_ and empty de-
                                           φιλοσοφίας

   ceit, according to the traditions of _human_ s, according to the ele-
                                        ἀνθρώπων

   ments _of_ (the) _world_ and not according to Christ (Col. 2:8).
          κόσμου

Lesson Six

English Words That Were Created from Greek Words

Find the Greek word in the second column that reminds you of an English word in the first column. Print that Greek word on the long blank provided. Then select the definition below which corresponds to the English word, and print the letter of the definition in the short blank. Copy these Greek words in your dictionary.

f 1. phonetics φωνη   τοπος (place)
c 2. galactic γαλακτος   σκολιος (crooked)
h 3. phosphorescent φως   φωνη (sound)
a 4. arterio-sclerosis σκληρος   γαλακτος (of milk)
d 5. topical τοπος   φοβος (fear)
g 6. neon νεος   φως (light)
b 7. phobia φοβος   σκληρος (hard)
e 8. scoliosis σκολιος   νεος (new)

   a. Hardening of arteries.   **b.** The fear of something.   **c.** Pertaining to our galaxy, the "Milky Way."   **d.** Placed into categories.   **e.** Curvature of the spine.   **f.** Study of the sounds of languages.   **g.** A rare gas named after its "new-ness."   **h.** Glows in the dark.

n 9. plastic πλαστος   κλεπτω (steal)
l 10. anthracite ανθρακος   ορθος (straight)
i 11. necromancy νεκρος   δενδρον (tree)
p 12. kleptomaniac κλεπτω   πλαστος (formed)
m 13. dendrite δενδρον   γραμμα (letter)
o 14. acoustics ακουω   ανθρακος (coal)
k 15. grammar γραμμα   νεκρος (dead)
j 16. orthodontist ορθος   ακουω (hear)

   i. The forbidden occult practice of attempting to contact the dead.   **j.** One who straightens teeth.   **k.** Study of language rules.   **l.** A type of coal.   **m.** Branch-like end of a nerve cell.   **n.** Substance that can be formed into any desired shape.   **o.** Science of sound.   **p.** Habitual thief.

x 17. Thanatopsis _θανατος_   κρανιον (skull)

q 18. leukocyte _λευκος_   μεγας (large)

u 19. gerontology _γερων_   μελας (black)

w 20. idiosyncracies _ιδιος_   εσωτερος (inner)

s 21. esoteric _εσωτερος_   γερων (old)

v 22. melanoma _μελκς_   ιδιος (self)

r 23. megaphone _μελας_   θανατος (death)

t 24. cranium _κρανιον_   λευκος (white)

y 25. trauma _τραυμα_   τραυμα (wound)

q. White blood cell.   r. Device that makes sounds louder.   s. Secrets known only to an inner group.   t. Head-bone.   u. Medical practice for the aged.   v. Tumor containing dark pigment.   w. My personal quirks.   x. A poem giving the author's thoughts about death.   y. We use this word for the condition brought on by shock.

(The Good Samaritan) approached and bandaged his _wound_ s with oil (Luke 10:34). (See Exercise One, #25.)   τραύματα

Scriptures

1. You have need (of) ___milk___, not solid food (Heb. 5:12).
   γάλακτος

2. Jesus said, "___I___ am the _light of_ the _a world_" (John 8:12).
   ἐγώ   φῶς   κόσμου

3. I looked and heard the _sound_ of many angels around the
   throne (Rev. 5:11).   φωνὴν
   θρόνου

(The word for "throne" has an –ου ending because it comes after a preposition—"around." Do not add "of.")

Introducing a new capital letter: Γ is the capital of γ.

4. They came to a _place_ called _Golgotha_, which means _Place_
   τόπον   Γολγοθᾶ   Τόπος
   of the Skull (Matt. 27:33).
   Κρανίου

(Use the word "of" with the word that ends in -ου. There is no word for "a" in Greek, but we need to use this word so our translation sounds like smooth English: of a skull.)

5. . . . perfecting holiness _in_ the _fear_ _of_ _God_
   (2 Cor. 7:1).   ἐν   φόβῳ   Θεοῦ

6. . . . you have put off the old ___man___ with its practices, ___and___
ἄνθρωπον   καὶ

have put on the ___new___ . . . (Col. 3:9–10).
νέον

7. But when the kindness and ___love___ of mankind through generosity of God our Saviour ap-
φιλανθρωπία   Θεοῦ

peared, He saved us (Titus 3:4).

8. Master, I knew that you were a ___hard___ ___man___ (Matt. 25:24).
σκληρὸς   ἄνθρωπος

9. And I saw a ___great___ ___white___ ___throne___ and one seated on it . . . and
μέγαν   λευκὸν   θρόνον

I saw the ___dead___ both great and ___small___ standing before the
νεκρούς   μικρούς

___throne___, ___and___ ___book___s were opened (Rev. 20:11–12).
θρόνου   καὶ   βιβλία

10. (Jesus partook of flesh and blood) so that through ___death___
θανάτου

he might destroy him who had the power over of death, that is, the
θανάτου

___devil___, and free those who through ___fear___ of ___death___ were
διάβολον   φόβῳ   θανάτου

enslaved all their lives (Heb. 2:14–15).

Lesson Seven

More Cognates

Matching: Select the best definition for each Greek word. Keep your dictionary current.

___1. φαρμακεια

___2. οινος

___ 3. δεσποτης

___ 4. εθνικος

___ 5. θησαυρος

___ 6. αποστασια

___ 7. ναρδος

___ 8. μουσικος

___ 9. τραυμα

___10. καταστροφη

___11. πορνη

___12. ειδωλον

___ 13. σκολιος

___ 14. μαθητης

___ 15. σωμα

___ 16. μαγος

a. A perfume-like ointment: nard.

b. Means "wound"; we use it to refer to going into shock after an accident.

c. Crooked. We call a crooked spine scoliosis. Also used figuratively.

d. Prostitute; we made the word "pornography" from this.

e. Idol, false god. Combined with the Greek word for worship, λατρεια, we get the word meaning idolatry: ειδωλολατρεια.

f. μαθ in Greek referred to learning in general, not just to the highly disciplined subject we call by that name today (math). The word you're matching to means one under discipline; a learner; usually translated "disciple" in the New Testament.

g. This word means "body." Our English word psychosomatic means that our bodies are affected by the state of our minds.

h. One who makes sounds by singing or playing an instrument.

i. Refers to the race of the person; comes from the Greek word εθνος, which means "nation." Ethnic (often translated "Gentile").

j. Means "treasure"; we use it to refer to a book which is a treasury of words: a thesaurus.

k. This word originally referred to drugs mixed for magic; now we use it for a drugstore or pharmacy. The word φαρμακος is translated "sorcerer."

l. One who practices magic. Our term for the "wise men" who visited the child Jesus is a respelling of this word into English: Magi.

m. Wine

n. Tyrannical ruler: despot.

o. Apostasy (falling away from the faith).

p. Means "turned down," and refers to disasters like earthquakes where everything topples.

Exercise Two

A Special Use for the Letter "I"

Some languages pronounce the name "Jesus" differently than we do. For example, in German it's spelled "Jesus," but pronounced "yay-zoose." Greek also has the "y" sound in names where we're accustomed to the "j" sound. But Greek doesn't spell those names either with a "y" or with a "j." Greek uses the letter "i" for this purpose.

For example: Ιωβ. Pronounce it yōb. It's the Old Testament figure noted for his suffering. We call him "Job."

Identify

	Greek Pronunciation	Match to Meaning
__ 1. Ιακωβ	yah-kobe	a. Jesus
__ 2. Ιωνας	yoe-nass	b. Jacob
__ 3. Ιησους	yay-zoose	c. Jonah

Matching Names

Select the best definition for each Greek word.

__ 4. Ιερεμιας

__ 5. Ιησους

__ 6. Ιορδανης (pronounce your-dah-nace)

__ 7. Γενεσις

__ 8. Κορινθος

__ 9. Ναθαναηλ

a. Our Lord and Savior
b. A city to which Paul wrote two letters (after Romans in New Testament).
c. First book in the Bible; it means "beginnings" (lincage, generations).
d. The river that John the Baptist used for baptizing (Jordan).
e. A disciple whom Jesus saw beneath a tree (John 1:45–49).
f. Prophet located after Isaiah in the Old Testament.

__10. Ιουδαια

__ 11. Ιουδας

__ 12. Νικοδημος

__ 13. κορνηλιος

__ 14. ποντιος πιλατος

__ 15. θωμας

g. The doubting disciple.
h. The Roman governor who OK'd Christ's crucifixion.
i. A name for the Holy Land: Judea.
j. He came to Jesus by night (John 3).
k. He betrayed Christ for 30 silver pieces.
l. He was swallowed by a great fish.
m. Peter preached the gospel to him (Acts 10).

Match Pronunciation to Greek Names

___ 16. Ιησους   a. ye-re-mee-as

___ 17. Ιακωβ   b. yay-zoose

___ 18. Ιερεμιας   c. you-dye-ah

___ 19. Ιακωβος   d. ya-kobe

___ 20. Ιωαννης   e. ya-co-boss (This is the Greek word for "James")

___ 21. Ιουδαια   f. yo-on-ace (Greek for "John")

Exercise Three

Pronunciation Check

Select the correct pronunciation for each Greek word.

___ 1. Ιερουσαλημ*   a. Eye-row-salem   b. Yeh-rue-sah-lame

___ 2. Ιερεμιας   a. Ear-em-my-us   b. Yeh-rem-ee-us

___ 3. Ιησους   a. Yay-zoose   b. Ee-ayze-oose

___ 4. Ιορδανης   a. Yor-dan-us   b. Yor-dah-nace

___ 5. Ιωαννης   a. Eye-oh-annas   b. Yoe-on-ace

___ 6. Ιουδαια   a. You-die-uh   b. Yoe-day-uh

___ 7. Ιουδας   a. Yah-dass   b. Yew-dass

___ 8. Ιακωβ   a. Yah-cob   b. Yah-cobe

___ 9. Ιωνας   a. Yoe-nass   b. Yon-us

___ 10. Ιωβ   a. Ee-ob   b. Yobe

___ 11. φαρμακεια   a. farma-kaya   b. farma-key-uh

___ 12. θησαυρος   a. theos-ourus   b. thay-sour-us

___ 13. γενεσεως   a. Jen-ess-iss   b. Gen-ess-eh-oce

___ 14. μουσικος   a. moo-zee-koss   b. myu-zik-us

*means Jerusalem

Meaning Check

Select the best definition for each Greek word.

___ 15. φαρμακεια
___ 16. γενεσεως
___ 17. καταστροφη
___ 18. θεος
___ 19. φιλοσοφια
___ 20. προς
___ 21. φιλος
___ 22. λογος
___ 23. σοφια
___ 24. κοσμος
___ 25. θησαυρος
___ 26. φιλαδελφια
___ 27. αδελφος
___ 28. σωτηρ
___ 29. εθνων

a. love of wisdom
b. god or God
c. everything fallen down
d. of lineage, generation; related to Greek name
   for first book of the Bible.
e. has something to do with drugs; in Bible times,
   that would mean drugs in the occult.
f. friend, related to (love, friendship)
g. wisdom
h. world
i. word
j. treasure
k. forth
l. of nations or Gentiles
m. brother
n. savior
o. brotherly love

Scriptures

As you check your answers to the following in your Bible, you may be surprised at how these familiar cognates are sometimes used. Also, note a new capital letter: Δ = δ.

Matthew 1:1 _____ of the _____ of _____ Christ, son of _____ . . .
        βίβλος   γενέσεως   Ἰησοῦ   Δαυὶδ

There was a _____ sent from _____; his name was _____ (John 1:6).
      ἄνθρωπος   θεοῦ   Ἰωάννης

Outside are the dogs _____ the _____ s _____ the _____ s _____
           καὶ   φαρμακοὶ   καὶ   πόρνοι   καὶ

the murderers _____ the _____ s _____ those _____ ing _____
       καὶ   εἰδωλολάτραι   καὶ   φιλῶν   καὶ

doing falsehood (Rev. 22:15).

Servants, submit to your _____s with all _____, not only to the good
                          δεσπόταις   φόβῳ

. . . but also to the _____ (1 Pet. 2:18).
                     σκολιοῖς

Land of _____ _____ land of _____, by the way of the sea, beyond
        Ζαβουλὼν   καὶ   Νεφθαλίμ

the _____, _____ of the _____ . . . (Matt. 4:15).
    Ἰορδάνου   Γαλιλαία   ἐθνῶν

When you pray don't use vain repetitions as the _____s do (Matt. 6:7).
                                                ἐθνικοί

_____ took bread, blessed it and gave it to his _____s, saying, "Take,
Ἰησοῦς   μαθηταῖς

eat, this is my _____" (Matt. 26:26).
                σῶμα

Lesson Eight

Some Common Prepositions

Select the word from the word list that would best translate the preposition (under-lined word) in each sentence. Write the letter of the English word you've chosen in the short blank at the front of each sentence.

Word List

___ 1. θρονος is ἐν οικῳ

___ 2. βιβλος is ἐπι θρονῳ

___ 3. σκορπιος is entering εἰς οικον

___ 4. Ανθρωπος is leaning ἀντι οικου

___ 5. Ανθπωπος is walking προς οικον

___ 6. λεων is running δια οικου

___ 7. Δενδρον is growing παρα οικῳ

___ 8. σκορπιος is climbing ἐκ δενδρου

___ 9. Καμηλος is walking away ἀπο οικου

a. on _____

b. beside _____

c. in _____

d. from _____

e. through _____

f. out of _____

g. toward _____

h. against _____

i. into _____

Write the correct Greek preposition after each word in the word list, and add the new words to your dictionary.

45

In Part II of this book you will learn the endings that are put on nouns, and there will be a list of which endings to use after particular prepositions. For Part I, it is sufficient for you to grasp only the meaning of the words.

Sentences with Prepositions

Write the letter of each picture in front of the corresponding sentence.

__ 1. Δανιηλ is sitting επι θρονῳ.
__ 2. Δεσποτης is whipping someone εν οικῳ.
__ 3. Ειδωλ is placed παρα θησαυρῳ.
__ 4. Καμηλος is going απο οικου.
__ 5. λεων is lying παρα πετρα.
__ 6. Διαβολος is going εκ καρδιας.
__ 7. Καμηλος is going δια οικου.
__ 8. Γαβριηλ is going εις οικον.
__ 9. κρανιον is leaning αντι βιβλον.
__ 10. Μαθητης is coming προς δενδρον.
__ 11. λεων is coming εκ οικου.
__ 12. βιβλος is placed επι λιθῳ.
__ 13. προφητης is leaning αντι δενδρου.
__ 14. Διαβολος is coming εις οικον.
__ 15. Μαθητης is coming προς θησαυρον.

Scriptures Using Prepositions

Pronounce the Greek word and then write its English equivalent above it.

1. _____ ____ those days, _____ came _____ Nazareth (in)
      καὶ   ἐν   Ἰησοῦς [a]   ἀπὸ

   _____ _____ was baptized (by going) _____ the _____
    Γαλιλαίας   καὶ   εἰς   Ἰορδάνην [b]

   by _____. _____ immediately, coming up ____ of the
       Ἰωάννου [c]   καὶ   ἐκ

   water he saw the heavens opened . . . (Mark 1:8, 10).

   > Footnotes: Pronunciations of words starting with I:
   > a. Ιησους = yay-zoose; b. Ιορδανην = your-dah-nane; c. Ιωαννου = Yo-ah-new

2. Beloved, if our _____ condemn us not, we have boldness _____
              καρδία   πρὸς

   _____ (1 John 3:21).
    θεόν

3. . . . innumerable as the sand which is _____ the seashore (Heb.
   11:12).   παρὰ

4. . . . so that _____ death he might destroy him who had the power of
            δια

   death, that is, the _____, and free those who were held in slav-
              διάβολον

   ery by _____ of death _____ all their lives (Heb. 2:14–15).
      φόβῳ   δια

5. Don't you know that whoever was baptized ____ Christ _____
                             εἰς   Ἰησουν

   was baptized ____ his death? We are buried with him therefore ____
        εἰς   δια

   _____ _____ death, so that as Christ was raised _____
    βαπτίσματος εἰς   ἐκ

   the _____ _____ the glory of the _____, we also might walk
      νεκρῶν δια   πατρός

   ____ newness of life (Rom. 6:3–4).
    ἐν

Lesson Nine

Words Formed by Combining with Prepositions

Some of these combinations were actually formed by the Greeks; others are English words formed from Greek roots.

Put the word that appears after the plus sign in your dictionary.

Words formed with παρα, "alongside": Resultant English words:

___ 1. παρα + αλληλων (each other)
___ 2. παρα + γραφω (write)
___ 3. παρα + βαλλω (throw)
___ 4. παρα + νοια (mind)
___ 5. παρα + σιτος (food)
___ 6. παρα + εν + θεις (put)

a. Throwing an everyday example alongside a spiritual truth gives us a <u>parable</u>: παραβολη.

b. A creature that gets its food by living near another creature is called a parasite.

c. When a person's mind is beside itself with fear: paranoia.

d. Two lines which are alongside one another are parallel.

e. Writing this sign ¶ alongside a sentence = a new paragraph.

f. Putting words within brackets next to what they're explaining.

Words formed with επι, "on":

___ 7. επι + στελλω (send)
___ 8. επι + γραφω (write)
___ 9. επι + φανος (lantern)
___ 10. επι + δερμα (skin)
___ 11. επι + γλοττις (tongue)
___ 12. επι + δημος (people)
___ 13. επι + γραμμα (written)
___ 14. επι + ταφος (tomb)
___ 15. επι + κεντρον (center)
___ 16. επι + σκοπος (watcher)

g. Church festival about Jesus shining forth with the truth of who He is: epiphany. *επιφανεια

h. It hangs above your tongue: epiglottis.

i. Outer layer of skin: epidermis

j. Message sent on to someone: an epistle. *επιστολη

k. Inscription on statue: epigraph.

l. Words on a gravestone: epitaph.

m. Bishops watch over the church in the episcopal system. επισκοπος

n. A disease coming upon many at the same time: epidemic.

o. Writing upon a subject with a short witty poem: epigram.

p. Place above center of an earthquake: epicenter.

Refer to picture of prepositions on page 45 to work out these.

___ 17. εκ   + κεντρον (center)
___ 18. απο + στελλω (send)
___ 19. απο + γη (earth)
___ 20. απο + λογος (word)
___ 21. δια + μετρον (measure)
___ 22. δια + σπορα (seed)
___ 23. παρα + ουσια (being)
___ 24. αντι + νομος (law)
___ 25. αντι + θεις (placed)

q. Measurement through circle: diameter.

r. Point of orbit far from earth: apogee.

s. One who's sent out on a mission: emissary or apostle. αποστολος.

t. Theological term for Christ's coming to be with us: parousia. *παρουσια.

u. Antinomians feel we shouldn't pay attention to the law.

v. An eccentric is off center.

w. People scattered through the world like sown seed: diaspora.

x. One idea placed in contrast against another: antithesis.

y. Words to defend your view against criticism. apology. *απολογια.

Note: Underlined words appear in Greek forms in the New Testament. Asterisked* words are used on following pages. Put them in your dictionary.

Exercise Two

Guess the Meanings

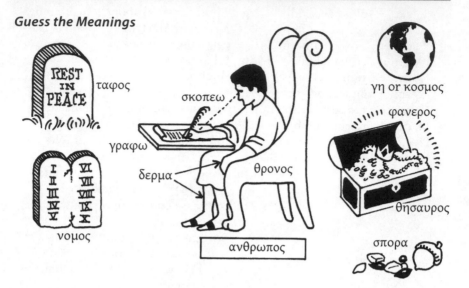

Write the appropriate Greek word on the long blanks.

man _____   law _____   see _____
write _____   treasure _____ shining _____
skin _____   seed _____   throne _____
grave _____   earth _____, _____

Exercise Three

Pronunciation Check

Select the correct pronunciation for each of these Greek words.

___ 1. αλληλους	a. pah-rah-bo-lay
___ 2. θησαυρους	b. yay-zoose
___ 3. επιφανεια	c. met-ray-teh
___ 4. θεω	d. theh-oh
___ 5. παρουσια	e. e-pee-fah-nay-ah
___ 6. Ιησους	f. gace
___ 7. λεγει	g. ah-lay-loose
___ 8. μετρειτε	h. leggay
___ 9. γης	i. pah-roo-see-a
___10. παραβοη	j. thay-sow-rooce

Meaning Check

Select the best definition for each of these Greek words.

__ 11. επι	k. against
__ 12. φανος	l. on
__ 13. επιφανεια	m. of God
__ 14. θησαυρος	n. torch
__ 15. παραβολη	o. of law
__ 16. θεου	r. parable; story of comparison
__ 17. νομου	s. treasure, storehouse
__ 18. λογος	t. shine upon
__ 19. εκ	u. out
__ 20. παρα	v. word
__ 21. απο	w. through
__ 22. δια	x. from
__ 23. αντι	y. next to
__ 24. παρουσια	z. Christ's coming

Scriptures

Pronounce the Greek words and write their English equivalents above them. Check answers in your Bible.

Don't lay up for yourselves _____ s _____ _____ (Matt. 6:19).
θησαυρούς   ἐπὶ   γῆς

For where your _____ is, there will your _____ be also (Matt. 6:21).
θησαυρός   καρδία

We know that whatever the _____ says, it says to those under the _____,
νόμος   νόμῳ

that every mouth may be stopped and the whole _____ be accountable to
κόσμος

_____; because by _____ s _____ no flesh shall be justified before
θεῷ   ἔργων   νόμου

Him (Rom. 3:19–20).

The Lord Jesus will destroy the lawless one by the _____ of his
_____ (2 Thess. 2:8).   ἐπιφανείᾳ
παρουσίας

Therefore comfort _____ with these _____s (1 Thess. 4:18).
ἀλλήλους   λόγοις

The greeting is in my hand: _____. This is my mark in every _____;
                          Παύλου   ἐπιστολῇ
this is how I _____ (2 Thess. 3:17).
             γράφω

_____, _____ of Christ _____, _____ the will ____ _____, to the
Παῦλος   ἀπόστολος   Ἰησοῦ*   διὰ   θεοῦ
saints in ____, faithful __ Christ ____; grace to you ____ ___peace___ ____
         Ἐφέσῳ   ἐν   Ἰησοῦ   καὶ   εἰπήνη**   ἀπὸ
____ our _____ ____ the Lord _____ Christ. Blessed be the _____ ____
θεοῦ   πατρὸς   καὶ   Ἰησοῦ   θεὸς   καὶ
_____ of our Lord _____ Christ (Eph. 1:1–3).
πατὴρ   Ἰησοῦ

*Ιησου pronounced Yay-zoo.
**ει and η in the same word: ειρηνη (ay-ray-nay).

Lesson Ten

More of the Alphabet

English Words:

αξ    ταξι    sounds like English x

Our word "doxology": comes from the Greek for δοξα (glory) + λογος = and means "words of glory." Now combine παρα plus δοξα and you get παραδοξα. English: _____

In English, we sometimes say "an" instead of "a," when the next word starts with a vowel. Greek makes a similar change with the preposition εκ (out of). When εκ comes before a vowel, it is written εξ instead.* The meaning stays the same:

εκ κοσμου = out of world; εξ οικου = out of house;

> εξ (out of) + οδος (way or path) = _____ (book of Bible)
> *in other words, an ς has been added to εκ, making εκς; then that word is respelled as εξ.

The Throat-Clearing Sound

This is the sound used in the German word "ach." It is written χ.

That looks like an "x"—but you know it can't be the "x" sound, because we just had the x-sound above, and it looked like this: ξ.

Now pronounce the famous German composer's name: Johann Sebastian βαχ.

53

Did you do OK? Then let's see how good you are at *starting* words with that sound:

Match to meanings at right—and no fair not attempting to pronounce the words:

___ 1. Χασμα

___ 2. Χριστιανος

___ 3. Χορος

___ 4. Χρονος

___ 5. Χερουβιμ

___ 6. Χαρτης

___ 7. Χαλδαιος

___ 8. Χαρακτηρ

___ 9. Χανααν

a. Greeks used this to refer to groups of dancers; we refer to singers with it, but we do base a word on it that means planning the steps for a dance: choreography.

b. a follower of the Lord Ιησους Χριστος.

c. a deep crack in the earth.

d. time; the basis for our word "chronology."

e. Chaldean (a person from south of Babylon).

f. Canaan (spelling influenced by the Hebrew original).

g. Means "exact likeness" in Greek; we use it to refer to distinguishing marks of personality.

h. Means "papyrus/paper" in Greek; for us, a map on paper.

i. Cherubim; certain types of angels.

Exercise Three

About the Word "Christ"

There's a Greek word, χρισει, which means anoint (pour oil on):

1. In the Old Testament the prophet Samuel takes oil and _____ David as king.
   χρίσει

2. In Luke 4:18, Jesus quotes Isaiah and applies it to Himself: "The Spirit of the Lord is upon me, because he has _____ (past tense) me to preach good news to the poor . . ."   ἔχρισεν

3. After the resurrection, the disciples knew Jesus was the anointed one, as shown by their prayer in Acts 4:27: . . . the people of Israel were gathered together against your holy servant Jesus, whom you didst

   _____.
   ἔχρισας

4. Χρίσειν, then, means "to _____." Someone who's been anointed is called a χριστός, spelled in English _____.
   This means the same as the Old Testament word "Messiah"—an anointed King who was to come, to save and rule God's people.

Exercise Four

The Word for "Grace"

χαρις means "grace": "For by χαριτι are you saved . . ." (Eph. 2:8). χαρισματα means "things you get by grace." See what your Bible does with 1 Corinthians 12:4—"Now there are varieties of χαρισματων, but the same Spirit."

From the word χαρισματα comes the English word _____, one who believes in the spiritual "gifts."

Exercise Five

The "PS" Sound

ψ is pronounced like ps.   English example: λιψ

If we turn to the Bible book after Job, we can read a ψαλμος.

ψυχικος (soulish), without the ος, is spelled in English as _____.

ψευδος (lie) is used in English words such as _____.

Scriptures

The first _____ _____ was made _____ a living _____ (1 Cor. 15:45).
          ἄνθρωπος   Ἀδὰμ   εἰς   ψυχὴν
You are ____ your _____ the _____, _____ you do the desires of your
       ἐκ   πατρὸς   διαβόλου   καὶ
_____. . . . When he speaks a _____, he speaks according to his own
πατρὸς   ψεῦδος
nature, because he is a _____ and the _____ of it (John 8:44).
                        ψεύστης   πατὴρ

Combinations of ψευδος with words you know:

2 Corinthians 11:26   In perils among _____s
                                         ψευδαδέλφοις

2 Corinthians 11:13   For such are _____s
                                       ψευδαπόστολοι

Matthew 7:15   Beware of _____s
                                    ψευδοπροφητῶν

Matthew 24:24   For there shall arise _____s
                                               ψευδόχριστοι

Words from the Previous Pages

Stir up the _____ _____ which is in you . . . (2 Tim. 1:6).
χάρισμα   θεοῦ

The _____s were first called _____s ____ _____ (Acts 11:26).
μαθητὰς   Χριστιανούς ἐν   Ἀντιοχείᾳ

_____ (capital δ) to _____ ____ the highest, _____ ____ ____
Δόξα   θεῷ   ἐν   καὶ   ἐπὶ   γῆς

_____, goodwill towards _____s (Luke 2:14).
εἰρήνη   ἀνθρώποις

Exercise Six

Another New Letter: ζ

ζ is pronounced like dz—as in "adz."

Match: *Select the correct translation for each of these Greek words.*

___ 1. ζῳον   (dzoe-on)   a. zeal
___ 2. ζηλος   (dzay-loss)   b. an animal. The word from
___ 3. ζηλωτης   (dzay-low-tace)   which we get "zoo"
                                    c. zealot

The capital of ζ is Z. The capital of λ is Λ.

Match: *Select the correct definition for each of these Greek words.*

___ 4. Ζεβεδαιος   (dze-bed-eye-oss)   d. Zacchaeus
___ 5. Ζακαριας   (dzah-kah-ree-ahss)   e. Lazarus
___ 6. Ζακχαιος   f. Zebedee
___ 7. Λαζαρος   (lodz-a-ross)   g. Zacharias
___ 8. Ζωη   h. life

Scriptures

_____ came ____ _____, where _____ lived, whom _____
Ἰησοῦς   εἰς   βηθανίαν   Λάζαρος   Ἰησοῦς

had raised ____ _____ (John 12:1).
           ἐκ   νεκρῶν

(No word "the" in the original before the last Greek word, but you can supply
it for the sake of smooth English.)

_____ if _____ through _____ cast out _____s, then
  Καὶ   ἐγὼ   Βεελζεβοὺλ   δαιμόνια

through whom do your sons cast them out? (Matt. 12:27).

_____ found _____ _____ said to him, "We have found the one
  Φίλιππος·   Ναθαναὴλ   καὶ

that _____ (____ the _____) _____ the _____s wrote about:
       Μωϋσῆς**   ἐν   νόμῳ   καὶ   προφῆται

_____, son of _____, _____ _____ (John 1:45).
  Ἰησοῦν   Ἰωσὴφ   ἀπὸ   Ναζαρέτ·

*Φ is the capital of φ.
**The two dots mean, "Pronounce the υ separately."

Lesson Eleven

Words about the Body

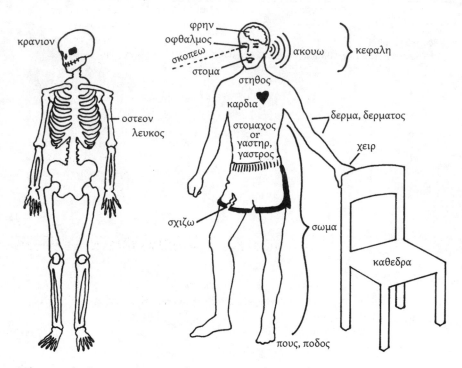

(The words that are in pairs above are two forms of the same word.)

Fill in the blanks with Greek words from the picture above.

see _____   stomach _____   skull _____
body _____   hear _____   stomach area _____
white _____   head _____   rip or tear _____
bone _____   brain _____   eye _____
mouth _____   chest _____   heart _____
skin _____   hand _____   chair _____
foot _____

Fill in the long blanks with Greek words from the picture on page 58. Select the best definition from the words in the right column for the English words in the left column.

__ 1. podiatrist _____
__ 2. phrenology _____
__ 3. ophthalmologist _____
__ 4. dermatologist _____
__ 5. hypodermic _____
__ 6. osteopath _____
__ 7. cathedral _____
__ 8. gastritis _____
__ 9. chiropractor _____
__10. schizophrenia _____ + _____
__11. stethoscope _____ + _____

a. adjusting joints by hand
b. under the skin
c. guessing mental ability from head-shape
d. instrument for making observations within the chest
e. foot-doctor
f. stomach cramps, inflammation
g. bone doctor
h. the mind seems to be torn into two personalities
i. eye doctor
j. this is the church where the bishop had his "seat," or headquarters
k. skin doctor

Exercise Two

The "H" Sound

The "h" sound is shown by a backwards comma over the first letter of a word that starts with a vowel:

ὡσαννα (hosanna) ἀλληλουια (hallelujah)

When an h sound is not wanted, the comma will go the other way:

ἀγαπη (means "love"), ἀνωθεν (means "again," "from above")

Match these Greek words with their English equivalents.

__ 1. ὁλος   a. hour
__ 2. ὡρα   b. Hebrew
__ 3. ὁδος   c. whole
__ 4. Ἑβραιος   d. path

Exercise Three

Write the Greek word in the long blank. Match the English words to the meanings below.

__ 1. holocaust   _____   ἡγεμων (governor)
__ 2. homogenized   _____   ὁμος (similar)
__ 3. eschatology   _____   ἑτερος (unlike)
__ 4. hegemony   _____   ὁλος (entire)
__ 5. Michael   _____   σχολη
__ 6. school   _____   Μιχαηλ
__ 7. heterodox   _____   εσχατος (final)
__ 8. homophonic   _____

a. Combined with γενος, "kind," it indicates mixing together until each sample of the material is of the same kind.   **b.** Study of the end-times as described in the Bible.   **c.** Combined with καυσις, "burning," it refers to mass slaughter of civilians.   **d.** Combined with φωνη, it is a musical term, meaning that all the sounds are happening at the same time, as chords.   **e.** The name of a head angel in the Bible.   **f.** Overlordship, taking the rule over.   **g.** Place for instruction.   **h.** Different from the accepted standards of church doctrine.

A _____ crying in the wilderness, prepare the _____ ____ _____
  φωνἠ   ὁδὸν   κυρίου
(Matt. 3:3).

(There is no "the" in the original before the last word but smooth English requires that you add one.)

Exercise Four

The Letter "U"

The U sound: Put lips like "oo" and try to say "ee." Scholars give various pronunciations ranging from "oo" in "book" to "u" in "unity."

The Greek word τυπος became English _____ (model or symbol).

Κμριος means "Lord" as in the liturgical song called the Kyrie. Opening a church song book, we'd sing a ὑμνος _____.

Paul warns Timothy to keep away from false μυθους _____.

In all these examples, Greek υ became English _____. But in the case of the Old Testament King δαυιδ, Greek υ became English _____.

Diphthongs with υ: ευ (pronounce "ewe") is a prefix meaning good. υι (wee) is found in the Greek word υἱός, which means "son" (pronounced hwee-oss).

Scriptures

Pronounce each Greek word and write its English equivalent above it.

If you are the _____ _____, command these _____s to become bread
(Matt. 4:3).   υἱός   θεοῦ   λίθοι

Let the _____ _____ indwell you richly, in all _____ teaching _____
        λόγος   Χριστοῦ   σοφία   καὶ
admonishing one another with _____s, _____s, and spiritual songs,
                              ψαλμοῖς   ὕμνοις
singing with _____ ____ your _____s to _____ (Col. 3:16).
            χάριτι   ἐν   καρδίαις   θεῷ

Exercise Five

Words with υ Which Became a "Y" in English

Select the best definition for each of these Greek words.

___ 1. αποκαλυψις
___ 2. αβυσσος
___ 3. τυραννος
___ 4. κηρυγμα
___ 5. κρυπτος
___ 6. μαρτυρ
___ 7. πρεσβυτερος
___ 8. δυναμις
___ 9. ψυχη
___10. φυσικος
___11. ψυχικος
___12. αποκρυφος
___13. υπνος
___14. γυμνασια
___15. δυναστης

a. This is a theological term, meaning "proclamation," from the word κηρυξ (announcer). Theologians use it to refer to the basic content of gospel message, with the English word "kerygma."

b. This word originally meant a "witness"; now we use it in particular to refer to those who lost their lives because of standing up for the truth. Martyr.

c. An oppressive ruler: tyrant.

d. A crypt is an underground room; means "hidden."

e. A form of κρυπτος, "hidden," plus απο, give us certain books that were found "hidden" and scattered in the Greek Old Testament, but were not part of the Hebrew original. Now published in a separate section. Apocrypha.

f. καλυψ, "covering," plus απο, "away from" = taking the cover off; revelation: apocalypse.

g. Power. Compare our word "dynamite."

h. An older person; source of the word "presbyterian," church rule by elders.

i. Soul: psyche.

j. Soulish: psychic.

k. Physical.

l. Means "sleep"; source of our word "hypnosis."

m. Training, discipline; became our word "gymnasium."

n. A great depth: abyss.

o. Means "ruler." Our word "dynasty."

Some Prepositions That Contain an υ

συν = with   ὑπο = under or by   ὑπερ = over or for

Scriptures

For you have died, and your life is hid _____ _____ _____ _____ (Col. 3:3).
                                        σὺν   χριστῷ   ἐν   θεῷ

Sin shall not rule over you, since you are not _____ _____ but _____
_____ (Rom. 6:14).   ὑπὸ   νόμον   ὑπὸ
χάριν

The _____ is not _____ his teacher, nor the servant _____ his _____
     μαθητὴς   ὑπὲρ   ·ὑπὲρ   κύριον
(Matt. 10:24).

<hr>

Exercise Six

Cognates with These Prepositions Used as Prefixes

Select the best definition for each of these Greek words.

___ 1. συναγωγη
___ 2. συνοδια
___ 3. hypnotism
___ 4. ὑπερβολη
___ 5. συνδρομη
___ 6. hypodermic
___ 7. hyperactive
___ 8. συμφωνια
___ 9. ὑποκριτης
___ 10. ὑποκρισις

a. A walking together, cooperation: synod (includes the word ὁδος, path).

b. A rushing together; we use the English derivative to mean a collection of symptoms: syndrome.

c. Over-active

d. Harmonious sounds; a form of συν plus φωνη became English "symphony."

e. Under the skin.

f. συν plus αγω (lead) gives us the word for a Jewish gathering place.

g. Outstanding; exaggeration; a term used in English literature: hyperbole. Add the Greek word ὑπερ to a form of βαλλω, "throw."

h. Comes from ὑπνος, which means "sleep."

i. hypocrisy

j. hypocrite

Lesson Twelve

Picture of a Field

Write the Greek words from the picture in the blanks.

1. Botany is the study of plants. Plants = _____
2. Greek word for rainbow became the name of a flower: _____
3. Chrysalis, the hard, gold-colored shell around a caterpillar which is turning into a butterfly, comes from this word meaning gold: _____
4. This flower name comes from the Greek word for star: _____
5. Helium; this element got its name because it was first discovered on the sun: _Sun = _____.
6. Seed: _____ _____
7. Crystal: _____
8. River: _____

63

9. Valuable substance we drill for in rocks (petroleum) comes from this word for rock: _____.

10. Air-filled (pneumatic) comes from this word which means wind or spirit: _____.

11. A hippopotamus is a horse _____ of the river _____.

12. Science of farming, agriculture, comes from the word for field: _____

Compound Words

Write the Greek words from the picture on page 63 that were combined to form these English words.

13. thermometer _____ + _____
14. anemometer _____ + _____
15. hippopotamus _____ + _____
16. astrology _____ + _____
17. astronomy _____ + _____
18. petrology _____ + _____
19. lithography _____ + _____
20. ichthyologist _____ + _____
21. chlorophyll _____ + _____
22. agronomy _____ + _____
23. dendrology _____ + _____
24. xylophone _____ + _____

Exercise Two

The Famous Secret Code of Early Christians

= ιχθυς

Write the English equivalent of each of these Greek words in the blanks.

ι is for Ιησους _____
χ is for Χριστος _____
θ is for θεου _____ _____
υ is for υιος _____
ς is for σωτηρ _____

Some Scriptures

It is important that you carefully pronounce each Greek word in this section because the scripture exercises are the only exercises from which you learn how to use accents. Of course, write in the English equivalents.

This then is the _____. The _____ is the _____ _____ (Luke 8:11).
    παραβολή   σπόρος   λόγος θεοῦ

The _____s of the _____ were for the _____ of the _____s
    φύλλα   ξύλου   θεραπείαν   ἐθνῶν
(Rev. 22:2).

ὑπακουω. The Greek word ακουω, "hear," plus ὑπο, "under," is usually translated "obey" in the New Testament. (This is not a cognate.) I enjoy this picturesque notion of "hearing and submitting" and this helps me remember the word.

Even the _____s and the sea _____ him! (Matt. 8:27).
    ἄνεμοι   ὑπακούουσιν

Here's the same concept in a noun form and a participle form (that is, an "-ing" word):

Though he were a _____, yet he learned _____ from the things he
    υἱός   ὑπακοήν
suffered, and by completing everything he became the source of salvation to all __those_____-ing him (Heb. 5:8–9).
    ὑπακούουσιν

Νικη was the name of the ancient Greek goddess of victory; there is a statue from ancient Greece with this name, and an American anti-aircraft missile of the 1950's was name after her.

This is the _____ that overcomes the world: our faith (1 John 5:4).
    νίκη

Can you put the word "victory" into verb form? You would get a word that means "to have victory," to "conquer," to "overcome." The following full quote includes both noun and verb forms based on νικη:

That which is born of God _____ the world; and this is the _____ which
    νικᾷ   νίκη
_____ the world, our faith (1 John 5:4).
    νικήσασα

Combine a verb form of νικη with ὑπερ (over), and the result is Romans 8:37:

But in all these things we _____ (literally, we "over-conquer") through him who loves us.
    ὑπερνικῶμεν

Exercise Three

Words Created from Greek Numbers

Write the Greek word in the long blank. Match the English words to the meanings below.

__ 1. dekameter   _____   πρωτος (1st)
__ 2. prototype   _____   δευτερος (2nd)
__ 3. hexagon   _____   τριτος (3rd)
__ 4. proton   _____   τεσσαρες (4)
__ 5. myriads   _____   πεντε (5)
__ 6. chiliasm   _____   ἑξ (6)
__ 7. decathlon   _____   ἑπτα (7)
__ 8. πεντεκοστη   _____   οκτα (8)
__ 9. δευτερονομος   _____   δεκα (10)
                                               δωδεκα (12)
                                               χιλιοι (1000)
                                               μυριαι (10,000)

a. A basic atomic particle.
b. A holiday 50 days after Easter: Pentecost.
c. Combined with μετρον, "measure," it means 10 meters.
d. The approach to end-times studies that sees Christ returning during the thousand-year time-span of Revelation 20. The equivalent term with a Latin root is millennialism.

e. Moses reads the law (νομος) to the people a second time at the end of their 40 years of wandering in this book of the Bible: Deuteronomy.
f. Combined with τυπος; it means "the first of its kind."
g. Combined with αθλεω (compete), it is an Olympic contest made up of ten events.
h. Lots and lots!
i. Six-sided figure.

Scripture Examples

Pronounce the Greek. Write in the English equivalent. Remember, if a word has a final "s" supplied, it is plural.

(Jesus speaking to his disciples:) You shall sit _____ _____ _____s
                                              ἐπὶ   δώδεκα   θρόνους

judging the _____ tribes of _____ (Matt. 19:28).
            δώδεκα   Ἰσραήλ

And the _____ part of the _____s was burnt (Rev. 8:7).
        τρίτον   δένδρων

(And I saw) _____ _____s burning with fire before the _____, which
            ἑπτὰ   λαμπάδες   θρόνου

are the _____ _____s ____ ____ (Rev. 4:5).
        ἑπτὰ   πνεύματα   θεοῦ

Exercise Four

Scientific Words

I. Geology

Match these Greek words with their English equivalents.

___ 1. αμεθυστος   a. Crystal
___ 2. χαλκηδων   b. Chrysolite
___ 3. χρυσολιθος   c. Topaz
___ 4. ορος   d. Amethyst
___ 5. σαπφειρος   e. Sapphire
___ 6. τοπαζιον   f. Chalcedony
___ 7. κρυσταλλος   g. This word means "mountain"; the geological word for mountain building is "orogeny."

II. Life Science

Select the best definition for each of these Greek words.

___ 8. ασπις
___ 9. νωτος
___ 10. χιτων
___ 11. φυτεια
___ 12. φυλη
___ 13. κητος
___ 14. συκομορεα
___ 15. γαμεω
___ 16. γενος
___ 17. θωραξ
___ 18. πλασσω, and related words πλασμα and πλαστος
___ 19. ορνις
___ 20. αυξω

h. A whale is a cetacean.
i. A type of tree: sycamore.
j. This word is used in classifying to label the major divisions of living things: phyla. In Greek it means "tribe."
k. Asp (a snake).
l. This word means "back." The elastic rod of cells in the embryo where the backbone is going to be is called a notochord.
m. A classification word for the next category above "species"; it means "kind." Genus.
n. This word means "marry," and is found in many scientific terms dealing with reproduction, such as "gamete."
o. This word means "plant," and is the last part of many terms used in botany, such as bryophyte, saprophyte.
p. A tunic (type of garment) became the name for a certain type of clam: the chiton.
q. Means "grow" in Greek; used to refer to the chemical substance at the growing edge of plant roots and stems: auxin.
r. Bird. Source of the word "ornithology."
s. Means "to form"; varieties of this word refer to the fluid part of substances, to an organized particle, as in chloro*plast*, and to "plastic" surgery.
t. The middle part of an insect's body; means "breastplate" in Greek.

Lesson Thirteen

Exercise One

Combining Throat-Letters

When there are two "throat-letters" (such as "g"), the first is pronounced like the "ng" in singer.

αγγελος means "messenger"

English version: _____

Pronounce the first γ like "ng."
Pronounce the second γ like a *hard* g.

Exercise Two

Combining Prefixes with αγγελος

__ 1. αρχη (chief) + αγγελος = αρχαγγελος
__ 2. ευ (good) + αγγελιον (message) = ευαγγελιον

Match to correct explanation above.

    a. good news
    b. a chief angel—archangel

Example of ευ + αγγελος

As a Noun	__ 3. ευαγγελιον (good message)
As a Verb	__ 4. ευαγγελιζω (give a good message)
Another Noun	__ 5. ευαγγελιστης (one who gives a good message)

Match to these English translations (commonly used in Bible):

    a. proclaimer   b. gospel   c. preach

Exercise Three

Changing to English Letters

In the blank write the appropriate English word.

ευαγγελιστης (good-message-giver) Take off the ending (ης), change υ to v, and write γγ as ng, and you get: _____

ευαγγελιζω (tell good news) Change the last letter to a silent e: _____

Now try Luke 2:10–11: Pronounce the Greek and translate into English.

And the _____ said (to the shepherds), "Do not fear; for behold, I
          ἄγγελος

_____ to you about a great joy which will be to all the people."
εὐαγγελίζομαι

I am not ashamed of the _____, for it is the _____ ____ _____
                       εὐαγγέλιον   δύναμις   θεοῦ

unto salvation for all who believe (Rom. 1:16).

Exercise Four

Other Words Formed with αρχη ("Chief" or "Old" or "Beginning")

Select the best definition for each of these Greek words.

___ 1. πατριαρχης   a. We use this term to mean someone who plans a
___ 2. αρχαιος   building; in Greek it means the master builder.
___ 3. αντιχριστος   b. Patriarch: an honored male ancestor.
___ 4. αρχιτεκτων   c. Archaic
                    d. A powerful figure of the end-time who sets him-
                       self against Jesus.

Pronounce the Greek and translate into English.

According to the _____ ____ _____ given to me, I laid a foundation as a
                 χάριν   θεοῦ

_____ _____; others built upon it. . . . No other foundation can be
σοφὸς   ἀρχιτέκτων

laid besides the one that is laid, who is _____ _____ (1 Cor. 3:10–11).
                                         Ἰησοῦς   Χριστός

Exercise Five

Words with αι Which Became e When They Were Taken into English

Match these Greek words with their English equivalents.

___ 1. αιων   a. demon
___ 2. Αιγυπτος   b. gangrene
___ 3. δαιμων   c. Egypt
___ 4. αινιγμα   d. eon
___ 5. γαγγραινα   e. enigma (puzzle)
___ 6. αἱρετικος   f. heretical
___ 7. αἱμα   g. <u>hemo</u>globin (means "blood")

First John, Chapter One

The blanks in the following quotation are for words you have learned so far; sometimes the meanings might be variations of the meanings you have so far associated with these words.

That which was _____ the _____, which we heard, which we saw with
             ἀπ' *   ἀρχῆς

our _____s, what we beheld and our _____s touched, concerning
    οφθαλμοῖς   χεῖρες

the _____ of _____—_____ the _____ appeared, ____ we saw ____
   λόγου   ζωῆς   καὶ   ζωὴ   καὶ   καὶ

_____ ____ announce to you the eternal _____ which was with the
μαρτυροῦμεν   καὶ   ζωὴν

_____ _____ shown to you—what we saw and heard we announce also to
πατέρα   καὶ

you so that you also may have fellowship with us. ____ our fellowship is with
                                   καὶ

the _____ ____ with his _____ _____. ____ these things (we)
   πατρὸς   καὶ   υἱοῦ   Ἰησοῦ   Χριστοῦ   καὶ

_____ so that our joy might be full. ____ this is the _____ which we
γράφομεν   καὶ   ἀγγελία

heard _____ him ____ announce to you: that _____ is _____ _____ dark-
     ἀπ' *   καὶ   θεὸς   φῶς   καὶ

ness is not in Him at all. If we say that we have fellowship with Him _____
                                            καὶ

walk ____ darkness, we lie and do not do the truth. But if we walk ____ the
    ἐν   ἐν

_____ as He is ____ the _____, we have fellowship with _____ ____
φωτὶ   ἐν   φωτὶ   ἀλλήλων   καὶ

the _____ of _____ his _____ cleanses us _____ all sin.
   αἷμα   Ἰησοῦ   υἱοῦ   ἀπὸ

* Contraction of απο.

Exercise Six

Reviewing the Doubled Throat-Letters

1. γγ (English "ng – g") αγγελος, "messenger"
   Spell in English: _____

2. γχ (English nch) αγχυρα
   Spell in English: _____
   Also spelled αγκυρα

3. γξ (English nx) λαρυγξ
   Spell in English: _____

Scriptures

Rejoice as you share in the suffering _____ _____, so that you may also
                                            Χριστοῦ

be glad at the _____ of his _____ (1 Pet. 4:13).
             ἀποκαλύψει   δόξης

My _____ and my _____ was not with enticing _____s of _____
   λόγος   κήρυγμά   λόγοις   σοφίας
. . . (1 Cor. 2:4).

They did not find any, though many _____s came forward (Matt.
26:60).   ψευδομαρτύρων

They ordained _____s in every church (Acts 14:23).
            πρεσβυτέρους

_____ rebuked it, and the _____ went out (Matt. 17:18).
 Ἰησοῦς   δαιμόνιον

Which hope we have as an _____ of the _____ (Heb. 6:19).
                ἄγκυραν   ψυχῆς

Their _____ is an open _____ (Rom. 3:13).
    λάρυγξ   τάφος

Exercise Seven

Capital Letters

Guess which capital letters and small letters go together. Check your answers below.

1. __ H	a. ρ
2. __ Θ	b. φ
3. __ P	c. η
4. __ Φ	d. θ
5. __ Λ	e. σ
6. __ Π	f. δ
7. __ Σ	g. λ
8. __ Δ	h. π
9. __ Ξ	i. ω
10. __ Y	j. ξ
11. __ Ω	k. γ
12. __ Γ	l. υ

The Greek Letters

Caps	Small	Name	Sounds like	What each letter was changed to when Greek words were written in English
A	α	ἄλφα	f<u>a</u>ther	a
B	β	βῆτα	b	b
Γ	γ	γάμμα	hard g	both hard and soft g
Δ	δ	δέλτα	d	d
E	ε	ἒ ψιλόν	p<u>e</u>t	e
Z	ζ	ζῆτα	a<u>dz</u>	z
H	η	ἦτα	<u>ei</u>ght	e or long e
Θ	θ	θῆτα	<u>th</u>ink	th
I	ι	ἰῶτα	p<u>i</u>n or mach<u>i</u>ne	i or y or j
K	κ	κάππα	k	k/c, both hard and soft
Λ	λ	λάμβδα	l	l
M	μ	μῦ	m	m
N	ν	νῦ	n	n
Ξ	ξ	ξῖ (ksee)	ta<u>x</u>i	x
O	ο	ὂ μικρόν	l<u>o</u>g	o
Π	π	πῖ	p	p
P	ρ	ῥῶ	r	r
Σ	σ & ς	σίγμα	s	s
T	τ	ταῦ	t	t
Y	υ	ὖ ψιλόν	like German u*	y or v or u
Φ	φ	φῖ	f	ph
X	χ	χῖ	like German a<u>ch</u>	ch
Ψ	ψ	ψῖ	ps	ps
Ω	ω	ὦ μέγα	n<u>o</u>te	o or long o

*Put lips like "oo" and say "ee."

Combinations

In γγ, γχ, and γκ speak the first γ like "ng." αυ like "cow," ευ like "feud," ου like "food," υι like "wee." αι like "aisle," ει like "eight."

Accents ˇˆ all sound the same. ʽ = breathe hard, like h sound. ʼ = don't make h sound.

Lesson Fourteen

For Practice with Capital Letters

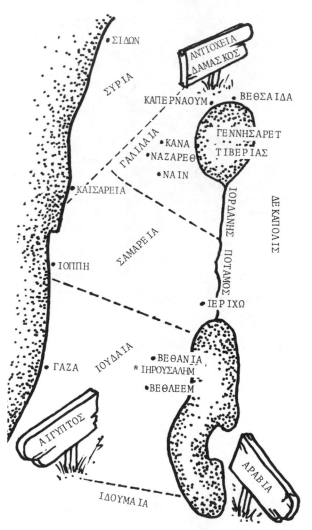

Here are the place names in English. Find them and copy in Greek small letters on your own sheet of paper.

Seas
Tiberias
Gennesaret

River
Jordan River

Regions
Syria
Galilee
Decapolis
Samaria
Judea
Idumaea

Cities
Jerusalem
Caesarea
Capernaum
Sidon
Antioch
Damascus
Bethsaida

Towns:
Bethlehem
Bethany
Jericho
Cana
Nazareth
Nain
Joppa
Gaza

Countries
Egypt
Arabia

Books of the New Testament

For practice with capital letters.

Number them in the order they occur in the Bible. Then write them out using small Greek letters.

I. Gospels and Acts

1. ΚΑΤΑ ΜΑΡΚΟΝ   4. ΠΡΑΞΕΙΣ ΑΠΟΣΤΟΛΩΝ

_____   _____

2. ΚΑΤΑ ΙΩΑΝΝΗΝ   5. ΚΑΤΑ ΜΑΘΘΑΙΟΝ

_____   _____

3. ΚΑΤΑ ΛΟΥΚΑΝ

_____

The word κατα means "according to." The word πραξεις reminds me of the word "practices." The word αποστολων means "of apostles."

II. Letters of Paul

1. ΠΡΟΣ ΕΦΕΣΙΟΥΣ   7. ΠΡΟΣ ΚΟΡΙΝΘΙΟΥΣ Β

_____   _____

2. ΠΡΟΣ ΓΑΛΑΤΑΣ   8. ΠΡΟΣ ΤΙΜΟΘΕΟΝ Β

_____   _____

3. ΠΡΟΣ ΦΙΛΗΜΟΝΑ   9. ΠΡΟΣ ΘΕΣΣΑΛΟΝΙΚΕΙΣ Α

_____   _____

4. ΠΡΟΣ ΡΩΜΑΙΟΥΣ   10. ΠΡΟΣ ΤΙΜΟΘΕΟΝ Α

_____   _____

5. ΠΡΟΣ ΤΙΤΟΝ   11. ΠΡΟΣ ΘΕΣΣΑΛΟΝΙΚΕΙΣ Β

_____   _____

6. ΠΡΟΣ ΚΟΛΟΣΣΑΕΙΣ   12. ΠΡΟΣ ΚΟΡΙΝΘΙΟΥΣ Α

_____   _____

13. ΠΡΟΣ ΦΙΛΙΠΠΗΣΙΟΥΣ

_____

The word προς means "to." The letters α and β are used where we would use I & II, or 1 & 2.

III. Hebrews to the end

1. ΠΕΤΡΟΥ Α

   _____

2. ΙΩΑΝΝΟΥ Β

   _____

3. ΙΟΥΔΑ

   _____

4. ΙΑΚΩΒΟΥ

   _____

5. ΑΠΟΚΑΛΥΨΙΣ ΙΩΑΝΝΟΥ

   _____

6. ΙΩΑΝΝΟΥ Γ

   _____

7. ΠΡΟΣ ΕΒΡΑΙΟΥΣ

   _____

8. ΙΩΑΝΝΟΥ Α

9. ΠΕΤΡΟΥ Β

   _____

Note that the breathing marks (' and ') are not used sometimes in capital letter writing, so there is nothing to designate that "Hebrews" starts with an h.

Many of these end with -ου, for "of"; (Letter) "of James" is the intended meaning.

Remember the 3rd letter of the Greek alphabet is γ.

This is the end of Part I.

You have:

1. Become "at home" with the Greek alphabet and pronunciation.*
2. Seen dozens of Greek words that remind you of English words.
3. Learned a few Greek words that are not like English: και (and), οικος (house), and the prepositions (εν, απο, επι, etc.).
4. Seen that Greek words change their endings. In the next part you will find out why and how.
5. Seen the derivation of a great many religious and technical terms.

Many additional "cognates" will be found scattered throughout the coming pages.

In Part II you will learn:

1. Endings for nouns which show their purpose in the sentence.
2. How to make the word "the."
3. How to use adjectives and show which nouns they describe.
4. Which endings are to be used after certain prepositions.
5. How to make the present-tense endings of verbs.
6. How to make and translate entire sentences.

But that sounds like grammar!

You have absorbed some Greek grammar already:

1. You have seen that the ου ending tells you to translate with the word "of" (unless another preposition is already there).
2. You have learned that there is no word for "a" in Greek, but that you can include it in translating at times.
3. You have learned that a small letter ι is found under the last letter of certain words following certain prepositions: εν οικῳ   εν λαμπᾳ

---

*There are a number of systems of pronunciation in use today in various schools. The system used in this book is that used by J. Gresham Machen in his *New Testament Greek for Beginners*.

Part II

INTRODUCING ENDINGS

In Part II, you will learn:

1. Eight endings to put on a verb, and the resulting meanings.

2. Eight endings to put on a noun, and the significance of each ending for the noun's place in the sentence.

3. That adjectives and the word "the" make use of these same noun endings.

4. That the words following a preposition make use of these same endings.

5. Some of the essential technical terms used in Greek grammar.

6. To use a chart illustrating other noun and adjective endings that perform the same purposes as the eight endings you will actually learn.

7. Common pronouns (he, they, etc.).

Since you will be concentrating on endings, this section will use a small number of Greek words, with which you will become very familiar.

Lesson Fifteen

A Review of Some Familiar Terms

Match each word in the sentences below to the descriptions found at the right.

1. John lifts stones.

   ____ ___ _____

   a. noun—name of a person, place, or thing.
   b. verb—action word.

2. The man lifts heavy rocks over

   ___ ___ ___ ____ ____ ___

   his head.

   __ ___

   a. noun
   b. verb
   c. adjective—describes a noun.
   d. preposition
   e. pronoun—takes the place of a noun.
   f. definite article

   Which noun in the sentence is "plural" (more than one)? _____.
   Which nouns are singular? _____, _____.

3. John gave Tom a large book.

   —,__ __ —,__ __ __ —,__

   a. noun
   b. verb
   c. adjective

   Use of nouns
   d. subject—who did the action.
   e. direct object—what the action was done to.
   f. indirect object—who received the direct object.

   The verb in the sentence is in _____ tense.
   (Present or past or future?)

4. John's friend gave Tom a new

_____ _____   ___ ___

book inside the library.

a. preposition
b. prepositional phrase
c. adjective

Use of nouns
d. subject
e. possessive—indicates belonging to.
f. indirect object
g. direct object
h. object of the preposition

Related Words

(Recognizing similar meanings despite differences in some letters).
What do these five words have in common:

Give   Gave   Gift   Giver   Given

There isn't a single letter they have in common except the "G," and yet we know they have something in common: they share a single basic meaning. They all have something to do with giving.

The same thing can happen in Greek. The purpose of this page is to open your eyes to some connections between words that might not seem obvious at first. The two words λεγω and λογος are related to each other, just as "give" and "gift" are related to each other. In this case, they both have something to do with "speaking." λεγω is a verb, and can be translated "speak" or "say." λογος is a noun, and is usually translated "word." The only letters they have in common are λ and γ, but they share the same general meaning.

Translate the words related to λογος in the following sentences.

Exercise Two

Four of these blanks are for verbs and the other two are for nouns.

1. Verily, verily I _____ unto you.
   λεγω

2. Thy _____ is a lamp unto my feet.
   λογος

3. Now He _____ to us, "Today is the day of salvation."
   λεγει

4. What do you _____?
   λεγεις

5. Jesus answered them, _____, "Take heed to all my _____s."
   λεγων   *λογους*

Exercise Three

Words Related to "καλ"

Words based on the root καλ have something to do with "calling."

Fill in the blanks with suitable English translations.

1. I _____ unto you.
   καλω
2. Whoever _____ on the name of the Lord shall be saved.
   καλει

Endings on Verbs

Greek can say "I call" with only one word: καλω

The ω on the end reveals that the subject of the sentence is "I."

The Greeks also have a word for "I" (εγω) which they can use as an option, for the sake of emphasis.

Therefore, "I call" can be either καλω or εγω καλω.

In a similar way, "you call" can be either καλεις or συ καλεις, and, "he calls" can be either καλει or αυτος καλει.

You have just seen three verb-endings:

Verbs end with ω when the subject is "I";

end with εις when the subject is "you"; and

end with ει when the subject is "he," "she," or "it."

These verb endings are called "personal endings."

"I" is called "first person,"

"You" is called "second person," and

"he," "she", and "it" are called "third person."

The word καλει is termed the "third person singular" of the verb καλεω.

You have also just seen three pronouns, which you should now add to your dictionary:

εγω means "I."

συ means "you."

αυτος means "he."

When the subject of your sentence is a noun, use the "third person" ending (-ει):

Man calls = ανθρωπος καλει
Mans speaks = ανθρωπος λεγει
God speaks = θεος λεγει
God wills = θεος θελει

Be sure these words are in your dictionary:

καλω = I call
λεγω = I speak or I say
θελω = I will (or want or wish)

Exercise Four

Drill on Verb-Endings

Matching: Match these Greek words with their English translations.

I. __ 1. θελω   a. you want
   __ 2. θελεις   b. I want
   __ 3. θελει   c. he wants

II. __ 4. λεγω   a. he says
    __ 5. εγω λεγω   b. I say
    __ 6. λεγει
    __ 7. αυτος λεγει

III. __ 8. καλω   a. I want
     __ 9. εγω λεγω   b. he calls
     __10 θελω   c. apostle calls
     __11 καλεις   d. I call
     __12. λεγεις   e. prophct wants
     __13. συ θελεις   f. you say
     __14. αυτος καλει   g. disciple says
     __15. λεγει   h. you want
     __16. θελει   i. I say
     __17. αποστολος καλει j. he wants
     __18. μαθητης λεγει   k. you call
     __19. προφητης θελει l. he says

Plural Verb-Endings

"First person singular" is "I"; therefore, "first person plural" is "we" (many of us).

"We speak" = λεγομεν

"Second person plural" indicates "more than one of you"; if you were from Texas, you would say "you-all"; in Shakespeare's time, you would use the word "ye."

"Ye speak" = λεγετε

"Third person plural" is "they."

"They speak" = λεγουσι

(You will learn the pronouns "we," "ye," and "they" on a later page.)

The Plural Endings Then Are:

Verbs end with ομεν when the subject is "we,"
        with ετε when the subject is "ye," and
        with ουσι when the subject is "they" or a plural noun.

Examples with Plural Nouns as Subjects

Men call = ανθρωποι καλουσι
Brothers say = αδελφοι λεγουσι
Angels want = αγγελοι θελουσι
Lepers throw = λεπροι βαλλουσι
Apostles write = αποστολοι γραφουσι

(Did you notice that the -οι ending makes a *noun* into a plural?)

This Diagram Shows All the Endings

Verb Endings

When Subject Is	Singular	Plural	
1st Person (I)	-ω	-ομεν	(we)
2nd Person (you)	-εις	-ετε	(You all or ye)
3rd Person (he, she, it)	-ει	-ουσι	(They)

Set aside a few pages in your dictionary to copy the charts of endings, and to list the endings in alphabetical order for quick reference.

A letter ν is often added after the third person endings for smooth connections to the following word.

Exercise Five

Pronunciation Check

Match these Greek words with their pronunciations.

___ 1. λογους   a. law-goose   b. low-gauss
___ 2. λεγεις   a. leg-ice   b. leg-ace
___ 3. καλουσι   a. caw-Lucy   b. caw-lousy
___ 4. αυτος   a. ow-toss   b. aw-toce
___ 5. εγω   a. ee-go   b. egg-oh
___ 6. θελομεν   a. Thell-omen   b. Thell-aw-men

Meaning Check

Match these Greek words with their translations.

___ 7. αυτος λεγει   c. man says
___ 8. εγω λεγω   d. he says
___ 9. ανθρωπος λεγει   e. we say
___ 10. ανθρωπος βαλλει   f. I say
___ 11. καλουσι   g. man throws
___ 12. λεγομεν   h. they throw
___ 13. βαλλουσι   i. they call
___ 14. καλεις   j. you call
___ 15. θελετε   k. ye want

Two Other Endings

Another common ending is used when talking about the action in general, without any subject. We do this in English by using two words: "to call." The Greek equivalent is one word: καλειν = to call. This is called the "infinitive." One infinitive ending is -ειν.

One final ending. The "participle" is a complex subject in Greek grammar. For now, add "-ing" to your translation when you come across a Greek verb ending in -ων. Example: λεγων = saying.

Sentence Illustrating Several Verb Forms

θεος	λεγει,	λεγων,	θελω	καλειν	ανθρωπους
God	speaks,	saying,	"I want	to call	men."

The example above consists of four (4) verbs and two (2) nouns.

Circle the four (4) verbs.

The reason you do not recognize the ending on "men" is that we have not yet talked about noun-endings, only verb-endings.

Lesson Sixteen

Scriptures Using the Verb Forms You Know

Pronounce in Greek, translate, and check yourself.

(Jesus fell on his face, praying:) _____ _____, my _____, if it is pos-
καὶ λέγων πάτηρ
sible, remove this cup _____ me; nevertheless, not as _____ _____ but
ἀπ᾽ ἐγὼ θέλω
as ____ (Matt. 26:39).
σύ

If then _____ _____ him _____, how is he his _____ (Matt. 22:45)?
Δαυὶδ καλεῖ κύριον υἱὸς

It is not good <u>to take</u> the children's bread _____ _____ it to the dogs
(Mark 7:27). λαβεῖν καὶ βαλεῖν

Think not _____ among yourselves, <u>we have</u> _____ as our _____,
λέγειν ἔχομεν Ἀβραάμ πατέρα
for _____ to you that _____ is able <u>to raise up</u> children of _____ ____
λέγω θεὸς ἐγεῖραι* Ἀβραάμ ἐκ
these _____s (Matt. 3:9).
λίθων**

(The master of the vineyard answered,) "Is it not lawful for me <u>to do</u> what
_____ with my own?" (Matt. 20:15). ποιῆσαι*
θέλω

_____ no one _____ _____ wine into old wine-skins (Mark 2:22).
καὶ βάλλει νέον

---

* -αι is another "infinitive" ending—note the word "to" in the translation.

**ων here does not indicate a participle because λιθος is a noun.

(Pilate answered:) "Which of the two _____ that I release unto you?" They
$\underset{\theta \acute{\epsilon}\lambda\epsilon\tau\epsilon^1}{}$

said, "_____." _____ _____, to them, "What shall I do with _____ called
$\underset{\beta\alpha\rho\alpha\beta\beta\tilde{\alpha}\nu}{}$ $\underset{\Pi\iota\lambda\tilde{\alpha}\tau\varsigma\ \lambda\acute{\epsilon}\gamma\epsilon\iota^2}{}$ $\underset{\text{'}I\eta\sigma o\tilde{\nu}\nu}{}$

_____?" _____, "Crucify him" (Matt. 27:21–22).
$\underset{\chi\rho\iota\sigma\tau\acute{o}\nu}{}$ $\underset{\lambda\acute{\epsilon}\gamma o\upsilon\sigma\iota\nu^3}{}$

Examples of Verb Endings from First John

Perfect love _____ out fear (1 John 4:18).
$\underset{\beta\acute{\alpha}\lambda\lambda\epsilon\iota}{}$

_____ to you, children, because your sins have been forgiven (2:12).
$\underset{\Gamma\rho\acute{\alpha}\phi\omega}{}$

And _____ these things to you so your joy may be full (1:4).
$\underset{\gamma\rho\acute{\alpha}\phi o\mu\epsilon\nu}{}$

New Verbs Are Introduced before Some of the Following Passages

_____ = I have.
$\underset{\check{\epsilon}\chi\omega}{}$

The one who confesses the Son _____ the Father also (1 John 2:23).
$\underset{\check{\epsilon}\chi\epsilon\iota}{}$

If our hearts condemn us, _____ boldness with God (3:21).
$\underset{\check{\epsilon}\chi o\mu\epsilon\nu}{}$

I have written these things to you that ye may know that _____ eternal
life (5:13).
$\underset{\check{\epsilon}\chi\epsilon\tau\epsilon}{}$

The one _____ the Son _____ the life; the one not _____ the Son _____
$\underset{\check{\epsilon}\chi\omega\nu^4}{}$ $\underset{\check{\epsilon}\chi\epsilon\iota}{}$ $\underset{\check{\epsilon}\chi\omega\nu}{}$ $\underset{\theta\epsilon o\tilde{\nu}}{}$

_____ not the life (5:12).
$\underset{\check{\epsilon}\chi\epsilon\iota^5}{}$

1. θελετε is "ye will," but since this is a question, translate as "will ye" or "do ye will" (or, "do ye want," or "do ye wish").

2. Your Bible might translate this as a past tense; Matthew uses present tense in the original as part of his dramatic style.

3. This is the ending ουσι, and the ν is added at the end just for smoothness in the sentence, as we sometimes say "an" instead of "a."

4. Word for word = The one having. A common translation in a case like this would be "He who has" or "the one who has."

5. Word for word = has not the life. You could translate, "does not have the life."

_____ = I remain
μένω

The anointing which you received from him _____ in you, and _____ no
                                         μένει   ἔχετε

need that anyone should teach you (1 John 2:27).

Everyone _____ in him does not sin (3:6).
         μένων

_____ is love, and the one _____ in love _____ ____ _____, _____
Θεὸς   μένων   μένει ἐν θεῷ   καὶ

_____ _____ in him (4:16).
θεὸς   μένει

_____ = I do.
ποιῶ

Everyone _____ sin also _____ lawlessness (1 John 3:4).
         ποιῶν   ποιεῖ

You are of your father the devil, and _____ _____ the desires of your
father (John 8:44).   θέλετε   ποιεῖν

Lesson Seventeen

Pronounce in Greek; translate into English.

μισῶ = I hate.

Do not wonder, brothers, if the _____ _____ you (1 John 3:13).
            κόσμος   μισεῖ

γινώσκω = I know.

_____ is greater than your _____ s _____ _____ all (1 John 3:20).
Θεός   καρδίας   καὶ   γινώσκει

And in this _____ that _____ in us—he has given us his Spirit
(1 John 3:24). γινώσκομεν   μένει

In this _____ that _____ in him and he in us (1 John 4:13).
        γινώσκομεν   μένομεν

In this _____ the Spirit _____ (1 John 4:2).
        γινώσκετε   θεοῦ

βλέπω = I see.

_____ another law in my members . . . (Rom. 7:23).
Βλέπω

And why _____ the speck in your brother's eye . . . ? (Matt. 7:3).
        βλέπεις

(Remember, there is no special ending for questions, just the question mark. You have to use correct English to make it sound like a question.)

You have used βάλλω, "throw." Now put the preposition εκ in front as a prefix:

But the Pharisees said, "_____ the demons through the prince of the
                        ἐκβάλλει

_____ s" (Matt. 9:34).
δαιμονίων

And calling the _____ _____s to himself, he gave them authority

δώδεκα   μαθητὰς

_____ unclean spirits (Matt. 10:1).v

ἐκβάλλειν

And if _____ through <u>Beelzebub</u> _____ the _____s, through

ἐγώ   βεελζεβοὺλ   ἐκβάλλω   δαιμόνια

whom do your sons _____? (Matt. 12:27).

ἐκβάλλουσιν

Verses Related to Nouns and Adjectives You Know

Pronounce in Greek; translate into English.

_____ is related to the noun _____, "love."

ἀγαπῶ   ἀγάπη

Remember the comma above the α simply means, "Do not make an h sound."

Examples from 1 John:

If anyone says, "_____ _____," and hates his _____, he is a liar
(1 John 4:20).   ἀγαπῶ   θεόν   ἀδελφὸν

The one not _____ _____ in death (1 John 3:14b).

ἀγαπῶν   μένει

The one _____ that he is in the light, and _____ his brother, is in the

λέγων   μισῶν

darkness; the one _____ his _____ _____ in the light (1 John 2:9–10).

ἀγαπῶν   ἀδελφὸν   μένει

Beloved, love one another, because love is of God, and everyone _____ is
born of God and _____ God (1 John 4:7).   ἀγαπῶν

γινώσκει

Here is the same sentence showing the nouns used for "beloved" and "love":

_____, love one another, because _____ is of God, and everyone

Ἀγαπητοί   ἀγάπη

_____ is born of God . . . (1 John 4:7, 8).

ἀγαπῶν

The following sentence shows that some verbs change the ο in ομεν to an ω.
(More details on these changes in Part V.)

In this _____ that _____ the children (of) _____, when

γινώσκομεν   ἀγαπῶμεν   θεοῦ

_____ _____ (____)_____ his commands (1 John 5:2).

ἀγαπῶμεν θεὸν καὶ   ποιῶμεν

The following example shows that some nouns change the vowel at the point where the stem and the ending connect. You would expect the word to end with ετε:

Woe to you Pharisees, because _____ the upper seats in the syna-
gogues . . . (Luke 11:43).   ἀγαπᾶτε

_____ = I like or love (notice resemblance to φιλος, "friend," and φιλια,
φιλεω

"love" or "friendship").

The father _____ the Son and shows him everything which _____ (John 5:20).
         φιλεῖ   ποιεῖ

Exercise One

Guessing at Related Verbs

Pronounce these Greek words; translate into English.

On the blank in front of each scripture, put the letter of the noun or verb from the word list on page 92 that is related to one of the verbs in the quotation.

____ 1. For ___ _____ about them that ___ _____ a zeal for God, but
          μαρτυρῶ   ἔχουσιν

not according to knowledge (Rom. 10:2). (Did you understand the word
that ended with ν? It was the ουσι ending with ν added.)

____ 2. Behold, ___ _____ you as sheep in the midst of wolves (Matt.
10:16).   ἀποστέλλω

___ ___ ____ 3. The _____ _____ wherever __ _____, and
                   πνεῦμα   πνεῖ   θέλει

__ _____ the _____ of it (John 3:8).
ἀκούεις   φωνὴν

____ 4. Now ___ _____ in part and ___ _____ in part . . .
             γινώσκομεν   προφητεύομεν
(1 Cor. 13:9).

____ 5. One and the same _____ _____ all these things, distributing
                          πνεῦμα   ἐνεργεῖ
to each as he wills (1 Cor. 12:11).

____ 6. You put a lamp on a stand, _____ ___ _____ on all those in the
_____ (Matt. 5:15).   καὶ   λάμπει
οἰκίᾳ

_____ 7. Having _____s __ _____ not, and having ears ___ _____
        οφθαλμοὺς βλέπετε   ἀκούετε

not (Mark 8:18).

Word list of related nouns:

a. πνευμα   d. ενεργεια   g. "hear" *a verb from Part I*

b. λαμπας   e. προφητης   h. θελημα (will, wish, desire)

c. μαρτυρ   f. αποστολος

Verb Possibilities Summarized

Verb construction is complicated and will be explained in Part V. This page will survey the possibilities and introduce the terminology you will need to use a reference book.

    I. First there are the six personal endings:

	Singular	Plural
1st Person	I throw	we throw
2nd Person	you throw	ye throw
3rd Person	he throws	they throw

These can also be translated: I am throwing, you are throwing, etc.

Remember, each of these is only one word in Greek. βαλλει = He is throwing

    II. The example above is in present tense. There is also future tense (I will throw, you will throw, etc.), and there are four different kinds of past tense. Simplified listing:

        Imperfect—I was throwing, etc.

        Aorist—I threw. A simple statement without reference to when it happened. The most common form for past.

        Perfect—I threw. An act in the past with results still occurring in the present. (Example: "Jesus died and rose." We would put "died" in the aorist, because it was a single act; we would put "rose" in the perfect, because although it happened in the past, He is still risen.)

        Pluperfect—I had thrown, etc.

Multiplying the 6 tenses x the 6 persons = 36 different looking verbs, each with a different meaning.

Example: "throw," in third person imperfect = he was throwing.

    III. All 6 tenses listed above are in active voice. All 36 possibilities can also be found in passive voice (I am being thrown, etc.) and in middle voice (I am throwing myself, etc.), adding up to 108 different constructions.

Example: Second person singular aorist passive: You were thrown (one word in Greek)!

IV. All possibilities given so far are in indicative mood.
There are also:

> **Imperative** mood, for commands: "Throw"!
>
> **Subjunctive** mood. Many uses: one example would be to show possibility: (if) I should throw.
>
> **Optative** mood. Also many possibilities. Example: I would throw.
>
> **Infinitive** mood. "To throw."

These moods are not found in all tenses, so we don't have to multiply 108 x 5.

Example: Third person plural perfect subjunctive: They should have thrown.

V. Participles (such as –en and –ing words) occur in present, future, aorists, and perfect. Participles can be used with an adverbial sense, or less commonly as adjectives or nouns, and each can get many different endings.

Do not try to remember the facts on this page now. This page was included only to round off the introduction to verb endings, and to show you what is coming in Part V.

Lesson Eighteen

Four Uses for Nouns

Subjects

Shown in English by coming first in the sentence.
Shown in Greek by having the ending -ος. ανθρςπος λεγει = man says.

If subject is plural, the ending to use is -οι.
ανθρωποι λεγουσι = men say.

Possession

Shown in two different ways in English:

1. With an ending (apostrophe s):
2. By using the word "of":

God's law = law of God

Shown in Greek in one way: The ending ου. λογος θεου = word of God
= (God's word).

Exercise One

Translating

In this workbook, we will always use the word "of" when we see the ου ending. Try these:

I.
___ 1. ανθρωπος θεου   a. house of man

___ 2. οικος ανθρωπου   b. book of Mark

___ 3. βιβλος Μαρκου   c. man of God

If possessor is plural, use ending -ων.
οικος ανθρωπων = house of men.

(ων looks like the participle ending you learned earlier. If ων ends a noun, it designates possessive plural; if ων ends a verb, it designates a participle.)

Object

Shown in English by coming after the verb: Paul helped Mark.
Shown in Greek by the ending ov: Παυλος helped Μαρκον.

II.

___ 4. Παυλος helped ανθρωπον   a. Paul helped Philip

___ 5. Παυλος helped Μαρκον   b. Paul helped Mark

___ 6. Παυλος helped Φιλιππον   c. Paul helped man

If object is plural, use ους.
παυλος helped ανθρωπους = Paul helped men

Since meanings are shown by endings, word order can be mixed up without obscuring the meaning of the sentence:

"ανθρωπον helped παυλος" and "ανθρωπον παυλος" helped both mean, "Paul helped man."

III. Using all three endings

___ 7. ανθρωπος θεου saw Πετρον   a. Man saw house of Peter

___ 8. ανθρωπος saw οικον Πετρου   b. Peter saw house of God

___ 9. Πετρος saw οικον θεου   c. Man of God saw Peter

IV. Using plurals and mixing up word order

___ 10. οικον ανθρωπων saw Πετρος   a. Peter saw houses of man

___ 11. οικους ανθρωπου saw Πετρος   b. Men saw houses of Peter

___ 12. οικους Πετρου ανθρωποι saw   c. Peter saw house of men

Indirect Object

Shown in two ways in English:

1. Using the word "to": Peter gave the book to Mark.
2. Using a special word order; putting the word in between the verb and the object: Peter gave Mark the book.

Shown in one way in Greek: The ending ω. We will call this ending the dative ending, and we will always translate by using the word "to."

Πετρος λεγει Μαρκω = Peter speaks to Mark

For plural, use οις. ανθρωποις = to men

V. Matching:

___ 13. εγω gave ανθρωπω   a. Peter gave to Timothy

___ 14. Τιμοθεος gave Παυλω   b. Timothy gave to Paul

___ 15. Πετρος gave Τιμοθεω   c. I gave to man

All four endings:

Φιλιππος	gave	βιβλον	Μαρκου	Παυλω
Philip		book	of Mark	to Paul
Subject		object	possessive	dative

Exercise Two

Chart of Noun Endings

	Singular	Plural
Subject	-ος	-οι
Possessive (use "of")	-ου	-ων
Dative (use "to")	-ω	-οις
Object	-ον	-ους

Matching

Match these Greek words with their English equivalents.

___ 1. θεου   a. to man

___ 2. Μαρκω   b. of God

___ 3. Παυλου   c. to men

___ 4. βιβλων   d. of books

___ 5. βιβλοις   e. to Mark

___ 6. ανθρωπω   f. of Paul

___ 7. ανθρωποις   g. of men

___ 8. ανθρωπων   h. to books

Words after prepositions use these same endings.

Sentences using singulars and plurals:

ανθρωποι		βιβλους	νομων	λεπροις	εν οικω
men	gave	books	of laws	to lepers	in house
Subject	Verb	Object	Possessive	Dative	Prepositional Phrase

Μαρκος	θελει	γραφειν	λογους	νομου	ανθρωποις	θεου
Mark	wants	to write	words	of law	to men	of God
Subject	Verb	Infinitive	Object	Possessive	Dative	Possess
	Verbs					

Exercise Three

Pronunciation Check

Match the Greek with its pronunciation.

____ 1. λογος   a. low-goce   b. law-gawce
____ 2. λογου   a. log-goo   b. low-go
____ 3. λογω   a. log-go   b. low-go
____ 4. λογον   a. low-gov   b. log-gone
____ 5. λογοι   a. log-goo   b. log-goi
____ 6. λογων   a. law-gone   b. log-own
____ 7. λογοις   a. log-goose   b. log-oice
____ 8. λογους   a. log-oce   b. log-goose

Meaning of Nouns with Endings

Match the Greek with the best translation.

____ 9. λογοις   a. to word
____ 10. λογοι   b. to words
____ 11. λογω   c. of words
____ 12. λογος   d. word (subject)
____ 13. λογου   e. word (object)
____ 14. λογον   f. words (subject)
____ 15. λογων   g. words (object)
____ 16. λογους   h. of word
____ 17. θεου   i. to men
____ 18. θεω   j. of men
____ 19. ανθρωποις   k. to God
____ 20. ανθρωπων   l. of God

Verbs Plus Nouns

Match the Greek with the best translation.

___ 21. γραφω λογους   m. to write word
___ 22. γραφει λογους   n. I write word
___ 23. γραφω λογον   o. I write words
___ 24. γραφειν λογον   p. he writes words
___ 25. λεγει Μαρκῳ   q. to speak words
___ 26. λεγω Μαρκῳ   r. I speak words
___ 27. λεγειν λογους   s. I speak to Mark
___ 28. λεγω λογους   t. he speaks to Mark

Exercise Four

Scriptures Using Noun Endings

In each set of parentheses, write two letters. First, write a capital letter indicating whether the ending of the word indicates that the word is:

S (subject)   D (dative)
P (possessive)   O (direct object)

Then write a small s or p to indicate singular or plural. For smooth English, you may add the words "a" and "the" to the sentences.

1. Follow me and I will make you fishers _____ . (Matt. 4:19).
                                            ἀνθρώπων ( )

2. Glory _____ in the highest . . . (Luke 2:14).
        θεῷ ( )

3. If _____ _____ him _____, how is he his _____?
     Δαυὶδ   καλεῖ   κύριον ( )   υἱὸς ( )
(Matt. 22:45).

4. _____ about them that _____ _____ _____
    Μαρτυρῶ   ἔχουσιν   ζῆλον ( )   θεοῦ ( )
(Rom. 10:2).

5. The Kingdom of heaven is similar _____ who sowed
good seed . . . (Matt. 13:24).   ἀνθρώπῳ ( )

6. _____ _____, and according to our law he ought to die, be-
   ἔχομεν   νόμον ( )
cause he made himself _____ _____ (John 19:7).
             υἱὸν ( )   θεοῦ ( )

7. _____ _____ are upon the righteous (1 Pet. 3:12).
  Ὀφθαλμοὶ (   )   Κυρίου (   )

8. Whoever has left houses or _____ or sisters or father or
                               ἀδελφοὺς (   )
  mother or children or _____ for my name's sake . . . (Matt.
                         ἀγροὺς (   )
  19:29).

9. While he was still far from the house, the centurion sent _____,
  _____ to him . . . (Luke 7:6).   φίλους (   )
  λέγων

10. They ordained _____ in every church (Acts 14:23).
                  πρεσβυτέρους (   )

11. Ye received it not as _____ _____, but as it is in
                         λόγον (   )   ἀνθρώπων (   )
  truth: _____ _____ (1 Thess. 2:13).
         λόγον (   )   θεοῦ (   )

12. Do not lay up for yourselves _____ upon earth (Matt. 6:19).
                                 θησαυροὺς (   )

13. He went away from them about the cast _____ (Luke 22:41).
                                          λίθου (   )

14. _____ wore a garment made from hairs _____ (Matt. 3:4).
    Ἰωάννης   καμήλου (   )

Lesson Nineteen

Sentences with Noun and Verb Endings

Translate into English on a separate piece of paper, and check answers on answer page. You'll need to refer to the charts on the previous pages. After you have completed this, then start with the English sentences and try to translate the odd-numbered sentences back into Greek.

A. Subject − Verb − Object
1. ανθρωποι βαλλουσι λιθους.
2. αδελφος γραφει λογους.

B. Subject − Verb − Dative
3. θεος λεγει Φιλιππω.
4. αδελφοι λεγουσι λεπροις.

C. Pronoun subject − Verb − Dative
5. εγω γραφω Μαρκω.
6. αυτος γραφει Παυλω.

D. Subject "understood" − Verb − Object
7. βαλλω λιθον.
8. γραφεις λογους.

E. Subject − Verb − Object − Possessive
9. αδελφοι γραφουσι νομον θεου.
10. Μαρκος λεγει λογον ανθρωπων.

F. Subject − Verb − Dative − Possessive
11. δουλος (slave) γραφει ανθρωποις θεου.
12. λεπροι λεγουσι δουλοις Παυλου.

G. Subject "understood" − Verb − Object − Possessive − Dative
13. λεγομεν λογους θεου ανθρωποις.
14. λεγουσι λογον νομου Φιλιππω.

H. Subject "understood" – Verb – Infinitive – Object
    15. θελω λεγειν λογους.
    16. διδασκει (he teaches) γραφειν λογους.

I. Subject – Verb – Object – Prepositional Phrase
    17. Κορνηλιος γραφει βιβλον εν οικω.
    18. θεος αγαπει ανθρωπους εν κοσμω.

J. Subject – Verb – Dative – Prepositional Phrase
    19. δουλοι λεγουσι σκορπιω επι οικω.
    20. Νικοδημος γραφει αδελφω επι λιθω.

K. Subject – Possessive – Verb – Object – Possessive – Dative – Possessive
– Prepositional Phrase – Possessive
    21. ανθρωποι θεου γραφουσι λογους βιβλου αδελφοις Παυλου εν οικω
        προφητων.
    22. αδελφοι λεπρων λεγουσι λογους θεου ανθρωποις θεου εν οικω
        θεου.

Lesson Twenty

Adjectives

The adjective gets the same ending as the noun it is describing.

> good man = καλος ανθρωπος
> bad law = κακος νομος

If the noun is plural, the adjective also must have the plural ending.

> good laws = καλοι νομοι
> bad men = κακοι ανθρωποι

If the adjective describes the object of the sentence, it gets the same ending as the object. In this example, it is plural:

> God gives us good things = θεος gives us καλους λογους

A Special Usage for Adjectives

Sometimes the adjective appears without a noun. You have to supply a word like "one" or "thing" as you translate:

> good one writes = καλος γραφει
> good ones speak = καλοι λεγουσι
> God gives us good things = θεος gives us καλα

The adjective ἁγιος means "holy." The backwards comma above the first letter means you are to pronounce an h sound, so the word is pronounced "hah-gee-aws."

> holy man speaks = ἁγιος ανθρωπος λεγει
> holy one says = ἁγιος λεγει
> holy ones write = ἁγιοι γραφουσι
> God speaks to holy ones = θεος λεγει ἁγιοις

In most English Bible translations, "holy ones" is translated by the word "saints."

Examples of the Ways Adjectives Are Used

Pronounce the Greek; translate into English.

1. Adjective coming before noun: I see _____ _____ in my members . . . (Rom. 7:23).
   ἕτερον   νόμον

2. Adjective after noun: I looked, and behold, _____ _____ . . . (Rev. 6:2).
   ἵππος   λευκός

3. Adjective without noun—you have to add a word, such as "thing": They were told not to hurt the earth, nor any _____ . . . (Rev. 9:4).
   χλωρὸν

4. A noun and an adjective on each side of the word "is." Since "is" is treated like an equal sign, both must get a subject ending: This _____ is _____ (John 6:60).
   λόγος   σκληρός

5. "Shall be" is a future form of "is": Many of the _____ shall be
   πρῶτοι
   _____, and the _____ _____ (Matt. 19:30).
   ἔσχατοι   ἔσχατοι   πρῶτοι

Exercise One

Scriptures with Adjectives

Translate; circle every adjective.

1. If anyone builds on the foundation _____, silver, _____
   χρυσόν   λίθους
   _____, wood, hay, stubble . . . (1 Cor. 3:12).
   τιμίους

2. Glory be forever _____ _____ _____ _____ _____ _____.
   μόνῳ   σοφῷ   θεῷ*   διὰ   Ἰησοῦ   Χριστοῦ
   _____ (Rom. 16:27).
   Ἀμήν

3. Many _____ shall be _____ and many _____ _____
   πρῶτοι   ἔσχατοι   ἔσχατοι   πρῶτοι
   (Matt. 19:30).

4. He said _____, "How much do you owe?" (Luke 16:7).
   ἑτέρῳ

5. _____ _____ _____, _____, followed, _____ . . .
   Καὶ   ἄλλος   ἄγγελος   δεύτερος*   λεγων
   (Rev. 14:8).

6. But inwardly you are full _____ _____ (Matt. 23:27).
   νεκρῶν   ὀστέων

*Have you noticed that all the words that go together end the same? But you only have to say "of" or "to" once for the entire group.

7. Among the lamps I saw someone _____ _____ _____
   (Rev. 1:13).   ομοιον   υἱὸν   ἀνθρῶπου

Some Adjectives Which Are Related to Words You Already Know

In the first blank, write the small letter from the list of Greek words you know; in the second blank, write the capital letter corresponding to the meaning of the adjective.

Adjectives	Words You Know	Adjective Definitions
__ __ 1. λαμπρος	a. ψευδος (lie)	A. wise
__ __ 2. χρυσεος	b. εθνος (nation, Gentile)	B. false
__ __ 3. σοφος	c. ψυχη (the animal self)	C. shining (use twice)
__ __ 4. ψυχικος	d. σοφια (wisdom)	D. psychic (not spiritual)
__ __ 5. εθνικος	e. χρυσος (gold)	E. national, ethnic
__ __ 6. ψευδης	f. λαμπας (lamp)	F. golden
__ __ 7. φανερος	g. φανος (torch)	

The Word "The"

The word "the" is a letter t plus the same ending as the noun it is with:

θεος λεγει τον λογον = God speaks the word

Exception. When "the" appears with the subject, it does not have a letter t. "The" with a singular subject is ὁ, pronounced "haw." "The" with a plural subject is οἱ, pronounced "hoi."

ὁ	ανθρωπος	gave	καλους	βιβλους	τω	αδελφω
the	man	gave	good	books	to the	brother

Careful: τω is not the word "to." It is the word "the," with the dative ending to go with the word αδελφω.

Different Customs. The Greeks use the word "the" in places we don't expect, such as before names. When translating, we simply leave out the "the" in conformity with English usage.

ὁ θεος λεγει τῳ Πετρῳ	=	The God speaks to the Peter (literal).
	=	God speaks to Peter (good translation).

As is the case with adjectives, the word "the" is sometimes used alone, without a noun. You have to add a word like "one" or "thing" so it makes sense.

Examples:
With a prepositional phrase:

ὁ εν τῳ οικῳ λεγει   =   The one in the house speaks

With a participle:

ὁ λεγων αγαπα   =   The one speaking loves; or the speaking one loves; or as a paraphrase acceptable in translating: He that is speaking loves.

1. "The" with a noun: God so loved _____ _____ (John 3:16).

τὸν   κόσμον

2. "The" with an adjective: Paul, apostle of Christ Jesus, _____ _____ in Ephesus . . . (Eph. 1:1).

τοῖς

ἁγίοις

3. With the word "is": ____ _____ is ____ _____ (Matt. 13:38).

ὁ   ἀγρός   ὁ   κόσμος

A Special Adjective Placement

A common Greek usage is for an adjective to come after a noun, each with its own word "the" (all endings need to match). When you translate, say the word "the" once, then the adjective, then the noun:

ὁ θεος ὁ ἁγιος	=	The God the holy (word for word)
	=	The holy God (translation)

4. Into the lake burning with fire, which is ____ _____ (Rev 21:8).

ὁ   θάνατος   ὁ   δεύτερος

The slot after the second "the" can be filled with entire phrases:

5. ὁ ανθρωπος ὁ λεγων λογους μενει εν τω οικω τω μικρω.

Word for word:
The man the saying words remains in the house the small.

With adjectives placed correctly in front of nouns:
The saying-words man remains in the small house.

Smooth English:
The man who is saying words remains in the small house.

Scriptures with Nouns and "The"

_____ _____ is _____ _____; the good seed is _____ _____ of the Kingdom
 Ὁ   ἀγρός   ὁ   κόσμος   οἱ   υἱοὶ
(Matt. 13:38).

. . . did not so much as lift _____ _____ into heaven . . . (Luke 18:13).
                              τοὺς   οφθαλμοὺς
. . . not seeing the brightness _____ _____ (Acts 26:13).
                                τοῦ   ἡλίου
He spoke a rebuke _____ _____ and to the sea (Matt. 8:26).
                  τοῖς   ἀνέμοις
Then I saw _____ _____ in the vision; . . . and the heads _____ _____
           τοὺς ἵππους   τῶν   ἵππων
as heads of lions (Rev. 9:17).

Because he makes _____ _____ of him rise on the evil and the good . . .
(Matt. 5:45).   τὸν   ἥλιον

Everything in the world . . . lust of flesh, lust _____ _____ (1 John 2:16).
                                                 τῶν   οφθαλμῶν
Which is greater, _____ _____ or the temple that sanctifies ____ _____?
(Matt. 23:17).   ὁ   χρυσὸς   τὸν   χρυσόν

Exercise Three

Adjectives and "The"—Matching

__ 1. ὁ καλος ανθρωπος   a. The good man (object)

__ 2. οἱ ανθρωποι οἱ καλοι   b. The good men (object)

__ 3. του καλου ανθρωπου   c. to the good men

__ 4. των καλων ανθρωπων   d. The good man (subject)

__ 5. τῳ ανθρωπῳ τῳ καλῳ   e. of the good men

__ 6. τοις καλοις ανθρωποις   f. to the good man

__ 7. τον καλον ανθρωπον   g. of the good man

__ 8. τους καλους ανθρωπους   h. The good men (subject)

Fill in the correct word for "the"; then, match to meaning:

_____ 9. ἁγιος θεος __   i. to the holy men

_____ 10. κακου ανθρωπου __   j. to the bad man

_____ 11. κακῳ ανθρωπῳ __   k. of the good men

_____ 12. ἁγιον ανθρωπον __   l. of the bad man

_____ 13. κακοι ανθρωποι __   m. the holy God (subject)

_____ 14. καλων ανθρωπων __   n. the bad men (object)

_____ 15. ἁγιοις ανθρωποις __   o. the holy man (object)

_____ 16. κακους ανθρωπους __   p. The bad men (subject)

Lesson Twenty-One

Guessing Meanings

Write the Greek word in the blank:

αριθμοι

1 πρωτος 2 δευτερος 3 τριτος 7 αλλος

μεγας μεσος μικρος αλλος

οικος ναος αλλος πληρης κενος μεσος αλλος

ταφος νεκρος

first _____	large _____	temple _____
second _____	small _____	grave _____
third _____	other _____	dead _____

full _____	numbers _____
medium _____	
empty _____	

All the words above are adjectives, except three which are nouns.
Write (n) after the nouns.

Exercise Two

Match the Greek with their English equivalents.

Verbs

___ 1. γραφω   a. I throw
___ 2. σκοπεω   b. to call
___ 3. βαλλω   c. calling
___ 4. ακουω   d. I write
___ 5. λεγει   e. I call
___ 6. καλεω   f. I see
___ 7. καλειν   g. I hear
___ 8. καλων   h. he says

Nouns and Adjectives

___ 9. ἁγιος   i. grace
___ 10. καλος   j. good
___ 11. κακος   k. holy
___ 12. λαμπρος   l. bad
___ 13. νεκρος   m. anointed one
___ 14. αλλος   n. dead
___ 15. χαρις   o. shining
___ 16. χριστος   p. other

Match meanings to these adjectives. English derivatives are given as hints.

___ 17. ιδιος   q. hidden (cryptic)
___ 18. ὁμοιος   r. entire (holistic)
___ 19. εσχατος   s. only (monocle)
___ 20. χρυσος   t. young (nepotism)
___ 21. ἑτερος   u. made of earth or clay (ceramic)
___ 22. νηπιος   v. other (heterosexual)
___ 23. κεραμος   w. last (study of last things: eschatology)
___ 24. κρυπτος   x. golden (chrysalis)
___ 25. μονος   y. own (idiosyncrasy)
___ 26. ὁλος   z. similar (homogenous)

Exercise Three

Sentences with Adjectives

See if you can guess the meaning of the new words through the pictures. Answers are on page 316.

1. ὁ πρωτος ανθρωπος, εν τῳ οικῳ, λεγει λογον.
2. ὁ δευτερος ανθρωπος γραφει λογους εν τῳ ναῳ.
3. ὁ τριτος ανθρωπος σκοπει τον νεκρον ανθρωπον.
4. ὁ πρωτος ανθρωπος βαλλει τον μικρον λιθον εν τῳ οικῳ.
5. ὁ δευτερος ανθρωπος ακουει τον λογον του πρωτου ανθρωπου.
6. ὁ αλλος ανθρωπος σκοπει τον κενον ταφον.
7. οἱ ανθρωποι βαλλουσι σκληρους λιθους.
8. ὁ αδελφος γραφει σκολιον λογον.

9. Μαρκος λεγει σκληρον λογον του νομου τοις ἁγιοις αδελφοις.
10. λεγομεν καλους λογους του ἁγιου θεου τῳ αποστολῳ.
11. λεγουσι νεον λογον θεου τοις σοφοις ανθρωποις.

Scriptures

Pronounce the Greek and translate.

This is a _____ _____; who is able _____ it? (John 6:60b).
       σκληρός   λόγος   ἀκούειν

For ____ _____ _____ _____ is _____—and you are that temple!
   ὁ   ναὸς   τοῦ   θεοῦ   ἅγιος
(1 Cor. 3:17).

The demons cried, _____, "What have you to do with us, _____ of Naza-
                λέγων   Ἰησοῦ
reth? . . . I know who you are—____ _____ _____ _____!" (Mark 1:24).
                               ὁ   ἅγιος   τοῦ   θεοῦ

Exercise Four

Scriptures with Adjectives and "The"

Circle the adjectives; pronounce the Greek; translate.

A. Adjectives Describing Nouns

What shall it profit _____ if he should gain _____ _____
                       ἄνθρωπος   τὸν   κόσμον

_____ . . . (Matt. 16:26).
   ὅλον

He is a debtor to keep _____ _____ _____ (Gal. 5:3).
                        ὅλον   τὸν   νόμον

. . . which was not made known _____ _____ _____ _____ as is
                                τοῖς   υἱοῖς τῶν   ἀνθρώπων

now revealed _____ _____ _____ of him and prophets in the
             τοῖς   ἁγίοις   ἀποστόλοις

Spirit (Eph. 3:5).

In the glory of his Father ____ _____ _____ _____ (Luke 9:26).
                           καὶ τῶν   ἁγίων   ἀγγέλων

Who can forgive sins if not _____ ____ _____? (Luke 5:21).
                            μόνος   ὁ   θεός

B. Adjectives without Nouns

Add words like "one" or "thing" if needed to make sense.

You have taken off the old _____ and put on _____ _____ (Col. 3:9–10).
                           ἄνθρωπον   τὸν   νέον

How are ____ _____ raised up? (1 Cor. 15:35).
        οἱ   νεκροί

I know who you are: ____ _____ _____ _____ (Mark 1:24).
                    ὁ   ἅγιος   τοῦ   θεοῦ

_____ ____ _____ blew the trumpet (Rev. 8:7).
καὶ   ὁ   πρῶτος

Servants, submit to your masters, not only to the good ones but also ____
_____ (1 Pet. 2:18).   τοῖς
σκολιοῖς

We believe in God who raises _____ _____ (2 Cor. 1:9).
                             τοὺς   νεκρούς

That you ministered _____ _____ and still minister (Heb. 6:10).
                    τοῖς   ἁγίοις

Lesson Twenty-Two

Pronouns

The word "he" (αυτος) changes its endings, like a noun does. If you use the noun endings, you can construct forms like αυτω (to him) and αυτου (of him).

Example: οικος αυτου = house of him (you can say, "his house").

The plural of "he" would be "they"; continuing with the chart, you can make αυτων (of them) and αυτοις (to them).

Example: οικος αυτων = house of them (their house).

The same possibilities exist for "I," with its plural, "we"; and for "you." These charts show all the possibilities. Notice that you can tell, in Greek, whether you are talking about one "you" or several, which you cannot do in English unless you use a word like "ye" or "you-all."

	I	We			You	
	Singular	Plural			Singular	Plural
Subject	εγώ	ἡμεῖς*		Subject	σύ	ὑμεῖς
Possessive	μου	ἡμῶν		Possessive	σοῦ	ὑμῶν
Dative	μοι	ἡμῖν		Dative	σοί	ὑμῖν
Object	με	ἡμᾶς		Object	σέ	ὑμᾶς

Examples

λεγει μοι = he says to me

οικος ημων = house of us
            = our house.

*pronounced "hay-mace"

Examples

λεγει σοι = he says to you

οικος ὑμων = house of you
            = your house

Exercise One

I. Matching

__ 1. ἡμιν   a. to me
__ 2. ἡμεις   b. of me (my)
__ 3. ἡμας   c. we (subject)
__ 4. ἡμων   d. of us
__ 5. μοι   e. to us
__ 6. μου   f. us (object)

II. Matching:

__ 7. ὑμεις   a. to you (sing.)
__ 8. συ   b. of you (sing.)
__ 9. σοι   c. you (subject, plur.)
__ 10. ὑμιν   d. of you (plur.)
__ 11. ὑμων   e. to you (plur.)
__ 12. σου   f. you (subject, sing.)

Sometimes you will see the forms starting with μ with an ε in front: εμε means the same as με.

III. Scriptures

Pronounce the Greek and translate.

1. Grace _____ and peace from God the Father _____ (Eph. 1:2).
   ὑμῖν   ἡμῶν

2. And _____, being dead in the trespasses and sins _____ . . .
          ὑμᾶς   ὑμῶν
   (Eph. 2:1).

3. _____ is the peace _____ (Eph. 2:14).
      Αὐτὸς   ἡμῶν

αυτος can also mean "self" or "himself":

ὁ θεος αυτος λεγει = God Himself says

Scriptures Using Pronouns

Pronounce the Greek and translate.

_____ zeal __ __ _____ __ _____ has consumed _____ (John 2:17).
'Ο   ζῆλος τοῦ οἴκου σου   με

_____ , _____ _____ __ _____ will _____ __ _____ ,
Παῦλος   ἀπόστολος Χριστοῦ Ἰησοῦ διὰ θελήματος θεοῦ

__ _____ to the ones being ___ _____ _____ faithful __ _____
τοῖς   ἁγίοις τοῖς οὖσιν ἐν Ἐφέσῳ καὶ πιστοῖς ἐν Χριστῷ

_____ : _____ _____ __ _____ __ _____ __ _____ _____ _____
Ἰησοῦ   Χάρις ὑμῖν καὶ εἰρήνη ἀπὸ θεοῦ πατρὸς ἡμῶν καὶ

_____ _____ _____ . Blessed be __ _____ ___ _____ __ ___
κυρίου Ἰησοῦ Χριστοῦ   ὁ   θεὸς καὶ πατὴρ τοῦ

_____ __ ____ _____ _____ . The one blessing _____ ____ every
κυρίου ἡμῶν Ἰησοῦ Χριστοῦ   ἡμᾶς ἐν

spiritual blessing ___ ___ heavenlies ___ _____ __as__ he chose ____ ____
         ἐν τοῖς   ἐν Χριστῷ καθὼς   ἡμᾶς ἐν

_____ . . . (Eph. 1:1–4).
αὐτῷ

For _____ _____ transforms __ __ _____ of light (2 Cor. 11:14).
    αὐτὸς ὁ ζατανᾶς   εἰς ἄγγελον

Did you consider translating αυτος as "himself"?

__ _____ _____ ____ _____ ____ shows ___ ___ everything which _____
ʹΟ πατὴρ φιλεῖ τὸν υἱὸν καὶ   αὐτῷ   αὐτὸς

_____ (John 5:20).
ποιεῖ

In the following two examples, the words above the brackets are being used as adjectives would be used: following the nouns, and with a word "the" of their own. Grasp the overall idea, and put the entire thought into good English.

_____ was _____ (Luke 15:25).
ʹΟ υἱὸς αὐτοῦ ⌐ὁ πρεσβύτερος⌐   ἐν ἀγρῷ

Why _____ ____ splinter _____, but
    βλέπεις τὸ*   τὸ* ἐν τῷ οφθαλμῷ τοῦ αδελφοῦ σου

do not notice the ____ ____ ____ _____ beam? (Luke 6:41).
         ἐν τῷ ἰδίῳ** ὀφθαλμῷ

   * another word for "the"
   ** one's own

Everyone coming _____ ____ ___ _____ ____ _____ _____ _____ __
        πρός με καὶ ἀκούων μου τῶν λόγων καὶ

_____ _____, I'll show you what he is _____ (Luke 6:47).
ποιῶν αὐτούς   ὅμοιος

A sower went out to sow ____ _____ _____ (Luke 8:5).
        τὸν σπόρον αὐτοῦ

_____ ____ that ____ are _____ (Matt. 16:18).
Λέγω σοι   σὺ   Πέτρος

Exercise Two

Endings after Prepositions

Since there are only eight types of endings, we have to use these same endings when writing a noun after a preposition.

θεω = to God, but εν θεω = in God, NOT "in to God"

___ 1. εν αδελφω   a. to brother
___ 2. αδελφω   b. in brother
___ 3. εις αδελφον   c. of brother
___ 4. προς αδελφου   d. towards brother
___ 5. αδελφου   e. into brother
___ 6. λεγει   f. to speak
___ 7. λεγειν   g. he speaks

Notice that the English word "to" is used for two completely different purposes: if the word is a verb, and ends with ειν, it is an "infinitive," and we use the word "to." If the word is a noun, and ends with ω, (or οις for plural), it is the dative or indirect object, and we again use the word "to" with it.

Exercise Three

Some prepositions have more than one meaning.
The meaning is revealed by the ending of the following word. (That word is called the "object" of the preposition.) Example: see #11, p. 116.

A. μετα ανθρωπου means _____ a man (because of the ου ending).
B. μετα ανθρωπον means _____ a man (because of the ον ending).

Preposition (with alternate forms)	Meaning if next word-ending looks like		
	Possessive	Dative	Direct Object
1. αμφι			around
2. ανα			up
3. αντι	instead of, against		
4. απο (αφ', απ')	from		
5. δια	through		because of
6. εις			into
7. εν		in	
8. εκ (εξ)	out of, from		
9. επι (εφ', επ')	on	near, on	about, against

10. κατα (καθ᾽)	down from		according to
11. μετα (μεθ᾽)	with		after
12. παρα	from the side	at the side	to the side, compared with
13. περι	concerning		near
14. προ	before		
15. προς	toward	near	toward
16. συν		with	
17. ὑπερ (English "hyper")	above		over
18. ὑπο (English "hypo")	by	under	during

English Words Formed from the Last Three Prepositions on the Chart

Match to the definitions at the right.

___ 1. synergism

___ 2. hypercritical

___ 3. hypodermic

___4. synchronize

___ 5. hyperbole

___ 6. hypothermia

a. under the skin (δερμα)

b. work (εργον) along with God

c. under-heated (θερμη is warmth)

d. to check time (χρονος) with one another

e. over-judging (κριτικος = able to judge; a judge is a κριτης)

f. over-throw: an exaggeration (βολη is a form of βαλλω)

Scriptures Using Prepositions

Check the ending of the noun following the preposition in order to determine which meaning of that preposition to use in your translation.

What did you go out to see? A reed shaken ____ ____? (Matt. 11:7).
      ὑπὸ   ἀνέμου

Use a little wine ____ ____ _____ and the frequent ailments ____ (1 Tim. 5:23).
      διὰ   τὸν   στόμαχον   σου

____ ____ _____ ____ ____ seasons _____, ____ no need ἐφ᾽ ἵπποις that I
Περὶ τῶν χρόνων καὶ τῶν καιρῶν ἀδελφοί ἔχετε
write ___ _____ (1 Thess. 5:1).
      ὑμιν

And the soldiers of heaven followed him ____ _____ _____ (Rev. 19:14).
                                          ἐφ᾽   ἵπποις λευκοῖς

_____ _____ _____ _____ _____ _____ ____ _____ (Matt. 23:34).
Εγὼ   ἀποστέλλω   πρὸς   ὑμᾶς   προφήτας   καὶ   σοφοὺς

And going out they went ____ _____ _____ (Acts 12:17).
                              εἰς   ἕτερον   τόπον

Drink _____ it, all of you (Matt. 26:27).
      ἐξ

Do not be overcome _____ _____ _____ (Rom. 12:21).
                         ὑπὸ   τοῦ   κακοῦ

Judas went ____ _____ _____ _____ _____ (Acts 1:25).
                εἰς   τὸν   τόπον   τὸν   ἴδιον

He showed me ___ _____ of the water of life, _____ as _____,
                ποταμὸν   λαμπρὸν   κρύσταλλον

going ___ ____ _____ _____ ____ _____ (Rev. 22:1).
       ἐκ   τοῦ   θρόνου   τοῦ   θεοῦ

Lesson Twenty-Three

Meanings of Prepositions

Why is it that prepositions mean different things in different situations? Some of these instances can be explained this way: The preposition has to make sense with the relationship that is already suggested by the ending of the noun. For example, we have been using the word "of" to translate when there is a possessive ending:

ὁ Ιησους is ὁ υἱος του ανθρωπου.

But what do we mean by this word "of"? We could hardly call it possession in this case—as though the man possessed the son. There is a different relationship there; but a relationship, nonetheless, and our English word "of" seems to cover the situation. (The man "generated" or "begat" the son—grammarians call this sense of the word genitive).

What would you do with the following sentence?

We are condemned του νομου

There is a relationship expressed here between law and condemnation, but the word "of" doesn't express this relationship adequately. What word would you use?

The Greeks, way back in the formative years of their language, long before Christ, asked themselves the same question. Part of the answer was the development of prepositions to clarify the shades of meaning meant by the noun ending. We would clarify the sentence above by writing:

δια του νομου or ὑπο του νομου

Thousands of years later, when someone set out to make a Greek/English dictionary, he would catch the sense of the entire sentence and then conclude—obviously δια and ὑπο can mean "by" or "through." Greek dictionaries will list a dozen or more words for many prepositions that seem to be the right word at various times. You can often reach the same conclusion just by using common sense.

Language is so complicated that for our purposes it is better just to see what is done, rather than to try to explain it. You will run across two results of the developments we have been describing:

1. You will see endings that don't seem to make sense according to the translating we have done so far:
   a. Do not get drunk οινῳ (Eph. 5:18). Here you would supply a preposition as you translate into English, but it won't be the preposition "to."
   b. Use a little οινῳ for your stomach and frequent ailments (1 Tim. 5:23). Here you can translate into English without using any preposition.
2. You will see prepositions that don't seem to fit their customary meaning:
   a. See that no one repay κακὸν ἀντὶ κακοῦ (1 Thess. 5:15).
   b. If anyone ἐν ὑμῖν should wander from the truth . . . (James 5:19).

The next section presents some of the many shades of meaning expressed by noun endings. You are not expected to memorize these possibilities, or to regard them as rules, but simply to realize that this explains why some of the endings and prepositions you will see are not translated with their simplest meaning.

More on Noun Cases—The Seven Cases

There originally were seven different case endings for seven different uses of nouns. The endings were simplified to four, but the seven uses can still be distinguished. In the following examples, the words in quotes can be stated by one Greek word just by using the right ending. In actual usage, a preposition (from, to, under, etc.) is often added—its function is to strengthen and clarify the tendency that the noun already has due to its endings.

The Seven Cases

A. Number one is what we have been calling the subject ending:

   1. Nominative—subject of sentence

B. The next two use what we have been calling the possessive ending:

   2. Genitive—possible meanings:
      a. possession
      b. relationship, or further definition
         baptism "of repentance" ("in view of repentance")
         the earnest "of (the) spirit"

      c. value: wheat "for a denarius"

      d. quality: this body "of sin"

      e. The word in the genitive can cause an action to the word being modified: obedience "of faith" (i.e., faith produces obedience).

      f. On the other hand, the main noun can cause action to the noun in the genitive: blasphemy "of the Spirit."

  3. Ablative—main idea: source, separation (answers the question "from where"? Also used for comparisons).

Examples:

    I will give him "of (the) manna" (a part of all the manna) (Rev. 2:17). All of you, drink "of it" (a part of it) (Matt. 26:27).

The phrase church "of God" makes sense whether regarded as a genitive (God's possession) or as an ablative (the church's) source is God.

C. The next three use what we have been calling the dative ending:

  4. Locative (compare English word "location")—answers the questions "Where?" "In what?"

Examples:

    "in (the) boat"; poor "in spirit"; baptized "in the Jordan."

Also used to express time: "on the (first) day"

  5. Dative—usually used about people who receive the action of the sentence. Varieties of meaning:

      a. indirect object

      b. object of such verbs as "trust."

      c. possessing something: The promise is "to you."

      f. reference: We died "to sin." (We died so far as sin is concerned.)

      g. personal interest: It is "to (the) advantage" of you that I go away (John 16:7).

  6. Instrumental (what "instrument" or tool is used to bring about the action of the sentence)—answers the questions "How?" "With what method?"

Examples:

    Partake "with thanks"; bound "with fetters"; killed "with (the) sword"; purchased "by blood."

Also association: They followed "him"
Also time: "about 400 years"

D. This one is the one we have been calling the direct object:

7. Accusative—answers questions like "To what extent?" "In what direction?" "How long?" "To what purpose?"

There is also an eighth usage, called vocative, used in speaking directly to someone. Example in English: *Father*, may I go out?

Example in Greek (Jesus is speaking to the Father): Πάτερ δίκαιε, . . . (translate: "Righteous father, . . .") (John 17:25).

These eight usages were found in the language which was ancestral to the Greek language (see charts on page 237–8 for more information).
Examples are taken from *Light from the Greek New Testament* by Boyce W. Blackwelder. Anderson, Indiana. 1958.

Examples of Possessive and Dative Endings

This first set of examples is from Ephesians Chapter One.

Words with Possessive Endings

1. Genitive use:

Blessed be the God and Father ___ ___ _____ ___ ____ _____
_____ (Eph. 1:3).   τοῦ   κυρίου   ἡμῶν   Ἰησοῦ
  Χριστοῦ

2. Ablative use:

God made known to you the mystery ___ ___ _____ ____ ____
(Eph. 1:9).   τοῦ   θελήματος   αὐτοῦ

> (The ending ατος is another type of possessive ending: θελήματος means "of will." The meaning here is that the source of the mystery is in God's will. The word αυτου is back to genitive meaning: It is His will.)

Words with Dative Endings

1. Dative use:

Paul is writing _____ _____ (to the saints) (Eph. 1:1).
                 τοῖς   ἁγίοις

2. Locative use (place) with the usage strengthened by the preposition εν:

Paul is writing to the saints ____ _____ (Eph. 1:1).
                              ἐν   Ἐφέσῳ

3. Instrumental use ("how" or "with what"). Here again the word εν is used, but our English word "in" doesn't begin to do justice to the relationship expressed:

God predestined us ____ _____ (Eph. 1:4).
                   ἐν   ἀγάπῃ

Some Additional Uses of Datives

1. Certain words regularly are followed by datives rather than direct objects (accusatives). One of these words is "believe":

Abraham believed _____ (Rom. 4:3).
                  θεῷ

If you do not believe _____ _____ _____ (Luke 1:20).
                      τοῖς   λόγοις   μου

"Believe" is also often followed by a prepositional phrase:

I believe _____ _____ _____.
          εἰς   τὸν   θεόν

2. A dative is sometimes used to tell when something happened:

Jesus healed ____ _____ (Luke 13:14).
             τῷ   σαββάτῳ

These many uses of noun endings will jump out at you as you look at actual scripture passages. A college text or course will go into much more detail, specifying these variations.

Examples of Prepositions with Various Meanings

And be not drunk with wine, but be filled ____ _____ (Eph. 5:18).
                                          ἐν   πνεύματι

Lest you dash _____ _____ _____ _____ ___ ___ (Matt. 4:6).
              πρὸς   λίθον   τὸν   πόδα   σου

_____ answered, "Pray _____ _____ _____ _____ _____ _____
Σίμων   ὑμεῖς ὑπὲρ   ἐμοῦ   πρὸς   τὸν   κύριον
that what you said will not happen _____ _____" (Acts 8:24).
                                   ἐπ᾽   ἐμὲ

Christ also suffered _____ sin, the righteous _____ the unrighteous
(1 Pet. 3:18).   περὶ   ὑπὲρ

The one who has blessed us _____ every spiritual blessing . . . (Eph. 1:3).
                         ἐν

Simeon said _____ Mary . . . (Luke 2:34).
            πρὸς

The one conquering shall not be hurt ____ _____ _____ _____
_____ (Rev. 2:11).   ἐκ   τοῦ   θανάτου   τοῦ
  δευτέρου

and if _____ ____ _____ _____ _____ s, ____ _____
      ἐγὼ   ἐν   βεελζεβοὺλ   ἐκβάλλω   δαιμόνια   οἱ   υἱοὶ

___ ___ ____ whom _____ (Matt. 12:27).
ὑμῶν   ἐν   ἐκβάλλουσιν

We announce ___ ___ the eternal _____ which was _____ ____ _____
(1 John 1:2). ὑμῖν   ζωὴν   πρὸς τὸν πατέρα

_____ ___ ____, if anyone ____ _____ should wander from the truth
 Αδελφοί   μου   ἐν   ὑμῖν
and someone brings him back (James 5:19).

Lesson Twenty-Four

The Noun Endings—Simplified Listing

You have learned eight endings for nouns, corresponding to four uses of nouns in a sentence, with singular and plural variations. The endings you have learned are only one of three different sets of endings. These sets of endings are called "declensions." You have learned the noun endings for the second declension (Roman numeral II on the chart below).

The words in capital letters at the left are the abbreviations for the correct terms for the four possible uses of nouns in a sentence.

What we have been calling

"subject"	is	termed	nominative case
"possessive"	is		genitive case
"dative"	is		dative case
"direct object"	is		accusative case

Singular	I*	II	III
Nom.	α or η or ης or ας	ος or ον	_ _ _ _ **
Gen.	ας or ης or ου	ου	ος or ως or ους
Dat.	ᾳ or ῃ	ῳ	ι
Acc.	αν or ην	ον	α or ν or ος or like Nom.
Plural			
Nom.	αι	οι or α	ες or εις or α
Gen.	ων	ων	ων
Dat.	αις	οις	σι
Acc.	ας	ους or α	ας or εις or η or ιν or α

* technical name: "first declension"
** no particular ending: words like φως, πατηρ

We are not going to learn all the details for how to attach these endings on to words. These details would be covered in a college course in Greek. We are going to learn how to use the chart to understand sentences in the Greek New Testament.

Let's begin by looking a little closer at column II. Three endings are given as alternates. These are used when the noun is listed in the dictionary as "neuter." For example, δενδρον happens to be a neuter noun. Its ending, ον, shows us that it is a second declension noun—it uses the endings from column II. If we want to say "trees," the form would be δενρδα. If we want to say "of a tree," there is no alternative listing, so we write δενδρου. If you ask, "How can you tell the difference between nominative and accusative with a second-declension neuter word?", the answer is "You can't." You have to determine it from the context of the sentence.

Example: The word εγρον (work) is a second declension neuter noun.

What does it profit if a man says he has faith, but has not _____?
(James 2:14).   ἔργα

With the ending α, εργα must be either nominative plural (subject) or accusative plural (direct object).

Since the subject of the sentence is "man," the word "works" must be the direct object (accusative), since that is the only other alternative.

It is a general principle about neuter words, of any declension, that the mom. and acc. will be the same, and their plurals will end with α.

Examining the Noun-Ending Chart

About the Chart as a Whole

One simplifying factor is that the genitive plural endings (ων) arc the same in all three declensions. Unfortunately, ων is also the ending you learned as a participle ending:

Jesus spoke, _____, "I do not require the approval _____ _____."
                λεγων   ανθρωπων

You know you cannot translate ανθρωπων with an "ing" because it is a noun.

Another simplifying factor is that all the dative endings have a letter ι— either full-size or small.

About the Third Declension

The following example uses a third declension word you know:

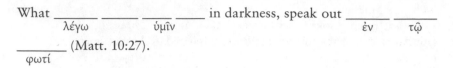

What _____ _____ _____ in darkness, speak out _____ _____
     λέγω   ὑμῖν   ἐν   τῷ
_____ (Matt. 10:27).
  φωτί

Most of the third declension words appear in a short version in the nominative singular, so that the real "stem" of the word appears only in the other forms. A dictionary will give you this information, by showing you what the word looks like in both nominative and genitive forms.

For example, "light" in the dictionary is listed as φως, φωτος n (the n tells us it is a neuter word). This means the genitive form of φως is φωτος, and the stem is φωτ (you find the stem by taking off the genitive ending). All the rest of the endings are to be hooked on to the stem. In the scripture example above, the dative ending ι was therefore hooked on to the stem φωτ, not on to φως or φω.

An Exception

In the following example, "light" is a direct object, so you would expect it to have one of the accusative endings:

. . . but on a lampstand, so those coming in may see the _____ (Luke 8:16).
                                                          φῶς

The reason it does not end as you would expect is that neuter words are written the same in both nominative and accusative.

Another Exception

The σ in the dative plural ending σι interacts with the stem of the word in a way that results in some of the stem letters being changed. This is no problem for you, however, since as soon as you see the ι at the end, you know you are dealing with a dative ending. (The ending ουσι would only be found on verbs, and the nominative plural endings are usually obvious just from the sense of the sentence.)

Third Declension Scripture Examples

> Dictionary entry: πατηρ, πατρος m, father (therefore stem is πατρ)

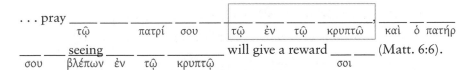

. . . pray ____ ____ ____ ____ — | τῷ ἐν τῷ κρυπτῷ |, ____ __ _____
      τῷ   πατρί   σου   καὶ ὁ πατήρ

___ ___ seeing ____ ____ _____ will give a reward ___ ___ (Matt. 6:6).
σου   βλέπων ἐν   τῷ   κρυπτῷ   σοι

The part in the box is an entire phrase which is used as an adjective.

> Word-for-word: to the father of you to the in-the-secret
> Placed in adjective position: to the in-the-secret father of you
> Smooth English: to your father in secret

The next example shows how the Greeks may add or change letters as they make connections between stem and endings (the η of πατηρ changed to ε).

They left the boat ____ ____ _____ ____ ___ and followed him (Matt. 4:22).
                              καὶ τὸν πατέρα αὐτῶν

This book will not go into all the rules about connecting stems and endings. That is a major subject for a full college course.

> Dictionary entry: παῖς, παιδός m & f, child or slave

("M & f" means the word can be used to designate either a boy or girl; the word is sometimes translated "child," sometimes as "slave.")

Then Herod slew all _____ _____ in Bethlehem . . . (Matt. 2:16).
                       τοὺς   παῖδας

All you need to notice is that one of the accusative plural endings was placed on the stem, which is shown in the second word of the dictionary ending to be παιδ. As a reconfirmation, the form of the word "the" used also indicates accusative plural.

The elder son called one _____ _____ _____ and asked what this might mean (Luke 15:26).   τῶν   παίδων

A Word about Cognates

Many of our English words which came from Greek are based on the stem of the word rather than on the nominative form. Our word "pedagogue" is made from the stem παιδ plus the word αγω (lead). So "pedagogue" means one who leads a child—a teacher.

The Greeks had already formed this particular word. Example:

Therefore ____ _____ _____ ____ ____ was constituted ____
       ὁ   νόμος   παιδαγωγὸς ἡμῶν   εἰς

_____ (Gal. 3:24).
 Χριστόν

. . . now that faith has come, no longer _____ _____ are we . . .
(Gal. 3:25).   ὑπὸ   παιδαγωγόν

The word "constituted" is treated like the word "is," with the nouns on both sides of it receiving nominative endings. When you translate, move the expression "was constituted" in between the word "law" and the word "pedagogue." By the way, what declension is the word παιδαγωγος? (second)

Another example: The Greek dictionary entry for "foot" is πους, ποδος. We did not make our word "podiatrist" from the nominative (πους) but rather from the stem (ποδ).

Examining Column I—First Declension

Before you react to how complicated this column looks, look at the bottom half—at least there are no alternatives for the plural endings. Notice that the genitive plural ending is the same as all the others, that the dative plural has an "ι" in it (but notice that the nominative plural does also), and that the accusative plural is the same as the first alternative listed for genitive singular (ας).

What about all those alternatives? All you need to know is that a word will not jump from one column to another. If the nominative form (found in the dictionary) ends with α, the other endings needed will be listed under the α. But what if the nominative ends with ης? A dictionary will tell you how to make genitive. From that point on there are no additional alternatives. Since there was an η in the nominative form, continue to use endings with η in them in dative and accusative.

Dictionary entry: **μαθητης**, ου *m, disciple, pupil, follower*

Then ____ ____ ____ ____ _____: "Behold the <u>mother</u> ____ _____."
   λέγει   τῷ   μαθητῇ   μήτηρ σου

And ____ that _____ __ _____ took her as his own (John 19:27, 28).
 ἀπ᾽   ὥρας   ὁ   μαθητὴς

(Dictionary entry for "hour" is ὥρα, ας. In our example it takes the genitive ending because it comes after the word απο).

Then ____ _____ _____ _____ _____ ____ _____ . . . (Matt. 9:37).
     λέγει   τοῖς   μαθηταῖς   αὐτοῦ

A simplifying factor about the first declension: the stem is found in all forms, even in the nominative.

Dictionary entry: γη, γης *f, earth*

Other (seed) fell on rocky ground where it had not much _____, and dried
                                             γῆν

up _____ not having much depth _____ _____ (Mark 4:5).
   διὰ   γῆς

Thy will be done, as in heaven, so ____ _____ (Matt. 6:10).
                                    ἐπὶ   γῆς

Dictionary entry: ζωη, ζωης *f, life* (ζωον *was "animal") from which we get the
      English word "zoo"*

Here is the word with the genitive ending, ης.

The hope _____ _____ eternal, which God who cannot lie has announced
      ζωῆς   αἰωνίου

_____ _____ _____ (Titus 1:2).
πρὸ   χρόνων   αἰωνίων

Lesson Twenty-Five

All the Forms of "The"

Singular	Masculine	Feminine	Neuter
Nominative (subject)	ὁ	ἡ	το
Genitive (possessive)	του	της	του
Dative	τῳ	τη	τῳ
Accusative (object)	τον	την	το
Plural			
Nominative	οἱ	αἱ	τα
Genitive	των	των	των
Dative	τοις	ταις	τοις
Accusative	τους	τας	τα

So far you have learned the "masculine" column. Those endings are second declension endings, except for the nominative singular, which is special. The neuter column is the same as the masculine column, except that:

1. the nominatives are special, and
2. the accusatives are the same as the nominatives.

This corresponds to the endings listed as neuter alternatives in the second declension column, except that the nominatives and accusatives end with ov for nouns, but with o for "the."

Examples with a Neuter Noun, ἐργον

If _____ comes, accept him, for he does ____ _____ ____ ____
    Τιμόθεος   τὸ   ἔργον   Κυρίου

_____(1 Cor. 16:10).

For this __ _____ _____ _____ was manifested, to destroy ____ _____
    ὁ   υἱὸς   τοῦ   θεοῦ   τὰ   ἔργα

____ ____ _____ (1 John 3:8).
  τοῦ   διαβόλου

130

The feminine endings are taken directly from the first declension column.

For where ____ _____ ___ _____ is, there also ____ _____
      ὁ   θησαυρός   σου   ἡ   καρδία

___ _____ shall be (Matt. 6:21).
σου

(Note that the word "the" and the noun will not necessarily rhyme, but they must correspond; they must be the right "gender" [masculine, feminine, or neuter] and the right "case" [nominative, genitive, etc.]).

| Dictionary entry: στομα, τος n, mouth | It is the subject of the sentence below. |

For out of the fullness ____ ____ _____ ____ _____ speaks (Matt. 12:34).   τῆς   καρδίας τὸ   στόμα

Which show ____ _____ ____ _____ _____ written ____ ____ _____
          τὸ ἔργον τοῦ   νόμου   ἐν ταῖς καρδίαις

_____ _____ (Rom. 2:15).
αυτῶν

Some dictionaries use the word "the" to indicate the gender of a noun, instead of the initials m, f, or n.

A dictionary entry for "love" is αγαπη, ης, ἡ. This indicates:

1. the genitive of αγαπη is αγαπης,
2. it is a feminine noun, because ἡ is the feminine form of "the."

Adjective Endings

Adjectives also use the endings on the noun-ending chart. Each adjective needs to use three sets of endings, so it can describe a masculine, feminine, or neuter noun. A Greek dictionary will indicate which columns (i.e., which declensions) to use with a given adjective by listing the nominative singular ending for all three possibilities.

For example, "new" in the dictionary is listed as follows: νεος, α, ον.

This means that a new man would be a νεος man, that a new woman would be a νεα woman, and that a new temple would be a ναον, "temple." In the case of this particular word, the masculine and neuter endings are from column II, and the feminine endings are to be taken from column I. If you want to say, "to new women," you would have to use the dative plural ending from column I, and write: to νεαις women. If you wanted to say "new temples" as the subject of your sentence, you would use the neuter variation from column II (the letter α) and write: νεα temples.

Repent and do ____ _____ _____ (Rev. 2:5).
                 τὰ   πρῶτα   ἔργα

The dictionary entry for "city" is πολις, εως, ἡ, which shows you it is a third-declension feminine noun. The entry for "holy" is ἁγιος, α, ον, which shows you it is an adjective, and the feminine forms of the adjective will use endings from the α column of first declension. I have left the following scripture in its original word order:

Then takes him __ _____ ____ ____ _____ _____ (Matt. 4:5).
              ὁ   διάβολος   εἰς   τὴν   ἁγίαν   πόλιν

The last three words go together. Although they do not rhyme, they are all accusative endings, as required following the preposition εις.

> Dictionary entry: πνευμα, πνευματος, το (=neuter) spirit

Then goes and brings along _____ _____ _____ worse than himself
(Matt. 12:45).
                   ἑπτὰ   ἕτερα   πνεύματα

In the next example, the adjective follows the noun, with its own word "the." The noun is feminine, so must take a feminine "the" and a feminine adjective. The dictionary entry for "good" is καλος, η, ον, showing us that the feminine endings will be from the η column. Finally, the preposition εις requires that the words following it have accusative case endings.

And other (seed) fell   εις   τὴν   γῆν   τὴν   καλήν (Mark 4:8)
    Word-for-word: _____ _____ _____ _____ _____
    Smooth English: _____

Do not grieve   τὸ   πνεῦμα   τὸ   ἅγιον   τοῦ   θεοῦ. (Eph. 4:30)
    Word-for-word: ____ _____ ____ _____ _____ ___ _____.
    Smooth English: _____.

In the next example, there is an adjective with no verb; it is neuter plural, so add "things."

In the day that God judges ____ ___ _____ ____ _____ (Rom. 2:16).
                      τὰ κρυπτά   τῶν ἀνθρώπων

Scriptures with First and Third Declension Endings

Remember that "he" was the word αυτος. In order to say "she," use the feminine endings of the word "the," making sure that each word starts with αυτ (αυτη, αυτης, etc.).

And his mother kept all these words _____ _____ _____ _____ (Luke 2:51).
ἐν   τῇ   καρδίᾳ   αὐτῆς

("The heart" has the dative endings because it comes after "εν." αυτης is genitive: of her).

I gave ____ _____ time to repent, but she does not wish to repent of the for-
αὐτῇ

nications ____ _____ (Rev. 2:21).
αὐτῆς

The same approach is used for neuter. To say "it," put αυ in front of the neuter endings on the "the" chart (p. 130).

If the words go together, as in the following example, they will all be in the same case, even if they might be in different declensions. In the example, both words are genitive, but the first word is third declension, so ends with "ος," while the second word is second declension, and ends with "ου":

Andrew, the brother _____ _____ (John 1:40).
Σίμωνος   Πέτρου

σαρξ, σαρκος = flesh (cognate to English *sarcophagus* when added to φαγος, "eater, glutton")

Since therefore ____ _____ share _____ ____ _____, he partook
τὰ   παιδία   αἵματος   καὶ   σαρκός

of the same . . . (Heb. 2:14).

The adjective μεγας (large, great) is an example of an irregular adjective.

The dictionary entry is μεγας, μεγαλη, μεγα. The accusative neuter is the same as the nominative μεγα; the masculine accusative is μεγαν. All the rest of the forms make use of the extra λ, as you see it in the feminine form. For example, the masculine genitive is μεγαλου.

In this example, the words are feminine, in accusative case:

And I heard behind me _____ _____ as a trumpet . . . (Rev. 1:10).
                                        φωνὴν   μεγάλην

Here the words are in dative, and tell "how" Jesus cried:

Jesus cried _____ _____, _____ (Matt. 27:46).
                      μεγάλη   φωνῇ   λέγων

The following are masculine, accusative:

And rolled _____ _____ to the door of the tomb (Matt. 27:60).
                      λίθον   μέγαν

Two adjective examples using first declension:

And seeking to establish _____ _____ righteousness . . . (Rom. 10:3).
                                      τὴν   ἰδίαν

If anyone strikes you on the cheek, turn to him also _____ _____
(Matt. 5:39).   τὴν   ἄλλην

Lesson Twenty-Six

Forms of the Verb "To Be"

Αυτος εστι means "he is."

Remove the αυτος, and εστι alone would still be translated "he is."
Put a noun before it, and the word εστι will be translated "is."

ὁ αποστολος εστι means "The apostle is."

Think of the word "is" as an equal sign. The word on the right side of the equal sign is not the direct object, but is the equivalent of the subject of the sentence. The word on the right side of the word "is" will have a nominative ending.

ὁ ανθρωπος εστι δουλος. The man is a servant.
(noun with nominative ending)

ὁ ανθρωπος εστι καλος. The man is good.
(adjective with nominative ending)

Sometimes the letter ν will be added to εστι in order to make a smooth connection to the word that follows:

ὁ ανθρωπος εστιν αποστολος. The man is an apostle.

Sometimes the word order will be different from English:

ὁ ανθρωπος δουλος εστιν. The man is a servant.

Check the following examples in your Bible:

ὁ ____ ____ ____ (1 John 1:5).
θεὸς φῶς ἐστὶν

ὁ ____ ____ ____ (1 John 4:8).
θεὸς ἀγάπη ἐστίν

The word with ὁ is the subject, and should begin the English version:

_____ _____ _____ _____ ___ _____ _____ _____
Κύριός   ἐστιν   τοῦ   σαββάτου   ὁ   υἱὸς   τοῦ   ἀνθρώπου
(Matt. 12:8).

Εγω ειμι means "I am."

_____ _____ ___ _____ _____ ___ _____ (Rev. 1:17).
Ἐγώ   εἰμι   ὁ   πρῶτος   καὶ   ὁ   ἔσχατος

If you remove the word εγω, you have to supply the word "I."

Ειμι καλος = I am good.

In the following example, the word order is not like English:

____ ____ ____ ____ (John 10:36).
Υἱὸς τοῦ θεοῦ εἰμι

This chart shows the forms of the verb "to be" in the present tense:

		Singular	Plural	Infinitive		English Equivalent		
Persons	1	ειμι	εσμεν	ειναι		(I) am	(we) are	to be
	2	εις or ει	εστε			(you) are	(you) are	
	3	εστι	εισι			(he) is	(they) are	

(ν sometimes added to third person)

Matching, to see if you can follow the chart:

__ 1. ειναι   a. he is
__ 2. εσμεν   b. to be
__ 3. εστιν   c. I am
__ 4. ειμι   d. we are

Scripture Examples

And I also ___ ___ _____ that ____ ____ _____, and upon this rock I
              σοι   λέγω   σὺ   εἰ   Πέτρος
will build my church (Matt. 16:18).

_____ _____ __ _____ one _____ (John 10:30).
Ἐγὼ   καὶ   ὁ   πατὴρ   ἐσμεν

_____ _____ _____ _____ ___ _____ to the good, but innocent _____
  Θέλω   ὑμᾶς   σοφοὺς   εἶναι   εἰς*

____ _____ (Rom. 16:19).
τὸ   κακόν

(Jesus said): _____ _____ from this world; _____ not _____ from this
                 ὑμεῖς   ἐστέ   ἐγώ   εἰμί

world (John 8:23).

  *This is the preposition "to," not the second person of "to be."

In the next example, the last word is an adjective with a third-declension ending, genitive case to match the word "God" which it is describing.

_____ _____ said, "____ ___ _ _____ _ _____ ___ _____
  Σίμων   Πέτρος   Σὺ   εἶ   ὁ   χριστὸς   ὁ   υἱὸς   τοῦ   θεοῦ

____ _____" (Matt. 16:16).
τοῦ   ζῶντος

Some samples of Greek word order that seem unusual to us:

Lord, I know that you _____ _____ _____ (Matt. 25:24).
                        σκληρὸς   εἶ   ἄνθρωπος

_____ _____ ____ ____ this (John 6:60).
  Σκληρός   ἐστιν   ὁ   λόγος

Some New Vocabulary

Find the meanings of these nouns by looking up the Bible passages.

_____ _____ ___ _____ _____ ____ _____ (John 11:25).
  Ἐγώ   εἰμι   ἡ   ἀνάστασις   καὶ   ἡ   ζωή

The word "the" is ἡ because the nouns are feminine. The noun chart shows that -η is a nominative ending in first declension. But the ending -ις is not found on the chart. The word happens to be third declension, in which nominatives end in various ways.

_____ _____ ___ _____ _____ _____ (John 6:35).
  Ἐγώ   εἰμι   ὁ   ἄρτος   τῆς   ζωῆς

The third and fourth words have nominative endings, but the word της is a genitive (possessive) form of "the," and the noun chart shows us that -ης is a genitive ending in the first declension. The literal translation of the last two words would be "of the life." Since we don't commonly use the word "the" with the word "life" in a sentence like this, we may omit the word "the" in the translation.

_____ _____ _ _____ (John 10:11).
Ἐγώ   εἰμι   ὁ   ποιμὴν ὁ   καλός

An example of a noun and an adjective, each with its own word "the." We rearrange the words to make good English. Word for word, it says "I am the shepherd the good."

ὁ _____ _____ _____ (John 3:33).
   θεὸς   ἀληθής   ἐστιν

Supplying the Form of "To Be" When It Is Lacking

The word εστι is sometimes omitted, and the meaning has to be added by the translator:

   Θεος εστι ἅγιος and θεος ἅγιος both mean "God is holy."

The problem is that with only two words—θεος and ἅγιος—you might not know whether to translate "God is holy" or "holy is God." To the rescue comes the word ὁ (the). It is used to point out which word is the subject. You can put the words in any order, and you will still know which one is the subject: the one with ὁ.

ὁ θεος ἅγιος and ἅγιος ὁ θεος both mean "God is holy."

ὁ ἅγιος θεος εστι καλος and ὁ ἅγιος θεος καλος both mean "The Holy God is good."

It will still mean the same if we mix up the word order, as long as we put ὁ in the right place: καλος ὁ ἅγιος θεος.

In the following scriptures, begin your translation with the word that has a form of "the."

_____ (John 4:24). ("Pneuma" means "spirit.")
πνεῦμα ὁ θεός

So that, on the one hand, ____ _____ _____ (Rom. 7:12).
                          ὁ   νόμος   ἅγιος

We know that _____ ____ _____ if anyone uses it lawfully (1 Tim. 1:8).
             καλὸς ὁ   νόμος

An opened _____ ____ _____ _____ (Rom. 3:13).
          τάφος ὁ   λάρυγξ   αὐτῶν

Special Placement of Adjectives Reviewed

This handy use of the word ὁ is complicated by the fact that there are two ways to place adjectives in a Greek sentence:

1. The adjective can go before the noun as we do in English.

   ὁ ἁγιος θεος = the holy God

2. The adjective can come after the noun—but in this case, each word must have its own ὁ.

   ὁ θεος ὁ ἁγιος = the God the holy = the holy God
   (If you would leave out that second ὁ, you would have "God is holy.")

Adjectives can be placed in that manner anywhere in the sentence. For example, here the object of the sentence has an adjective:

Μαρκος γραφει τον ἁγιον λογον and Μαρκος γραφει τον λογον τον ἁγιον both mean "Mark writes the holy word."

In actual scriptural examples, you will find cases where the adjective is placed after the noun, without those extra "the's." You will usually not get mixed up if you look at the sense of the entire sentence. If the sentence already has a verb, then you will know you cannot add the verb "is." Also, anytime "is" would be required, the main word on each side of the word "is" has to have the "subject" ending.

Matching

Match these Greek phrases with their English equivalents.

___ 1. ὁ θεος ἁγιος
___ 2. ὁ ἁγιος θεος
___ 3. Θεος εστι ἁγιος
___ 4. ἁγιος ὁ θεος
___ 5. ὁ θεος ὁ ἁγιος
___ 6. Θεος ἁγιος
___ 7. ὁ ἁγιος θεος εστι
___ 8. ὁ θεος ἁγιος εστι
___ 9. ὁ θεος ὁ ἁγιος εστι
___ 10. ἁγιος ὁ θεος εστι
___ 11. Εστι ὁ εθος ἁγιος
___ 12. Εστι ὁ θεος ὁ ἁγιος
___ 13. ὁ θεος ὁ ἁγιος εστι;
___ 14. ὁ θεος εστι ἁγιος;

a. The holy God is.
b. The holy God
c. Is the holy God?
d. God is holy.
e. Is the God holy?

The following sentence is a common form for a blessing, and translators have customarily inserted the word "be" rather than "is."

Check your Bible for the meaning of the first word.

_____ __ ____ ____ _____ ___ _____ _____ _____ . . . (Eph. 1:3).
Εὐλογητὸς   ὁ   θεὸς   καὶ   πατὴρ   τοῦ   κυρίου   ἡμῶν

Lesson Twenty-Seven

Examples Using Plural

οἱ ανθρωποι εισι καλοι and οἱ ανθρωποι καλοι both mean "the men are good."

Remember that when two parts of a sentence are connected by a form of "be," such as "is" or "are," both parts of the sentence have the nominative ending. If the subject is plural, the word after "is" will also have to have a plural ending.

ὁ πετρος και ὁ Ιωαννης αποστολοι = Peter and John are apostles

Matching

Match these Greek sentences with their English equivalents.

___ 1. Οἱ αδελφοι καλοι.   a. The good brothers are holy.
___ 2. Ο Πετρος και ὁ Παυλος αποστολοι.   b. The brothers are good.
___ 3. Οἱ καλοι αδελφοι ἁγιοι.   c. The holy brothers are good.
___ 4. Καλοι οἱ ἁγιοι αδελφοι.   d. Peter and Paul are apostles.

Examples Using "He" and "They"

___ 5. Αγιοι καλοι.   e. God is good.
___ 6. Αυτοι καλοι.   f. God Himself is good.
___ 7. Αυτος εστι καλος.   g. The holy ones are good.
___ 8. Καλος ὁ θεος.   h. He is good.
___ 9. Ο θεος αυτος καλος.   i. They are good.

First John, Chapter One

What you do NOT know are the connecting words like "as," which will be covered in Part III; the past tenses of the verbs, which will be explained in Part V; the words for the important religious concepts, which will be the subject matter of Part IV; and some additional vocabulary, which you would have to look up

in a lexicon. (This is the word we should be using, rather than "dictionary,"
for a Greek/English reference book.) Now let's find out what you do know:

That which was ____ _____, which we heard, which we saw
                  ἀπ' ἀρχῆς

_____, what we beheld ____ ____ _____ _____
τοῖς[1] οφθαλμοῖς ἡμῶν   καὶ   αἱ   χεῖρες ἡμῶν

touched ____ ____ _____ ____ ____ ——— ___ __ ____ appeared, ___
        περί τοῦ λόγου τῆς ζωῆς   καὶ ἡ ζωή   καὶ

we saw ____ _____ ____ announce ____ ____ ____ ____
       καὶ   μαρτυροῦμεν καὶ   ὑμῖν τὴν ζωὴν τὴν[2]

_____ which was ____ ____ _____ ____ shown ____ ____.
αἰώνιον[3]   πρὸς τὸν πατέρα καὶ   ἡμῖν

What we saw and heard we announce also ___ ___ so that also _____ may
                                         ὑμῖν   ὑμεῖς

have _____ ____ ____ ____ _ _____. ___ __ _____ of ours __ ____
     κοινωνίαν[5] μεθ' ἡμῶν καὶ ἡ κοινωνία   [4]   μετὰ τοῦ

_____ ____ ____ ___ ___ ____ _____ _____ ____. ____ these things
πατρὸς καὶ μετὰ τοῦ υἱοῦ αὐτοῦ Ἰησοῦ χριστοῦ Καὶ

_____ _____ so that the joy ___ ____ might be full. ____ this _____
γράφομεν ἡμεῖς   ἡμῶν   Καὶ   ἔστιν

__ _____ which we heard ____ _____ ____ announce ____ ____, that __
ἡ ἀγγελία   ἀπ' αὐτοῦ καὶ   ὑμῖν   ὁ

____ ____ _____ ____ darkness ____ ____ not _____ at all. If we
θεὸς φῶς ἔστιν καὶ   ἐν αὐτῷ   ἔστιν

say that _____ _____ ____ _____ ____ __ __ _____darkness walk,
         κοινωνίαν ἔχομεν μετ' αὐτοῦ καὶ ἐν τῷ

we lie and not _____ ____ _____. But if ____ ___ ____ we walk as
               ποιοῦμεν τὴν ἀγήθειαν   ἐν τῷ φωτί

_____ _____ __ ___ _____ _____ _____ ____ _____ ____
αὐτός ἐστιν ἐν τῷ φωτί κοινωνίαν ἔχομεν μετ' ἀλλήλων[6] καὶ

___ ____ _____ ___ ____ ____ ___ cleanses _____ ____ all sin.
τὸ αἷμα Ἰησοῦ τοῦ υἱοῦ αὐτοῦ   ἡμᾶς ἀπό

1. Dative ending with instrumental use: answers the question "with what?"
2. The adjective coming after the noun, each with its own word "the."
3. "Eternal." Cognate to "eon."
4. Add the word "is."
5. This word means "fellowship," from the word κοινον, "common": "having something in
common." Some churches have "koinonia" groups. A related word is κοινη—that is used for
the "common" Greek of the world at the time of Christ, as opposed to the "classical" Greek in
which the masterpieces of the 400's BC were written.
6. Related to αλλος, "other"; translate: "each other."

Part III

THOSE SMALL WORDS

The purpose of this section is that you become so familiar and fluent with the common small words of Greek that when you look at a sentence you will be able to grasp the basic flow of it, and only have to look up the verb and possibly a few of the nouns in a dictionary.

In Part III, you will learn:

1. More uses for the words "and" and "to."

2. The common negative words like "no" and "not."

3. Common connectives like "for," "but," and "therefore."

4. Common adverbs such as "badly."

5. Adding "more" and "most" to adjectives.

6. More pronouns used as adjectives: "this," "that," "who," etc.

Lesson Twenty-Eight

More Uses for the Word καὶ (And)

1. also

   Surely _____ you are one of them . . . (Matt. 26:73).

καὶ

   Since the children share in blood and flesh, he _____ partook of the
   same . . . (Heb. 2:14).

καὶ

2. even
3. yet, but nevertheless
4. very, truly, in fact
5. indeed
6. καὶ . . . καὶ = both . . . and

   _____ the tabernacle _____ all the utensils of worship he sprinkled

καὶ   καὶ

   with blood (Heb. 9:21).

7. και + εγω = καγω: and I

   _____ ____ _____ that ____ ___ _____ (Matt. 16:18).

κάγὼ σοι λέγω   σὺ εἶ Πέτρος

More Uses for the Word αυτος (He)

1. "self" when used without its own word "the":

   God himself = ὁ θεος αυτος or αυτος ὁ θεος

   For _____ _____ _____ ___ _____ _____ (Luke 20:42).

αὐτὸς   Δαυὶδ   λέγει ἐν βίβλῳ   ψαλμῶν

2. "same" when used with its own word "the":

The same God = ὁ αυτος θεος or ὁ θεος ὁ αυτος

And here it's used without a noun:

Since the children share in blood and flesh, he _____ partook ____ _____
_____ (Heb. 2:14).   καὶ   τῶν
αὐτῶν

The entire Scripture:

<u>Since therefore</u> _____ ____ _____ <u>shared</u> _____ _____ ___ __
'Επεὶ   οὖν   τὰ   παιδία κεκοινώνηκεν   αἵματος[1] καὶ

_____ ____ _____ <u>likewise</u> _____ <u>partook</u> ___ _____
σαρκός   καὶ   αὐτὸς   παραπλησίως[2]   μετέσχεν[3]   τῶν

_____ (Heb. 2:14).
αυτῶν

1. Genitive ending with the sense of "having a portion."
2. This is an adverb, saying something about the verb "partook."
3. This verb was made from μετα in the sense of "with," plus εχω, "have."

Exercise One

A great many Greek adverbs are adjectives with an ως ending; this ending then does not change. Can you guess the meaning of the following adverbs, which are related to adjectives you know:

___ 1. αλλως   a. well
___ 2. καλως   b. in the same way, likewise
___ 3. κακως   c. at all, wholly
___ 4. ὁλως   d. for the first time
___ 5. ὁμοιως   e. otherwise
___ 6. πρωτως   f. wrongly, badly

The Word "Not"

The two words commonly used are ου and μη. There are definite rules about when to use one or the other: ου is used with a verb which is making an ordinary statement of fact, and μη is used for verbs with other shades of meaning, and with infinitives and participles.

More joy over one repenting sinner than over ninety-nine others who _____
need _____ of repenting (Luke 15:7).   ου
ἔχουσιν

My children, _____ these things _____ so that _____ ye may sin
(1 John 2:1).   γράφω   ὑμῖν   μὴ

> You can see that it's going to take creativity on your part to translate these Greek sentences with negatives in them into English.

In the following sentence, the verb κρινω, "judge," is used. In its first appearance it is giving a command. In its last appearance, it is passive: "ye may be judged."

_____ so that _____ (Matt. 7:1).
Μὴ   κρίνετε   μὴ   κριθῆτε

The next example uses a participle: loving-one. The "the" goes with the participle, to produce "the loving-one." Then the negative is stuck between them:

_____ _____ ____ _____ (1 John 3:14).
ὁ   μὴ   ἀγαπῶν   μένει   ἐν   τῷ   θανάτῳ

Check your Bible to get an idea of how translators have needed many English words to bring out what is meant in cases like this.

Using two negative words in a sentence does not change the meaning to a positive, as it does in English; rather, it just adds emphasis:

Jesus answered his disciples: "_____ all these? _____ ____ ____ ____,
                 Οὐ   βλέπετε   Ἀμὴν   λέγω   ὑμῖν
_____ shall be left here _____ ____ _____ which ____ shall be cast
οὐ   μὴ   λίθος   ἐπὶ   λίθον   οὐ
down" (Matt. 24:2).

The preceding Scripture also gave you a chance to translate a question. Check your Bible.

Letters are added to the basic negative words when they come before vowels in order to provide smoothness in sound. The point is that whatever may be added, those little words ου and μη are noticeable, and always indicate something negative.

Having eyes _____ ____ having ears _____ (Mark 8:18).
          οὐ   βλέπετε   καὶ   οὐκ   ἀκούετε
They _____ submitted to the righteousness _____ _____ (Rom. 10:3).
     οὐχ   τοῦ   θεοῦ

Many different words combine with the negative words to produce very specific shades of meaning. Some samples to guess at:

So then you are _____ strangers and sojourners, but fellow-citizens . . . (Eph. 2:19).   οὐκέτι

There is therefore now _____ condemnation ___ ___ ___ ___ _____ _____ (Rom. 8:1).   οὐδὲν   τοῖς   ἐν   χριστῷ
Ἰησοῦ

Those Little Indefinite Words

Have you ever said, "I just want to praise the Lord?" What did you mean by the word "just"? Certainly you weren't referring to "justice," but you did add a certain flavor to your meaning.

Greek also has these little words. Two of them are γε and τε. Sometimes they're not even translated:

For τε I had not known lust, if the law had not said, "Don't covet" (Rom. 7:7).

These little words combine with other words, as well. In the next example, τε has combined with "not" to provide one of the many words used in Greek for "either . . . or" and "neither . . . nor" situations.

But whoever should speak against the Holy Spirit, it shall not be forgiven him, _____ in this age _____ in the age to come (Matt. 12:32).
οὔτε   οὔτε

A word with a little more weight, but still hard to translate, is μεν. In the next translation example it is in a sentence that has just summed up a paragraph, and means something Like "on the one hand, then." Again, it is often left untranslated.

So ____ _____ _____ _____ and the commandment is _____ and just
ὁ   μὲν   νόμος   ἅγιος   ἁγία
and good (Rom. 7:12).

The word αρα is still a little stronger, and usually gets translated, with the sense of "then, consequently, so."

_____, therefore, you are _____ strangers and foreigners . . . (Eph. 2:19).
ἄρα   οὐκέτι

Now, _____, no condemnation to those in Christ Jesus (Rom. 8:1).
ἄρα
(You have to add the word "is" in this sentence.)

This brings us to the two most common "little" words you will be coming across: γαρ and δε.

One thing that is unusual about them is their placement in the sentence; they always come second (even if they have to split up a noun from its word "the"), but when you translate, you always say them first.

Meaning

γαρ (which is γε + αρα) means "for."

δε can mean "and," "but," and various other shades of meaning, depending on how the sentence it is in is related to the preceding sentence.

_____ _____ am I ashamed of the gospel, power ____ ____ ____ _____ unto
Οὐ   γὰρ   γὰρ θεοῦ ἐστιν

salvation (Rom. 1:16).

_____ ____ _____ _____ ___ _____ _____ . . . (Luke 20:42).
Αὐτὸς γὰρ Δαυὶδ λέγει ἐν βίβλῳ ψαλμῶν

Who shall rescue me from the body of this death? Thanks ____ ____ ____
                                                         δὲ   τῷ   θεῷ

_____ _____ _____ ____ _____ ____ _____ . ____ therefore ____
διὰ   Ἰησοῦ χριστοῦ τοῦ κυρίου ἡμῶν ἄρα   αὐτὸς

____ ____ in my mind serve _____ _____ , ____ ____ flesh _____ of
ἐγὼ μεν*   νόμῳ θεοῦ   τῇ   δὲ* σαρκὶ νόμῳ

sin (Rom. 7:24–25).

*μεν . . . δε used for "on the one hand . . . on the other hand."

Lesson Twenty-Nine

ἵνα = in order that

_____ your father and mother, ____ it may be well ____ (Eph. 6:2–3).
Τίμα   ἵνα   σοι

My children, _____ these things to you _____ ye may not sin (1 John 2:1).
                 γράφω   ἵνα

He is faithful and righteous _____ he may forgive our sins and cleanse us . . .
(1 John 1:9).   ἵνα

ὅτι = that, because

If we say _____ ____ ____ ____ sin, we deceive ourselves . . . (1 John 1:8).
           ὅτι   οὐκ ἔχομεν

He ought to die, ____ he made himself _____ ____ ____ (John 19:7).
                 ὅτι   υἱὸν θεοῦ

____ ____ ____ ____ ____ ____ ____ ____ _____ (Matt. 16:18).
Κἀγὼ δέ   σοι λέγω ὅτι σὺ εἶ Πέτρος

We know ____ we have passed ____ ____ _____ ____ ____ ____ ____
         ὅτι   ἐκ τοῦ θανάτου εἰς τὴν ζωήν ὅτι

____ _____ ____ _____ (1 John 3:14).
ἀγαπῶμεν   τοὺς ἀδελφούς

ἀλλὰ = but

God so loved the world that he sent his only Son, _____ everyone believing in
                                                   ἵνα

him should not perish, _____ have _____ _____ (John 3:16).
                       ἀλλὰ   ζωὴν αἰώνιον

Look carefully how you walk: not as unwise _____ as _____ (Eph. 5:15).
                                           ἀλλὰ   σοφοί

$\boxed{\underline{ο\mathring{\upsilon}ν} = \text{therefore}}$

Everyone _____ who hears my words and keeps them is like a man . . . (Matt. 7:24).
                    οὖν

_____, _____, _____ ___ _____ strangers and foreigners . . . (Eph. 2:19).
  ἄρα   οὖν   οὐκέτι   ἐστὲ

Since, ____, ____ _____ share in flesh and blood, ____ _____ par-
Ἐπεὶ οὖν   τὰ   παιδία   καὶ   αὐτὸς

took ____ ____ _____ _____ he might destroy <u>the</u>
     τῶν   αὐτῶν ἵνα διὰ τοῦ θανάτου   τὸν

<u>one</u> ___ing the power ____ _____ . . . (Heb. 2:14).
       ἔχοντα   τοῦ   θανάτου

$\boxed{\underline{ὡς} = \text{as}}$

Forgive us our trespasses, _____ we forgive those who trespass against us (Matt. 6:12).
                            ὡς

If we walk in the light ____ _____ _____ ____ ____ _____ (1 John 1:7).
                        ὡς   αὐτός   ἐστιν ἐν τῷ φωτί

The adversary ____ ____ _____ _____ ____ _____ roaring walks about
              ὑμῶν διάβολος   ὡς λέων

seeking someone to devour (1 Pet. 5:8).

And there fell from heaven _____ _____ burning ____ _____
                           ἀστὴρ   μέγας   ὡς   λαμπάς
(Rev. 8:10).

$\boxed{\underline{καθώς} = \text{as (κατα + ὡς)}}$

Let not greediness be named among you, _____ is fitting _____ (Eph. 5:3).
                                        καθώς   ἁγίοις

We thank God constantly, ____ having received _____ you heard ____ _____
                         ὅτι   λόγον*   παρ' ἡμῶν

_____, you received ____ ____ _____ _____ _____ ____ _____
τοῦ θεοῦ*   οὐ λόγον ἀνθρώπων ἀλλὰ καθώς ἐστιν

in truth: _____ ____ ____ (1 Thess. 2:13).
          λόγον θεοῦ

*These words go together in the English translation.

> ὥστε = so as, that (made from ὡς + τε)

The son of perdition sets himself up against everything called God or worship-
ful, _____ to sit ____ ____ _____ ____ _____, claiming ____ ____ ____
     ὥστε   εἰς   τὸν   ναὸν   τοῦ   θεοῦ   ὅτι   ἔστιν

_____ (2 Thess. 2:4).
θεός

God so loved the world, _____ he gave his only Son . . . (John 3:16).
                            ὥστε

> οὕτως = so, thus

As a sheep before his shearers is dumb, _____ he opened not ____ _____
____ ____ (Acts 8:32).   οὕτως   τὸ   στόμα
αὐτοῦ

_____ ____ loved ____ ____ _____, _____ ____ _____ the only-
Οὕτως γὰρ   ὁ   θεὸς τὸν κόσμον ὥστε τὸν υἱὸν
begotten he gave, ____ everyone believing ____ _____ would not perish
            ἵνα   εἰς   αὐτὸν

_____ have eternal life (John 3:16).
ἀλλ᾽

> ἤ = or, than

Let none of you suffer ____ murderer ____ thief ____ evildoer . . . (1 Pet. 4:15).
                    ὡς   ἤ   ἤ
There will be more joy in heaven over one sinner repenting ____ over ninety-
nine righteous . . . (Luke 15:7).   ἤ

Distinguish ἤ (or) from ἡ (the, feminine) by the direction of the breathing
mark. The word for "the" starts with an h sound.

ἤ . . . ἤ is another way to say "either . . . or."

> εἰ = if

Save yourself, ____ _____ ____ ____ _____ _____ (Matt. 27:40).
          εἰ   υἱὸς   εἶ   τοῦ   θεοῦ

Distinguish "if" from "are" by the accent, found only on "are."

_____ _____ _____ of anyone which he has built _____, he'll receive a reward
εἴ   τὸ   ἔργον   μενεῖ
(1 Cor. 3:14).

Καὶ   εἰ   ἐγὼ   ἐν   βεελζεβοὺλ   ἐκβάλλω   τὰ   δαιμόνια   ,   οἱ   υἱοὶ
_____ ___ _____ whom _____? (Matt. 12:27).
ὑμῶν   ἐν   ἐκβάλλουσιν

εἰ with μὴ = except (if not)

A prophet is not without honor _____ in his own country (Matt. 13:57).
                                                        εἰ   μὴ

ἐάν = if

Whoever _____ he should speak _____ _____ _____ _____ _____ _____ ,
              ἐάν   λόγον   κατὰ   τοῦ   υἱοῦ   τοῦ   ἀνθρώπου
it will be forgiven him (Matt. 12:32).

Beloved , _____ __ _____ _____ condemn us, boldness _____ _____ _____
Ἀγαπητοί   ἐὰν   ἡ   καρδία   μὴ   ἔχομεν   πρὸς
_____ _____ (1 John 3:21).
τὸν   θεόν

A shorter version, _ἄν_ lends an "iffy" meaning to a sentence: (translated often by using the word "would").

Lord, if you had been here, _____ _____ have died my brother (John 11:21).
                                                 οὐκ   ἄν

κἄν = and if (και + εαν)

_____ _____ ___ _ _____ , ___ ____ it should behoove _____ _____ _____ to
λέγει   αὐτῷ   ὁ   Πέτρος   κἄν   με   σὺν   σοὶ
die, _____ _____ I will forsake! (Matt. 26:35).
        οὐ   μή   σε

νῦν = now. Also spelled νυνι

_____ _____ _____ condemnation ___ _____ _____ _____
Οὐδὲν   ἄρα   νῦν   τοῖς   ἐν   Χριστῷ   Ἰησοῦ
(Rom. 8:1).

Lesson Thirty

Pronoun-Adjective Combination: "this"

οὗτος = this

Use the endings on the noun chart

	Masculine	feminine	neuter
Nom.	οὗτος	αὕτη	τοῦτο
Gen.	τούτου	ταύτης	τούτου
	etc.	etc.	etc.

1. The difference between αὕτη (feminine form of "this") and αὐτή (feminine form of αὐτός, translated "she") is found in the breathing mark and the accent. The word we are now learning *has* an h-sound; the word for "she" does not.
2. The plurals are οὗτοι, αὗται, ταῦτα = "these"
3. Remember that in all neuters, the accusative forms are the same as the nominative forms. The other neuter forms (genitive and dative) are the same as the masculine forms.
4. All the masculine and feminine forms *except* the nominatives, which were described above, start with a τ. So for example, the masculine genitive will be τούτου; the feminine genitive (since it uses first declension endings) is ταύτης.

The word can be used to describe a noun: μυστήριον τοῦτο = this mystery; or without a noun, as in the following neuter plural: ταῦτα = these things.

Exercise One

Matching

The genders are mixed together here; identify the meaning of each Greek phrase.

___ 1. ταυτης   a. to these
___ 2. τουτῳ   b. this one (speaking of a man)
___ 3. τουτων   c. to this
___ 4. ταυταις   d. this thing
___ 5. τουτο   e. of this
___ 6. ταυτα   f. this one (speaking of a woman)
___ 7. αὑτη   g. these things
___ 8. οὑτος   h. of these

Scripture Examples

I do not want you to be ignorant about _____ _____ (Rom. 11:25).
                                        τὸ   μυστήριον   τοῦτο

____ _____ ___ _____ _____ in earthen vessels (2 Cor. 4:7).
Ἔχομεν   τὸν   θησαυρὸν   τοῦτον

____ __ _____, ____ ____ _____ _____ I will build ____ ____
σὺ εἶ Πέτρος καὶ ἐπὶ ταύτῃ τῇ πέτρᾳ   μου

the church (Matt. 16:18).

It shall not be forgiven him, _____ ___ _____ ____ _____ ____ ___
                              οὔτε ἐν τούτῳ τῷ αἰῶνι οὔτε ἐν

____ coming age (Matt. 12:32).
τῷ

Children ___ ___, ___ ___ ___ ___ ___ ___ ___ ye may sin (1 John 2:1).
         μου   ταῦτα γράφω ὑμῖν ἵνα μὴ

____ _____ _____ __ _____ which we heard from him (1 John 1:5).
καὶ ἔστιν αὕτη ἡ ἀγγελία

("This" has to be feminine to match "message.")

That he might destroy the one having the power ____ _____, _____
_____ ____ _____ (Heb. 2:14).   τοῦ θανάτου τοῦτ'
ἔστιν   τὸν   διάβολον

Why Is the Word "This" Important?

In Ephesians 2:8, where it says, "By grace are ye saved through faith, and that not of yourselves . . .," the word "that" is a form of the word we have just studied, οὗτος.

It is given in its neuter form, τοῦτο. In Greek, the passage goes:

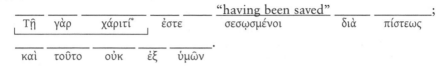

| Τῇ | γὰρ | χάριτί* | ἐστε | "having been saved" σεσῳσμένοι | διὰ | πίστεως ; |

| καὶ | τοῦτο | οὐκ | ἐξ | ὑμῶν . |

*Dative endings in the "instrumental" sense—i.e., "by what method?"

The question is, does the word τοῦτο refer to the word "grace," the word "saved," or the word "faith"? It has to refer to something "neuter."

The word faith happens to be feminine, so the sentence does not say that the "faith" is not of yourselves (although other scriptures may teach God as the author of faith); the word "grace" also happens to be feminine. The sense of the sentence is then that the entire process of salvation is not "of you," but is a gift of God.

Numbers

The number "one" is completely different in the three genders:

	Masculine	Feminine	Neuter
Nom.	εἷς	μια	ἕν
Gen.	ἑνός	μιας	ἑνός
Dat.	ἑνι	μια	ἑνι
Acc.	ἕνα	μιαν	ἕν

Nominatives are differentiated from the prepositions εις and εν because the number "one" has the h sound.

The following sentence uses all three genders:

For there is ____ _____ ___ ___ _____, _____ ____ you were
             ἓν   σῶμα   καὶ ἓν πνεῦμα   καθὼς   καὶ

called ____ _____ hope of your calling; ____ _____, ___ faith, ____
       ἐν   μιᾷ   εἷς   κύριος   μία   ἓν

_____, ___ _____ ___ _____ _____ __* ___ ___ ___
βάπτισμα   εἷς θεὸς καὶ πατὴρ πάντων   ὁ* ἐπὶ πάντων

____ ___ _____ ___ __ _____ (Eph. 4:4–5).
καὶ διὰ πάντων καὶ ἐν πᾶσιν

*This is an example of the word "the" without a noun; translate "the one."

_____ ____ _ _____ ____ _____ (John 10:30).
Ἐγὼ   καὶ   ὁ   πατὴρ   ἕν   ἐσμεν

Through the disobedience ___ ___ _____ _____ many were made
sinners (Rom. 5:19).   τοῦ   ἑνὸς   ἀνθρώπου

There is no "a" or "an" in Greek; when they felt a need for a word like that,
they would use number one.

   It is interesting to note how some of the words that mean "no" are combinations of the basic negative words with number one, as if to mean: not one!
Example: ουδεις, ουδεν.

Two

         δυο or δυω   in nom. and acc.
         δυσιν or δυσι   in gen. and dat.

_____ _____ can _____ _____ serve; __ ___ ___ ____ he'll hate ___ ___
Οὐδεὶς   δυσὶ κυρίοις   ἢ γὰρ τὸν ἕνα   καὶ τὸν

_____ love, __ _____ be devoted to ___ ___ _____ despise (Matt. 6:24).
ἕτερον   ἢ ἑνὸς   καὶ τοῦ ἑτέρου

Three

         τρεις   in nom. and acc.   (τρια for neuter)
         τριων   in gen.
         τρισι   in dat.

You who cast down the temple and rebuild in ____ _____ days, save yourself . . . (Matt. 27:40).   ἐν   τρισὶν

The brethren came as far as the Appian Forum and _____ _____
(Acts 28:15).   Τριῶν   Ταβερνῶν

All

παν is cognate with a phrase like "Pan-American Highway"—a road that goes
all through North and South America.
   Here are the forms for each gender:

	Masculine	Feminine	Neuter
Nom.	πας	πασα	παν
Gen.	παντος	πασης	παντος

The genitive shows you the stem, which the rest of the endings are attached to. You can see that the masculine is using third declension endings, and it will use that ντ in all the rest of its forms. For example, the dative will be παντι.

Something unusual happens in third declension words when you get to the dative plural. The σι ending from the noun chart interacts with the stem and changes it. In this case, the dative plural turns out to be πασι.

Exercise Two

Matching (All Genders and Numbers Mixed Together)

Match these various forms of παν with their respective meanings. Refer to the chart on page 124.

__ 1. πασης   __ 5. παντος   a. to all
__ 2. παντων   __ 6. πασων   b. of all
__ 3. παση   __ 7. παντι
__ 4. πασι   __ 8. πασαις

Scriptures

God . . . sent his Son _____ _____ believing in him would not perish . . .
(John 3:16).   ἵνα   πᾶς

If I know _____ _____ (1 Cor. 13:2).
            μυστήρια   πάντα

Slaves, submit ____ _____ _____ ____ _____ (1 Pet. 2:18).
               ἐν   παντὶ   φόβῳ   τοῖς   δεσπόταις

__ ____ _____ _____ ____ _____ ____ _____ shows _____ _____ what
ὁ   γὰρ   πατὴρ   φιλεῖ   τὸν   υἱὸν   καὶ   πάντα   αὐτῷ

_____ _____ (John 5:20).
αὐτὸς   ποιεῖ

Blessed be God . . . who has blessed us ____ _____ spiritual blessing (Eph. 1:3).
                                         ἐν   πάσῃ

He'll forgive our sins and cleanse _____ _____ _____ unrighteousness
(1 John 1:9).   ἡμᾶς   ἀπὸ   πάσης

There are seven related adverbs, all of which start with παντ.

Example: παντως = by all means

I have become all things to all men, _____ _____ I might save some
(1 Cor. 9:22).   ἵνα   πάντως

Same sentence, including two forms from page 157:

_____ _____ I have become _____, ____ _____ I might save some.
τοῖς   πᾶσιν   πάντα ἵνα   πάντως

The adjective πολυς, "much," gets endings similar to those of μεγας given in
Part II, 133–34.
The lexicon entries are: πολυς   πολλη   πολυ

Some fell on the rocks, where they did not have ____ _____ and dried up
(Matt. 13:5).   γῆν πολλήν

A related adverb is πολλακις, "frequently."

Lesson Thirty-One

Self

"I myself" would be ἐγὼ αὐτός. If a girl was talking, ἐγὼ αὐτή. For the other cases, these two words combine to make a new word.

Gen.:   εμου + αυτου = εμαυτου, "of myself"

This new word appears in all genders in all the remaining cases:

	Masculine	Feminine	Neuter
Gen.	εμαυτου	εμαυτης	εμαυτου
etc.			

The same treatment is given to σεαυτου (yourself) and ἑαυτου (himself).

The one speaking in tongues builds up _____ (1 Cor. 14:4).
   ἑαυτὸν

You who cast down the temple and rebuild it in three days, save _____
(Matt. 27:40).   σεαυτόν

If I rebuild the things I tore down, I make _____ a transgressor (Gal. 2:18).
   ἐμαυτὸν

According to our law he ought to die ____ ____ _____ _____ he made
(John 19:7).   ὅτι υἱὸν θεοῦ ἑαυτὸν

If we say we have no sin, we _____ deceive (1 John 1:8).
   ἑαυτοὺς

This example is in the accusative plural, "themselves," though to make sense in English we translate it as "ourselves."

A Different Word Meaning "Our"

	Masculine	Feminine	Neuter
Nom.	ἡμετερος	ἡμετερα	ἡμετερον
	etc.	*etc.*	*etc.*
	2nd declension	1st declension	2nd declension

And _____ fellowship is with the father (feminine to match "fellowship").
       ἡμετέρα

Same sentence (you have to add the word "is"):

_____ __ _____ __ _____ _____ _____ ____ _____ (1 John 1:3).
Καὶ   ἡ κοινωνία   ἡ ἡμετέρα   μετὰ   τοῦ   πατρὸς

> εκεινος = that. An adjective.

	Masculine	Feminine	Neuter
Nom.	ἐκεῖνος	ἐκείνη	ἐκεῖνο

(The man who finds the treasure) goes, sells all _____ and buys ____ _____
_____ (Matt. 13:44).   ἔχει   τὸν   ἀγρὸν
ἐκεῖνον

And the woman was saved _____   _____ _____ (Matt. 9:22).
                         ἀπὸ   τῆς   ὥρας   ἐκείνης

Related adverbs: ἐκεῖ, "there";   ἐκεῖθεν, "from there" (thence);   ἐκεῖσε,
"to there."

Asking Questions

The English word "who" can have two meanings:

1. to start a question, as in "Who did this?"
2. to relate one part of a sentence to another, as in, "The man who did this is not here."

These two uses are expressed by two totally different words in Greek. The second use is called a "relative pronoun," and will be taken up on page 162. The first use—the word used for asking a question—is the topic of this page and the next.

The endings are all third declension, and they are all identical to that declension except for the usual neuter exceptions:

	singular		plural	
	masculine & feminine	neuter	masculine & feminine	neuter
Nom.	τίς	τί	τίνες	τίνα
Gen.	τίνος	same	τίνων	same
Dat.	τίνι	same	τίσι	same
Acc.	τίνα	τί	τίνας	τίνα

Scriptures

The man with an unclean spirit cried, _____, "___ ___ ___ ___ ___ ___
                                               λέγων   Τί   ἡμῖν   καὶ   σοί*

_____ _____? Have you come to destroy us? I know ___ ___ ___, __
Ἰησοῦ   Ναζαρηνέ   σε   τίς   εἶ   ὁ

___ ___ ___ _____" (Mark 1:24).
ἅγιος   τοῦ   θεοῦ

*Literally, "What to us and to you, Jesus Nazarene?" It is interesting to see how translators have tried to turn that phrase into something that makes sense in English.

___ ___ _____ ___ splinter ___ ___ ___ ___ ___ ___
Τί   δὲ   βλέπεις   τὸ   τὸ   ἐν   τῷ   ὀφθαλμῷ   τοῦ   ἀδελφοῦ

___, ___ ___ ___ your _____ beam ___ notice? (Matt. 7:3).
σου   τὴν   δὲ   ἐν   τῷ   σῷ   ἀφθαλμῷ   οὐ

Indefinite Pronoun

. . . has the same forms as τίς, above, except without any accents. Translate as "some," "a certain," "anyone," "someone," etc.

_____ ___ ___, _____ ___ ___ _____ wanders from the truth and
Αδελφοί   μου   ἐάν   τις   ἐν   ὑμῖν

___ brings him back . . . (James 5:19).
τις

The enemy ___ ___ _____ ___ _____ roaring walks seeking _____
        ὑμῶν   διάβολος   ὡς   λέων   τινα
to devour (1 Pet. 5:8).

The Relative Pronoun

ὅς relates one word of a complete sentence to another, explanatory portion. English example: The relative pronoun is underlined twice.

The man <u>who</u> <u>hears words</u> stays in the house.

The entire part underlined can be removed, and you'll still have a complete sentence. The part underlined is called the "dependent clause."

Same sentence in Greek:

ὁ ανθρωπος <u>ὃ</u> <u>ακουει λογους</u> μενει εν τῳ οικῳ

The relative pronoun must have masculine, feminine, and neuter forms to go with the noun it follows, and must exist in all cases so it can fill a function in its part of the sentence. Almost all the forms look like the word "the" without any τ. The only way you can differentiate from "the" in its feminine nominative singular form is through the accent:

the = ἡ (no accent)   who = ἥ (the same thing happens in nom. plurals)

The neuter is easy to differentiate because the neuter "the" has a τ, but the neuter relative pronoun does not (ὅ). The masculine form was given in the first Greek example, above (ὅς). Notice it is like the noun endings you learned at the beginning of Part II.

In the following example, the word for "who" is masculine, to fit the subject of the sentence, but it is in the accusative case, so it can be the direct object in its own part of the sentence, the part underlined. The subject of the part underlined is "you":

ὁ ανθρωπος <u>ὃν</u> <u>ακουεις</u> μενει εν τῳ οικῳ

The correct translation of the double underlined word is "whom": "The man whom you hear stays in the house."

Λιθον <u>ὃν</u> <u>the builders rejected</u> has become the cornerstone (Matt. 21:42).

If the relative pronoun refers to a word which is neuter in English, translate with "which" or "that," as in the example above.

The basic rule of thumb about case for the relative pronoun has exceptions. Sometimes the relative pronoun is in the same case as the word it is relating to:

The man speaks to the apostle whom you hear
ὁ ανθρωπος λεγει τω αποστολω ᾧ ακουσεις

Sometimes the noun is missing, and so the relative pronoun has to be translated:

ὅς = he who   ἥ = she who   or for neuter, ὅ = that which

Example

ὅ was from the beginning, ὅ we have heard, ὅ we have seen with our eyes, ὅ we beheld and our hands touched, regarding the word of life . . . (1 John 1:1).

_____ _____ shall speak _____ _____ ____ ____ ____ _____, it shall
Καὶ   ὃς ἐὰν   λόγον   κατὰ   τοῦ   υἱοῦ   τοῦ   ἀνθρώπου

be forgiven _____; _____ should speak _____ ____ ____ _____ ____,
            αὐτῷ   ὃς δ'   κατὰ τοῦ πνεύματος τοῦ ἁγίου

it shall not be forgiven ___ ____, ____ __ ____ _____ ____ age _____ ____
                         αὐτῷ   οὔτε ἐν τούτῳ τῳ αἰῶνι οὔτε   ἐν

____ coming one (Matt. 12:32).
τῷ

Scriptures with Relative Pronouns

Draw a line under the relative pronoun, and a box around its part of the sentence.

__ ____ ____ _____ ____ _____ ____ _____ shows _____ __ _____
Ο γὰρ   πατὴρ φιλεῖ τὸν   υἱὸν   καὶ πάντα   αὐτῷ ἃ αὐτὸς
_____ (John 5:20).
ποιεῖ

The relative pronoun is neuter plural to match παντα ("all things").

____ ____ ____ ____ _____ _____ __ he has built, he'll receive a reward
Εἴ   τινος   τὸ   ἔργον μενεῖ ὅ
(1 Cor. 3:14).

Neuter singular to go with "work" (εργον).

Genitive Example

Transforming themselves into ministers of righteousness, ___ ___ the end
shall be _____ ___ ___ _____ ___ _____ (2 Cor. 11:15). ὧν
      κατὰ   τὰ   ἔργα   αὐτῶν

The hope of life eternal, ____ God who cannot lie announced . . . (Titus 1:2).
                  ἥν

Feminine accusative, not because it has anything to do with women, but because the word "life," which the ἥν has to go with, happens to be a feminine
noun. But English doesn't consider it feminine, so translate ην as "which."

_____ ___ ___ ___ _____ _____ _____ ___ _____, I agree _____ ___ _____
Εἰ   δὲ   ὃ   οὐ   θέλω   τοῦτο   ποιῶ   τῷ νόμῳ ὅτι καλός
(Rom. 7:16).

   (Did you add the word "is"?)
   There is no noun for ὅ to relate to, so add the word "that": "that which."

Relative Pronouns—Why Are They Important?

Titus 3:5: (He saved us) by his own mercy through the <u>washing of rebirth</u>
                                            λουτροῦ παλιγγενεσίας

and "<u>making-new again</u>" of the Holy Spirit, _____ he shed upon us bounte-
   ἀνακαινώσεως   πνεύματος ἁγίον,   οὖ

ously through Jesus Christ . . .

   The question is, "What did he shed upon us bounteously? The washing?
The rebirth? The renewal? The Spirit?

   The relative pronoun could be masculine or neuter, so that leaves out rebirth
and renewal, which happen to be feminine. Washing and Spirit are both neuter,
so either one could be the answer; the translator would probably pick Spirit,
since it is closer to the relative pronoun. Notice also that the relative pronoun
is genitive, with the sense of "of whom" or "of which," just as in English we
use the word "of" when we are talking about a "portion" of something: (I
would like a glass *of* water).

   The passage then could be translated: ". . . washing of rebirth and renewal
of the Holy Spirit, 'of whom' he shed upon us richly through Jesus Christ . . ."
That is, Jesus has shed upon us a portion of the Holy Spirit.

Another Relative Pronoun

Combine the one you just learned (ὅς) with the word τις and you get ὅστις, "whoever" or "whatever."

Πᾶς   οὖν   ὅστις   ἀκούει   μου   τοὺς   λόγους   τούτους   καὶ   ποιεῖ

_____ is like a wise man _____ built _____ ____ ____ ___ ___
αὐτούς   ὅστις   αὐτοῦ   τὴν   οἰκίαν   ἐπὶ   τὴν

_____ (Matt. 7:24).
πέτραν

As you form this word in the various cases, actually combine the correct case of ὅς with the right form of τις. For example, genitive would be οὗ + τινος = οὗτινος. Nominative plural would be οἱ + τινες = οἵτινες.

There shall be more joy in heaven over one sinner repenting than over ninety-nine righteous _____ have no need of repentance (Luke 15:7).
                     οἵτινες

Feminine, ἡ + τις to go with the feminine word "life" in the following sentence:

We announce to you the eternal life _____ was with the Father (1 John 1:2).
                                        ἥτις

In Greek:

We announce ____ ____ ____ ____ ____ _____ _____ was _____
               ὑμῖν   τὴν   ζωὴν   τὴν   αἰώνιον   ἥτις   πρὸς

____ _____ (1 John 1:2).
τὸν   πατέρα

Lesson Thirty-Two

Some, More, Most: Comparing Adjectives

σοφος means "wise." It can receive endings to fit masculine, feminine, and neuter in all cases:

	Masculine	Feminine	Neuter
Nom.	σοφος λογος	σοφη κεφαλη "head"	σοφον δωρον "gift"
Gen.	σοφου λογου	σοφης κεφαλης	σοφου δωρου

etc.

To change to "wiser," add τερ + the case ending.

	Masculine	Feminine	Neuter
Nom.	σοφωτερος λογος	σοφωτερα κεφαλη	σοφωτερον δωρον
Gen.	σοφωτερου λογου	σοφωτερας κεφαλης	σοφωτερου δωρου

etc.

1 Corinthians 1:25: ὅτι τὸ μωρὸν τοῦ θεοῦ σοφώτερον τῶν ανθρώπων εστίν.

To change to "wisest," add τατ + the case ending.

	Masculine	Feminine	Neuter
Nom.	σοφωτατος λογος	σοφωτατα κεφαλη	σοφωτατον δωρον
Gen.	σοφωτατου λογου	σοφωτατας κεφαλης	σοφωτατου δωρου

Jude 20: Build yourselves up on your ἁγιωτάτη faith.

Other types of adjectives are found which use ιων for the er ending and ιστος for the est ending.

Example: κακο = bad, κακιων = worse, κακιστος = worst

(Words that end in ων use "Type III" noun endings—see chart, page 124).

Luke 1:3 (The dedication of the book of Luke:) . . . to write to you, κράτιστε θεόφιλε.

(κρατος = strength, used here as a common word of greeting. The ε ending is used when talking directly to someone.)

There are also expressions which have the word "more" in them:

ποσῳ μαλλον = how much more (literally "by how much," "rather")

____ ____ ____ know how to give good gifts to your children, _____
Εἰ   οὖν ὑμεῖς   πόσῳ μᾶλλον

_____ in heaven will give good things to those asking _____
ὁ   πατὴρ   ὑμῶν   αὐτόν
(Matt. 7:11).

Exercise One

English Words with Varied Meanings

I. Four uses for the English word "that"
Match the sentence to the explanation at the right.

___ 1. I came that they might have life.
___ 2. I wrote that book
___ ___ 3. The man that came to our door entered.

a. A relative pronoun—which "relates" an explanatory group of words to a noun. Greek ὅς and its forms.

b. As a connective between two complete sentences; Greek words like ἵνα, "in order that."

c. A pronoun used to point out a certain noun. Greek: εκεινος.

d. A round-about way to translate a Greek participle. Literally: the saying man. Smooth English: The man that is speaking.

II. Three uses for the word "to"

     ___ 4. I came to church.
     ___ 5. I spoke to Peter.
     ___ 6. I want to go home.

e. Infinitive—a verb form with no subject ending. Greek endings ειν or αι.

f. A preposition, such as πρός or εις.

g. Indirect object; Greek dative.

These are just two examples of ways that Greek can be very precise. Greek verb structures also lead to precision, as we will be seeing in Part V. Here's just one example:

"You shall come."

In English, you wouldn't know whether I meant you were going to come in the future, or whether I was commanding you to come. In Greek, the difference would be obvious because two different endings would be used.

First John, Chapter One

The connecting words and the rest of the pronouns you have learned are now included:

___ __ was ___ ___, __ we heard, __ __ we saw _____,
  ὅ[1]   ἀπ᾽ ἀρχῆς ὅ   ὅ   τοῖς ὀφθαλμοῖς[2] ἡμῶν

___ __ we beheld ____ ___ ___ ___ touched ___ ___ ___ ___
  ὅ   καὶ αἱ χεῖρες ἡμῶν   περὶ τοῦ λόγου τῆς

_____—___ __ ___ appeared ___ we saw ___ _____ ___ an-
ζωῆς καὶ ἡ ζωὴ   καὶ   καὶ μαρτυροῦμεν καὶ

nounce ___ ___ ___ ___ _____ ___ was ___ ___ ___
  ὑμῖν τὴν ζωὴν τὴν αἰώνιον ἥτις   πρὸς τὸν πατέρα

___ appeared ___—__ we saw ___ heard we announce ___ __ ___,
καὶ   ἡμῖν ὃ   καὶ   καὶ ὑμῖν ἵνα

___ _____ _____ may have ___ _____. __ __ _____ __
καὶ ὑμεῖς κοινωνίαν   μεθ᾽ ἡμῶν Καὶ ἡ κοινωνία δὲ

___ _____ ____ ___ _____ ___ ____ ___ ___ _____ Ἰησοῦ
ἡ ἡμετέρα μετὰ τοῦ πατρὸς καὶ μετὰ τοῦ υἱοῦ αὐτοῦ

_____. ___ _____ _____ ____ ___ __ _____ ____ might be
Χριστοῦ Καὶ ταῦτα γράφομεν ἡμεῖς ἵνα ἡ χαρὰ[3] ἡμῶν

full. ___ _____ ____ __ _____ ___ we heard ___ _____ ____ an-
  Καὶ ἔστιν αὕτη ἡ ἀγγελία ἣν   ἀπ᾽ αὐτοῦ καὶ

nounce ___, ___ ___ ____ ___ ___ ___ ___ ___ ___ ___ ___
  ὑμῖν ὅτι ὁ θεὸς φῶς ἐστιν καὶ σκοτία[4] ἐν αὐτῷ οὐκ

_____. ____ we say ____ ____ ____ ____ ____ ____ ____ ____
ἔστιν   οὐδεμία[5]   Ἐὰν   ὅτι   κοινωνίαν   ἔχομεν   μετ'   αὐτοῦ   καὶ

____ ____ ____ walk, we lie ____ ____ ____ ____ ____ ____ .
ἐν   τῷ   σκότει   καὶ   οὐ   ποιοῦμεν   τὴν   ἀλήθειαν   Ἐὰν

_____ we walk ____ ____ ____ ____ ____ ____ ,
δὲ   ἐν   τῷ   φωτὶ   ὡς   αὐτός   ἐστιν   ἐν   τῷ   φωτί

_____ , _____
κοινωνίαν   ἔχομεν   μετ'   ἀλλήλων   καὶ   τὸ   αἷμα   Ἰησοῦ   τοῦ   υἱοῦ

_____ cleans ____ ____ ____ sin. ____ we say ____ sin ____ __ ____ ,
αὐτοῦ   ἡμᾶς   ἀπὸ   πάσης   Ἐὰν   ὅτι   οὐκ   ἔχομεν

_____ we deceive ____ ____ ____ ____ ____ ____ ____ . ____ we
ἑαυτοὺς   καὶ   ἡ   ἀλήθεια   οὐκ   ἔστιν   ἐν   ἡμῖν   Ἐὰν

confess the sins __ ____ , faithful _____ ____ righteous ____ he may forgive
                 ἡμῶν   ἐστιν   καὶ   ἵνα

__ ____ the sins ____ cleanse _____ ____ _____ unrighteousness. ____ we
ἡμῖν   καὶ   ἡμᾶς   ἀπὸ   πάσης   Ἐὰν

say ____ ____ we have sinned, __ ____ ____ ____ __ ____ ____
     ὅτι   οὐχ   ψεύστην   ποιοῦμεν   αὐτὸν   καὶ   ὁ   λόγος   αὐτοῦ

_____ ____ __ _____ .
οὐκ   ἔστιν   ἐν   ἡμῖν

1. Relative pronoun, neuter: that which
2. Dative in "instrumental" sense = what we saw with
3. Joy
4. Darkness
5. ου + δε + μια (one) = not even once

Part IV

WORD STUDIES

After completing Part IV, you will:

1. Be familiar with dozens of the most important religious terms used in the Greek New Testament.

2. See connections between English words that are based on the same Greek word.

3. Understand basic meanings of religious terms through seeing the Greek words from which they are derived.

How to Use Part IV

In order to introduce you to many new words used in context in Bible passages, I have included words with endings that you do not know. I do not expect you to understand these endings, but simply to fill in the blanks with the basic meaning of each word. You will be able to tell, from the context, whether to translate it as a verb or a noun, etc.

The word studies are purposely included before you know more about endings and word-changes so that you will not translate them as academic exercises, but rather catch the general meaning and think of it immediately in terms of its English meaning. Being able to decipher endings is important, but it can wait. The first goal is a feel for the language.

On the other hand, when I use endings you do know, I expect you to translate them fully; so that, if two English words are needed to translate the Greek word, I have put two blanks there to remind you:

εστιν
<u>he</u> <u>is</u>

When dealing with a complicated verb ending, I have sometimes added extra words in the blank to give you a hint:

αμαρτητε   σωθησομαι
<u>ye may　　　　　</u>.   <u>shall be　　　　</u> -ed
         (sin)   (saved)

but if I felt you could fill in the right word because the passage was familiar, I did not give any hints.

The purpose of Part IV is to show you how translators struggle to put concepts into smooth English. Typically, I will give you the general meaning of a word, then give you a sentence that has that word in it. After you have tried to express the overall meaning in your own words, I expect you to look up the passage in a Bible and see what the translator did there. I intend that you be surprised as you do this, for you will find cases where you put a concept into ordinary, down-to-earth English, and then discover that a translator has used a more technical term or a lesser known word.

For example, you are going to be exploring some words based on οικος. Along the line, you'll find yourself translating a word based on οικος as "up-building, or building-up." When you look up this passage in a Bible, and find that the translator there chose to use the word "edify," I want you to exclaim to yourself—"Oh. So that's what 'edify' means."

In this fashion, I hope to lead you through many important New Testament religious concepts. Feel free to guess; don't worry about endings you don't know, and compare your efforts with a Bible.

Lesson Thirty-Three

Exercise One

Words Related to "καλ"

Words based on the root καλ have something to do with "calling."
Fill in the blanks with suitable English translations.

1. I _____ unto you.
   καλω

2. Whoever _____ on the name of the Lord shall be
   saved.   καλει

   (In the next word, the α is omitted between the κ and
   the λ, similar to our process of contracting.)

3. Many are _____, but few are chosen.
   κλητης

   (The ε in front of the next word makes it past tense, and
   the θ makes it "passive.")

4. You <u>were</u> _____ -ed by God.
   εκληθητε

   (I put "were" on the line because the one Greek word
   needs two words to be translated fully into English.)

5. God gave us a _____ to be holy.
   κλησις

6. Paul was the _____, specially selected by God to
   κλητος
   preach to the non-Jews.

> **Word List**
>
> called
> call
> calls
> called one
> calling
> caller

Exercise Two

You translated successfully above, through guesswork, without having to know
the rules about the endings you saw or whether the forms you were dealing with

174

were different words or the same words with different endings. This is the way we will proceed throughout Part IV; in Part V, we'll actually learn the endings.

Here are the words you translated, as they would be listed in an analytical lexicon, which lists all related words together (see below for abbreviations):

___ 1. καλεω fut. -εσω pass. aor. εκληθην to call, send for
___ 2. κλησις, εως f.,   a calling, an invitation
___ 3. κλητος, η, ον   called, invited

In the short blanks above, indicate whether each word listed is a (a) noun, (b) adjective, (c) verb.

Abbreviations used:

fut. =   future
pass. =   passive (when the action is done to the subject)
aor. =   aorist (a type of past tense)

Now try these Scriptures:

Let each one remain in ____ ____ _____ in which he was _____.
                          ἐν   τῇ   κλήσει   ἐκλήθη

_____ were you _____; don't let it matter to you (1 Cor. 7:20–21).
Δοῦλος   ἐκλήθης

(God, who is the one) saving us and _____ (with a) holy _____,
                                    καλέσαντος   κλήσει

not according to our works but according to his purpose (2 Tim. 1:9).

Exercise Three

Combining καλ with the Preposition εκ "out-of"

The result is a new word, εκκαλεω, meaning "call out" or "summon forth."

As a verb: A. I _____ the swimmers from the pool.
                   εκκαλεω

             B. God _____ believers from this sinful world.
                    εκκαλει

But when Greek changes this word into a noun, we don't have an English word that would make a good translation:

I belong to those _____.
                  εκκλησιων

"Callees" would be awkward. We could use a phrase like "called out ones" or "who have been called out." Unfortunately, even though this noun is so awkward to translate, it occurs often in the New Testament.

Check your translation for these passages:

1. Upon this rock I will build my _____ (Matt. 16:18).
   ἐκκλησίαν

(This word is also used to refer to Old Testament believers, as below.)

2. Moses was in the _____ in the wilderness (Acts 7:38).
   ἐκκλησίᾳ

(This word is also used to refer to secular gatherings, as below.)

3. And having said this, he dismissed the _____ (Acts 19:41).
   ἐκκλησίαν

The English word _____ comes from this word.

Bible translators then have chosen to translate the word that means "called out ones" or "gathering" by the word "church."

Exercise Four

What follows is the background of the English word "church":

Remember the word κυριος? If you are acquainted with the traditional liturgy, you might remember that the name for the first major "song" in the liturgy is _____ from the phrase "Lord have mercy": κυριε, ελεισον.

A related noun is κυριοτης, "lordship," "ruling authority," as in the sentence:

Seated at His right hand in the heavenlies, above all <u>chiefship</u> and authority
                                                      ἀρχῆς
and <u>power</u> and _____ and every name that is named . . . (Eph. 1:21).
   δυνάμεως   κυριότητος

The adjective related to κυριος is κυριακος, η, ον "pertaining to the Lord," as in

I was in the Spirit on the _____ day (Rev. 1:10).
   κυριακῇ

By a long process of language change, generalized here, let's see what generations of Anglo-Saxon and English believers did to that word.

Start with κυριακος.

1. Remove the ending (ος) and you get _____.
2. Contract by removing the ια and you get _____.
   (If you respell this word with i instead of u, you get a word used in Scotland.)
3. Soften the k's to ch's, and the result is _____.

Combining καλ with the Preposition παρα

An example of a concept that is difficult to translate.

παρα means "next to" or "alongside." The resulting word, παρακαλεω, is very common in the New Testament, but there is no single English word that translates it adequately. The basic meaning obviously is "call alongside," but what would you do with the a sentence like the following?

"I παρακαλω you to be careful."

A Greek dictionary lists words like "urge, beg, appeal." You could think of the concept as "call alongside to help, or as a friend."
This passage from Ephesians 4:1 uses the new word, as well as forms of the word for "call," from the previous pages:

I therefore, the prisoner of the Lord, _____ you to walk worthily of
                                        παρακαλῶ

the _____ with which you have been _____.
     κλήσεως   ἐκλήθητε

In the following passage, the word is best translated "comfort":

Blessed are those that mourn, for they shall be_____ (Matt. 5:4).
                                        παρακληθήσονται

Now try putting the idea into a noun:

. . . blessed be the God of all _____, the one who's _____
                                παρακλήσεως   παρακαλῶν

us in all our affliction, so we are able to_____ those in any affliction
                                            παρακαλεῖν

with the same _____ with which we ourselves were _____
                παρακλήσεως   παρακαλούμεθα

by God (2 Cor. 1:3–4).

The Greeks used another form of this word for "someone who brought help in legal matters": a "lawyer."

Before you put me in jail, let me call my παράκλητον.

Because He helps me, I can correctly call Jesus my παράκλητος.

In John 14:16, Jesus tells His disciples He'll be going away. Then He adds,

I will ask the Father, and He will give you another _____ to be
                                                    παράκλητον
with you forever, even the Holy Spirit.

Put together all these ideas of "being alongside in a helpful way," of "comforting and appealing," and of "standing in for us in the sense that a lawyer would," and you begin to see what a good choice of words it was for Jesus to call the Holy Spirit a παρακλητος—and also how difficult to put this term into English. You will find the English form of this word, "paraclete," in theological writings and hymns about the Holy Spirit.

Lesson Thirty-Four

A. Originally ἅγιος meant something "set apart" just for God—like the special cup set aside for use at communion.

1. . . . as _____ promised in the _____ Scriptures (Rom. 1:2).
   θεός   ἁγίαις

2. God said to Moses, "Loosen your sandals, you're standing on _____ ground" (Acts 7:33).
   ἁγία

Exercise One

In the two examples above ἅγιος is used as what: (noun, verb, adjective)?
In the next two examples, ἅγιος is still an adjective, but there is no noun for it to describe; you have to make one up; such as "person," "ones," "things," or "place"—that would make sense.

3. Do not give _____ to dogs (Matt. 7:6).
   ἅγιον

4. In the Old Testament, the blood of animals was brought into the _____ by the high priest as a sacrifice for sin (Heb. 13:11); but
   ἅγια

   _____ went into the _____ (the real one in heaven, not the copy
   Χριστὸς   ἅγια

   on earth), not with the blood of animals, but with his own blood, to get eternal redemption for us (Heb. 9:11–12).

B. Later, the same word ἅγιος was used to describe the character of God himself—for He is "set apart" from everything else. He is better, He is more special.

5. God says, "Ye shall be _____, for _____ am _____ (1 Pet. 1:16).
                            ἅγιοι   ἐγὼ   ἅγιος

6. Jesus prayed, "_____ _____, keep my disciples safe" (John 17:11).
                   ἅγιε   πάτηρ

This characteristic of God naturally applies to Jesus, too:

7. Signs and wonders were performed through the name of thy _____
   servant _____ (Acts 4:30).   ἁγίου
            Ἰησοῦ

8. The demons cried, "What have you to do with us, _____ of
                                                    Ἰησοῦ

   Nazareth? Have you come to destroy us? I know who you are—____
   _____ _____ ____ _____" (Luke 4:34).   ὁ
   ἅγιος   θεοῦ

The same word ἅγιος is used to describe the Spirit (πνευμα means both "wind" and "spirit").

9. If even you evil people know how to give good gifts to your children,
   how much more will the _____ in heaven give the _____
                          πατὴρ   ἅγιον

   _____ to those that ask Him? (Luke 11:13).
   πνεῦμα

10. The love of God has been poured into our _____ by the _____
                                             καρδίαις   Ἁγίου

    _____ which was given to us (Rom. 5:5).
    πνεύματος

C. The same word ἅγιος is used in worshiping God—telling Him that we
   know He is really special, "set apart" from all others:

11. Day and night (the creatures in heaven) never cease to sing, "_____
    _____ _____ _____ _____ Almighty" (Rev. 4:8).   ἅγιος
    ἅγιος   ἅγιος   κύριος   θεὸς

Now try turning ἅγιος into a verb—that is, "be holy."

12. Our _____ in heaven, _____ Thy name (Matt. 6:9).
        πάτερ   ἁγιασθήτω

Did you recognize this as the beginning of the Lord's prayer, and write the word "hallowed"? Or did you try to say it in your own words? If so, you might have discovered that you would have to write words both in front of and behind the words "Thy name" in order to translate that one Greek word into good English—you might have come up with something like "let your name be holy."

Besides "holy" and "hallowed," there are lots of other words that translators have used to try to get across the meaning of ἅγιος. A few examples: "consecrated," "sanctified," "saintly," "sacred." These words might help as you try to do the rest of this sheet.

13. Don't be afraid when people harm you for doing good; just
    _____ Christ as Lord in your hearts (1 Pet. 3:14–15).
    ἁγιάσατε

    (The meaning is "consider as being holy." The word "hallow" would fit here. Some translations use the word "reverence.")

D. Jesus followed God's will by "setting himself apart" for the special task of being crucified. He knew the end result would be that we would then be set apart in a special way as God's children:

14. Jesus prayed, "_____ _____ myself in behalf of my follow-
    Εγὼ ἁγιάζω

    ers, so that they also <u>may be</u> _____-ed in truth (John 17:19).
    ἡγιασμένοι

    (You might have written, "I set apart myself," and that would be good translating. Many translators used the word "sanctify," since it means the same thing.)

    (The η at the beginning of the last word is a substitute for α, and makes it into a past tense.)

E. As a result of Christ's death, God looks at us in a new way:

15. Jesus made peace between you and God through his death, in order
    to present you _____ before him, if you continue in the faith (Col.
    1:22).   ἁγίους

16. God chose us before the world began, to be _____ and pure be-
    fore him (Eph. 1:4).   ἁγίους

F. Besides looking at us as holy (set apart) just for Him and His kingdom, God also works His characteristics of holiness into our behavior.

17. You were evil, but you were washed, you were _____-ed, you were
    ἡγιάσθητε

    justified in the name of _____ and by the _____ ___ _____
    (1 Cor. 6:11).   Ἰησοῦ   πνεύματι θεοῦ

18. God disciplines us for our profit, so we may share his _____
    (Heb. 12:10).   ἁγιότητος

19. For the temple _____ is _____—and you are that temple (1 Cor.
    3:17).   θεοῦ   ἅγιός

Here the word ἅγιος is turned into a noun:

20. This is the will _____, your _____ (1 Thess. 4:3).
                      θεοῦ   ἁγιασμὸς

    (Most translators try to put it into one word, like "holiness" or
    "sanctification.")

G. God wants us to submit to his plan of building his holiness in us:

21. I beseech you, by the mercies of God, present your bodies as a living
    sacrifice, _____ and well-pleasing to God (Rom. 12:1).
               ἁγίαν

The end result is a type of person who is a blessing to others:

22. Paul writing to a young person named Timothy: "Be a pattern to the
    believers in speech, love, faith, and _____ (1 Tim. 4:12).
                                           ἁγνείᾳ

    (This happens to be a different word, but meaning is similar.)

H. Because God looks at us as holy (special, set apart just for Him)—and
   works holiness in us—the Bible calls believers "holy ones." That is just
   one word in Greek—the word ἅγιος with no noun of its own. You have to
   add in the word "ones."

Paul opens one of his letters:

23. Paul, to those who have been _____
                                 ἡγιασμένοις ἐν Χριστοῦ Ἰησοῦ
    who are now called _____ _____ (1 Cor. 1:1–2).
                        ἁγίοις

Translators customarily translate "holy ones" or "set-apart ones" as one
word: "saints."

Try the beginning of another letter:

24. _____, _____ ____ _____ _____ _____ the will
    Παῦλος,   ἀπόστολος   Χριστοῦ   Ἰησοῦ   διὰ
    ___ _____, to_the _____ who are ____ _____ _____ who
    θεοῦ   τοῖς   ἁγίοις   ἐν   Ἐφέσῳ   καὶ

are faithful ____ _____ _____ , grace to you _____ peace
       ἐν   Χριστοῦ   Ἰησοῦ   καὶ

_____ _____ our _____ _____ the _____ _____
  ἀπὸ   θεοῦ   πατρὸς   καὶ   κυρίου   Ἰησοῦ

_____ (Eph. 1:1–2).
  Χριστοῦ

Exercise Two

Summary

Six of the words below are good words to use in translating words related to ἁγιος. Cross out the ones that are NOT.

Holiness	Sanctification
Love	Word
Consecrated	Apostle
Peace	Lord
Saint	Sanctify
Faith	Holy

Lesson Thirty-Five

The πνεῦμα Word Family

πνεῦμα means both "wind" and "spirit." In the next sentence, it is used both ways:

1. Jesus said to Nicodemus, "The _____ blows wherever it wants

πνεῦμα   πνεῖ

to—so it is with everyone who is born of the _____" (John 3:8).

πνεύματος

In the King James translation, the word πνεῦμα was translated "ghost":

2. Jesus said, "Go and disciple all nations, _____ them in the

βαπτίζοντες

name of ____ _____ _____ _____ _____ _____ _____

τοῦ   πατρὸς   καὶ   τοῦ   υἱοῦ   καὶ   τοῦ

_____ _____" (Matt. 28:19).

ἁγίου   πνεύματος

The same word, πνεῦμα, might also refer to an evil spirit, or demon. In the following sentence the word ακαθαρσις is from καθαρσις, which means "clean." The α in front turns it into its opposite.

3. After Christ casts out a___demon___ the crowd cries, "What a mes-

δαιμόνιον

sage! With authority and power, he commands the _____

_____ and they come out!" (Luke 4:36).   ἀκαθάρτοις

πνεύμασιν

Now combine θεος (God) with πνευμα, and you get a word meaning "wind coming from God," or "God-breathed":

4. All Scripture is _____, _____ profitable for teaching

(2 Tim. 3:16).   θεόπνευστος   καὶ

184

Every human being is made up of spirit and body. When these two are separated, the result is death. Ezekiel wrote, "The body returns to dust, and the spirit returns to Him who gave it." The apostle James referred to this in the following passage:

5. For just as the body without the _____ is dead, so also
$$\pi\nu\epsilon\hat{\upsilon}\mu\alpha\tau\sigma\varsigma$$

<u>faith</u> without works is dead (James 2:26).
πίστις

The πίστις Word Family

Select a word family that would make sense in all three sentences:

1. I would like more πιστιν   (noun)
2. God is πιστος   (adjective)
3. I πιστευω in Jesus   (verb)

Translators have used the following English words to translate πιστις: "believe"; "belief"; "faith"; "faithful"; "trust"; "put trust"; "rely on."

As a noun:

1. ____ have _____ _____ _____.
   Εγω   πιστιν   εν   θεω

As a verb:

2. Whoever _____ and is baptized shall be saved.
              πιστευει

3. ____ _____ into _____.
   Εγω   πιστευω   εις   Ιησου

As an adjective:

4. _____ is _____. He won't let you be tempted beyond your
   Θεος   πιστος

   strength.

Going Deeper

The basic word in the family that πιστις comes from is πειθω, which means "persuade." The forms in the following blanks are based on this word:

5. Jesus said, "If they don't hear Moses and the prophets, neither <u>will</u> <u>they be</u> _____ if someone were to rise from the dead" (Luke 16:31). πεισθήσονται

6. Paul said, "I am _____ that nothing can separate us from the
        πέπεισμαι

   love of God" (Rom. 8:38).

   (Other translations use the word "convinced" for the passages above.)

7. Paul writes, "We are the true people of God, who worship God right from the spirit, and having put no _____in the flesh" (our own ways) (Phil. 3:3).   πεποιθότες

   (Other translations use the word "confidence" to translate this passage.)

8. Paul said, "God allowed us to suffer so we would not be putting _____ in ourselves, but in Him" (2 Cor. 1:9).
        πεποιθότες

9. How difficult for them that _____ in riches to enter the King-
                          πεποιθότες

   dom of heaven, thought the disciples (Mark 10:24).

   (Other translations use the world "trust" for these passages.)

Why would the Greeks pick a word for *faith* that is in a word family that means persuasion? This suggests to us that we don't believe because of "blind faith," but the Holy Spirit has actually persuaded us inside that God is real and that Jesus has died for our sins.

Some Words Based on οἶκος

Those who live in one are called οικειοι.

You are fellow citizens with the saints and _____ ___ _____ (Eph. 2:19).
                                          οἰκεῖοι   θεοῦ

   (This word is an adjective: οικειος, εια, ειον, "belonging to a house." You could translate "family member.")

Another example:

If anyone does not care for his own, and especially his _____, he has denied the faith (1 Tim. 5:8).   οἰκείων

Another word, οικετης, means "household slave," "domestic servant":

_____, submit ____ _____ _____ _____ ___ _____
οἱ   οἰκέται   ἐν   παντὶ   φόβῳ   τοῖς   δεσπόταις

(1 Pet. 2:18).

Now combine λαρα plus οικος.
         (alongside)

You are no longer _____, but fellow citizens with the saints and
                    λάροικοι

_____ ___ _____ (Eph. 2:19).
οἰκεῖοι   θεοῦ

Πάροικοι are those who are not part of the household—neighbor, sojourner, visitor, temporary resident, stranger. Here is the corresponding verb:

(On the road to Emmaus) Cleopas said to him, "____ _____ _____
                                                Σὺ   μόνος   παροικεῖς

in Jerusalem and do not know what has happened in these past days?"
(Luke 24:18).

Now combine κατα plus οικος.
         (down, inside)

. . . that Christ (may_____) in your hearts by faith (Eph. 3:17).
                κατοικῆσαι

The corresponding noun form:

In Christ you are built together into an _____ of God (Eph. 2:22).
                                          κατοικητήριον

(You could translate: an "indwelling-place.")

Now combine οικος plus νεμω (administer) = οικονομος (manager)
(from the parable of the unjust steward):

__ _____ said to himself, "What shall I do? My Lord wants to take
Ο   οἰκονόμος

away the _____ from me" (Luke 16:3).
          οἰκονομίαν

That latter word is hard to translate without being awkward—you could say "administration," "stewardship," "management." In the next passage, the word is applied to God as the one who manages the entire universe, who runs it, and keeps it in order and on schedule:

God made known the _____ of His will, for an _____ of
                          μυστήριον   οἰκονομίαν
the fullness of time, to head up all things in _____ (Eph. 1:9–10).
                                                                      Χριστῷ

Exercise One

English Derivative

If you can respell the word οικονομια cleverly enough, you'll come up with the word we use to apply to the financial order. Hint: replace the first two letters with an "e."

_____

A related Greek word, οικουμενικος which means related to the inhabited world, became the English word we use when talking about the "worldwide" unity of church bodies. What is it?

_____

Now combine οικος plus δομεω (build).

_____ _____ ____ _____ rejected has become the head of
   Λίθον   ὃν   οἱ   οἰκοδομοῦντες
the corner (Matt. 21:42).

> (The reason for the longer ending is that this example happens to be a participle: translate "those building.")

(To Christ on the cross:) "You, the one casting down _____ _____ _____
                                                              τὸν   ναὸν   καὶ
____ _____ days _____-ing, save _____, ____ _____ ____
 ἐν   τρισὶν   οἰκοδομῶν   σεαυτόν   εἰ   υἱὸς   εἶ
_____ _____" (Matt. 27:40).
 τοῦ   θεοῦ

He that speaks in tongues _____ _____ (1 Cor. 14:4).
                                    οἰκοδομεῖ   ἑαυτόν

(A common translation of the term is "edify." The fact that that word means "build up" can be seen if you notice the resemblance to the word "edifice," which means a building.)

Here's the corresponding noun, referring to the act of building:

God gave gifts for the _____ of the body of Christ.
                                    οἰκοδομήν

(This can be translated "edification," that is, "up-building.")

Now combine together ελι + οικος + δομεω.

You are the family of God, _____ on the foundation of the
                                    ἐποικοδομηθέντες

apostles and prophets . . . (Eph. 2:19–20).

(This is a past participle: having been built like a house upon.)

Here's the same passage in fuller form:

(You are) _____ _____ _____ _____ _____ ____ foun-
              οἰκεῖοι   τοῦ   θεοῦ   ἐποικοδομηθέντες   ἐπὶ   τῷ

dation ___ _____ _____ _____ _____ . . . (Eph. 2:19–20).
          τῶν   ἀποστόλων   καὶ   προφητῶν

Now combine συν plus οικος plus δομεω: "built together with."

In whom also you _____ into a dwelling place of God in Spirit
(Eph. 2:22).   συνοικοδομεῖσθε

Same passage in fuller form:

| _____ | _____ | _____ | _____ | _____ | _____ | _____ | _____ |
| ἐν | ᾧ | καὶ | ὑμεῖς | συνοικοδομεῖσθε | εἰς | κατοικητήριον | τοῦ |

| _____ | _____ | _____. |
| θεοῦ | ἐν | πνεύματι |

At this point, let's put all the words we've seen based on οικος into a complete passage (Eph. 2:19–22):

| _____ | _____ | _____ | _____ | _____ | _____ | _____, |
| ἄρα | οὖν | οὐκέτι | ἐστὲ | ξένοι[1] | καὶ | πάροικοι |

| _____ | _____ | _____ | _____ | _____ | _____ | _____ |
| ἀλλὰ | ἐστὲ | συμπλῖται[2] | τῶν | ἁγίων | καὶ | οἰκεῖοι |

| _____ | _____, | _____ | _____ | ____ | _____ | _____ |
| τοῦ | θεοῦ | ἐποικοδομηθέντες | ἐπὶ | τῷ | θεμελίῳ[3] | τῶν |

ἀποστόλων   καὶ   προφητῶν   , ὄντος[4]   ἀκρογωνιαίου[5]   αὐτοῦ[6]

_____ _____ , ___ __ _____ _____ , being fitted-
Χριστοῦ   Ἰησοῦ   ἐν ᾧ   πᾶσα   οἰκοδομὴ

together, grows _____ _____ _____ ____ _____ .
                        εἰς   ναὸν   ἅγιον   ἐν   κυρίῳ

(The rest of the passage is already quoted in full on page 189.)

1. Ever hear of xenophobia (hatred of foreigners)?
2. You probably know that a Greek city was called a πολις. Those who lived there would be called πολιται. The word συμ (with) has been put in front to indicate that you are city-members along with those who were there before you. Literal: "with-citizens."
3. Foundation
4. This is a participle of "is": translate "being."
5. Cornerstone
6. Of it.

Lesson Thirty-Six

Putting the Letter α in Front of a Word . . .

changes it to its opposite (just like "im" does in English: possible become "impossible").

Below are listed some real Greek words, with their meanings. Then the same Greek words, but with the letter α in front, are listed. Match to the English translations listed.

I. θεος—God   σβεστος—can be put out if on fire
   τομος—"can be divided-up"   γνωσις—knowledge

___ 1. αθεος
___ 2. ατομος
___ 3. ασβεστος
___ 4. αγνωστος

A. A fireproof material
B. Someone who is without God; compare our word "atheist."
C. At one time scientists thought they had found a particle so small it couldn't be divided any further, so they called it an "atom"; in Scripture, it's used for a small moment of time.
D. Someone who says he doesn't know whether there is a God— "agnostic." In New Testament times, the "Gnostics" claimed to have superior knowledge about how to make contact with the divine, over and above that which the ordinary person would know (and over and above that revealed in the life and message of Jesus Christ).

II. σοφος—wise   συμφωνος—in harmony (cf. Eng. "symphony")
    τιμος—honored   μαρτυρος—witness (cf. Eng. "martyr")

____ 5. αμαρτυρος   E. ignorant
____ 6. ατιμος   F. dishonored
____ 7. ασοφος   G. clashing
____ 8. ασυμφωνος   H. without witness

III. σιτος—food, wheat   μετρος—measure
     φοβος—fear   γραμμα—letter, learning (a "scribe" in New Testa-
                                       ment was called a γραμματευς)

____ 9. αφοβος   I. starving or fasting
____ 10. αγραμματος   J. uneducated
____ 11. αμετρος   K. brave
____ 12. ασιτος   L. infinite, boundless

IV. κακος—evil   καρπος—fruit
    φωνη—sound   νους—mind (dative is νοι)

____ 13. ανοια   M. unfruitful
____ 14. ακακος   N. thoughtless, insane
____ 15. αφωνος   O. silent
____ 16. ακαρπος   P. good

V. πιστις—faith   ψευδης—lie
   ψυχη—soul   λογος—word

____ 17. αψυχος   Q. truth
____ 18. αλογος   R. unbelieving
____ 19. απιστος   S. cold-hearted
____ 20. αψευδης   T. speechless

VI. θανατος—death   γαμος—married (cf. Eng. "monogamous")
    ορατος—visible   δυνατος—powerful, able (cf. Eng. "dynamite")

____ 21. αγαμος   U. invisible
____ 22. αδυνατος   V. impossible
____ 23. αορατος   W. single
____ 24. αθανασια   X. immortality

VII. In the following examples, an ν is placed after the α to make a smoother transition into the main word.

ὕδωρ—water (cf. Eng. "hydraulics")
ὑποκριτης—one who pretends to be what he is not (cf. Eng. "hypocrite")
αιτιον—cause, guilt
ωφελεω—be useful
ἁλς, ἁλος—salt
αξιος—worthy

___ 25. ανυποκριτος	Y.	sincere, genuine
___ 26. ανυδρος	Z.	useless (this is the scientific name of the mosquito that caused trouble during the building of the Panama Canal)
___ 27. ανωφελης		
___ 28. αναξιος		
___ 29. αναιτιος		
___ 30. αναλος	AA.	dry, desert
	BB.	innocent
	CC.	saltless, insipid
	DD.	unworthy

Exercise Two

Caution

Do not confuse words that start with αν with those that start with ανα, which means "from above" or "again." Examples of such words include:

1. ανα + γενναω (give birth to)	= ___ αναγενναω	a. sit up
2. ανα + καθεδρα (chair)	= ___ ανακαθιζω	b. refresh
3. ανα + κεφαλη (head)	= ___ ανακεψαλαιοω	c. cause to be reborn
4. ανα + ψυχη (soul)	= ___ αναφυχω	d. sum up
5. ανα + μνεια (mention)	= ___ αναμνησις	e. reminder

This last word, when spelled in English, is the technical term used to refer to the part of a communion prayer in which the first Lord's Supper is remembered: _____.

Scriptures Using Words That Start with α

When they saw the boldness _____ _____ _____ _____
                                                   τοῦ   Πέτρου   καὶ   Ἰωάννου

_____ perceived ____ _____ _____ _____ ____
καὶ   ὅτι   ἄνθρωποι   ἀγράμματοί   εἰσιν   καὶ

_____, they wondered (Acts 4:13).
ἰδιῶται

He will clear his threshing floor and gather _____ _____ ____ ____
                                                          τὸν   σῖτον   αὐτοῦ

_____ _____ storehouse, but the chaff he will burn with <u>fire</u> _____
εἰς   τὴν   ἀποθήκην   πυρὶ   ασβέστῳ
(Matt. 3:12).

Exercise Three

Note two more English cognates to words used above:

> _____: One who operates a storehouse for drugs,
> "drugstore."

> _____: Add "maniac" and you get a person who likes
> to set fires.

_____ _____ carefully how you walk, _____ _____ _____
Βλέπετε   οὖν   μὴ   ὡς   ἄσοφοι

_____ _____ _____ . . . (Eph. 5:15).
ἀλλ'   ὡς   σοφοί

_____ _____ _____ _____ _____ in his own coun-
Οὐκ   ἔστιν   προφήτης   ἄτιμος   εἰμὴ
try . . . (Matt. 13:57).

. . . the hope ____ _____ <u>eternal</u>, ____ announced _____
                  ζωῆς   αἰωνίου   ἥν   ὁἀψευδὴς θεὸς

_____ _____ _____ (Titus 1:2).
πρὸ   χρόνων   αἰωνίων

_____ ____ a lamb before his shearers (is) _____ _____ _____
Καὶ   ὡς   ἄφωνος   οὕτως   οὐκ

opened ____ _____ ___ _____ (Acts 8:32).
τὸ   στόμα   αὐτοῦ
Yet God did not leave himself _____ _____ (Acts 14:17).
ἀμάρτυρον

Some were convinced, some disbelieved; ____ _____ being <u>among</u>
ἀσύμφωνοι δὲ   πρὸς
<u>themselves</u> they departed (Acts 28:24–25).
ἀλλήλους

_____ ___ _____; _____ ___ ___ _____ _____ becomes,
Καλὸν   τὸ   ἅλας   ἐὰν   δὲ   τὸ   ἅλας   ἄναλον
how shall you season it? (Mark 9:50).

And if you are to judge __ _____, _____ ____ _____ of lesser
<u>judgments</u>? (1 Cor. 6:2). ὁ   κόσμος   ἀνάξιοί   ἐστε
κριτηρίων

Having purified _____ _____ ___ _____ by obedience to the truth _____
τὰς   ψυχὰς   ὑμῶν   εἰς
_____ _____ . . . (1 Peter 1:22).
φιλαδελφίαν   ἀνυπόκριτον

(Christ,) ____ _____ _____ _____ _____, firstborn
ὅς   ἐστιν   εἰκὼν   τοῦ   θεοῦ τοῦ ἀοράτου

_____ _____ creation, ____ ___ _____ were created _____
πάσης   ὅτι   ἐν   αὐτῷ   τὰ πάντα

___ _____ heavens ____ ___ ___ ___ _____, __ _____
ἐν   τοῖς   καὶ   ἐπὶ   τῆς   γῆς   τὰ   ὁρατὰ   καὶ

____ _____, <u>whether</u> _____ <u>or "lord-ships"</u> _____ <u>"chief-ships"</u>
τὰ   ἀόρατα   εἴτε   θρόνοι   εἴτε   κυριοτητες   εἴτε   ἀρχαὶ

_____ authorities . . . (Col. 1:15–16).
εἴτε

Lesson Thirty-Seven

δικαιος and Related Forms

This word is one of the most important in the Bible, and one of the richest in meaning. Rather than give a definition, you will gradually see the concepts contained in this word as you guess at meanings in the following Scriptures:

(Boss to workers:) "I'll pay you whatever is _____" (Matt. 20:4).
   (Basic meaning is "fair," "just right.")   δίκαιον

The following sentence refers to the "just right" result of unbelief:

Those who reject the gospel will pay the _____ of eternal destruction
(Jude 7).   δίκην
   (This "just right" result would be a penalty, or a just result.)

This characteristic of being "just right" is descriptive of God Himself:

(Jesus, addressing the Father in prayer:) "_____, the world
has not known Thee . . ." (John 17:25).   Πάτερ δίκαιε

Centurion, seeing Jesus die, said, "Surely, this man was _____" (Luke
23:47).   δίκαιος
   (Some use the word "righteous" to translate this characteristic.)

The word δίκαιος was used a lot in courtrooms. In God's courtroom, all of us have to admit:

There is not a _____ man, no, not one (Rom. 3:10).
   δίκαιος

Some people may try to appear okay on the outside, but that doesn't fool God:

You may_____ yourself before men, but God knows your heart
δικαιοῦντες
(Luke 16:15).

196

(You may have translated "seem righteous" or "pretend to be okay"; a common translation of the verb form of our word is "justify.")

No matter what we've done, we'll be guilty in God's courtroom:

No one <u>will be</u>_____ by works of the law (Gal. 2:16).
          δικαιωθήσεται

So God came up with another plan:

But now, apart from law, the_____ of God has been shown. . . . Though
                                          δικαιοσύνη
all have sinned and fall short of the glory of God, they <u>are</u>_____
                                                                    δικαιούμενοι
as a gift by grace through the redemption which is in Christ Jesus (Rom. 3:21, 23–24).

For example, Abraham was a sinner; but:

Abraham believed God, and it (his believing) was reckoned to him as
_____ (Rom. 4:3).
    δικαιοσύνην

This is for all of us:

Blessed is the man to whom God reckons _____ without works
(Rom. 4:6).   δικαιοσύνη

This quality is something we do not possess in and of ourselves; it has to be reckoned to us by God. That is why the verb forms which describe this concept are placed in the "passive" voice, which expresses action being done *to* the subject.

We reckon a man <u>to have been</u>_____ by faith without works (Rom. 3:28).
                          δικαιοῦσθαι

The believer who has been put right with God also sees this characteristic of "rightness" come forth in his life and can be described with this term:

The earnest prayer <u>of a</u>_____ <u>man</u> has great results (James 5:16).
                          δικαίου

For the Christian, it takes a definite purpose to bring the "rightness" which God has declared about you into the experiences of daily living:

Flee youthful passions, and pursue _____, faith, love, and
peace . . . (2 Tim. 2:22).   δικαιοσύνην

Exercise One

Summary

Six of the following words have something to do with translating the δικαιος
word family. Cross out the six that do NOT:

just	faith	righteousness
holy	justify	lordship
fair	saint	believe
love	right	justification

Dictionary references:

δικη, ης (feminine)	— noun:	justice, judgment
δικαιος, αια, αιον	— adjective:	just, righteous, fair
δικαιως	— adverb:	justly, fitly, properly
δικαιοσυνη, ης (feminine)	— noun:	justice, rightness
δικαιοω	— verb:	to make right, to justify
δικαιωμα, ατος (neuter)	— noun:	an act of justice, a sentence, a decree
δικαιωσις, εως (feminine)	— noun:	a declaration of justice
δικαστης, ου (masculine)	— noun:	a judge

Two verses from Romans 10:

3. Not knowing _____ ⌐_____⌐ _____ _____ _____
              γὰρ   τὴν   τοῦ   θεοῦ   δικαιοσύνην,

_____ _____ _____ _____ seeking to establish, ____
  καὶ   τὴν   ἰδίαν   δικαιοσύνην   τῇ

_____ _____ _____ _____ did submit;
 δικαιοσύνῃ   τοῦ   θεοῦ   οὐχ

4. end _____ _____ ____ (___) _____ _____ _____
      γὰρ   νόμου   Χριστὸς   εἰς   δικαοσύνην

____ ____ ____ believing one.
παντὶ τῷ πιστεύοντι

Under the bracket, the first "the" goes with "righteousness." In v. 4, you have to add the
word "is."

Words Related to δικαιος

Remember that the letter α in front of a word changes it to its opposite.

If we confess our sins, He is faithful and _____ to forgive our sins and
                                          δίκαιος

cleanse us from all _____ (1 John 1:9).
                     ἀδικίας

For Christ died, _____ for _____ (1 Pet. 3:18).
                  δίκαιος   ἀδίκων

God's wrath is revealed against the _____ of men who suppress the
                                                 ἀδικίαν
truth in _____ (Rom. 1:18).
         ἀδικίᾳ

The words that start with κ in the following Scriptures are all related to the
concept "judge."

Jesus said, I do nothing on my own; as I hear, ____ ____, and my _____
is _____ (John 5:30).   κρίνω   κρίσις
   δικαία

God has set a day _____ the earth in _____ (Acts 17:31).
                   κρίνειν   δικαιοσύνη

Christ didn't revile in return, but put the whole matter into the hands of the
_____ -ing _____ -ly (1 Pet. 2:23).
κρίνοτι   δικαίως

_____ _____ _____, _____ ____ ye may be _____; ____ _ ____
Μὴ   κρίνετε ἵνα   μὴ   κριθῆτε   ἐν ᾧ γὰρ

_____ -ment _____, ye shall be _____ -ed, _____ ____ _
κρίματι   κρίνετε   κριθήσεσθε   καὶ ἐν ᾧ

_____ ____ _____, it shall be _____ -ed ____ ____ (Matt. 7:1–2).
μέτρῳ   μετρεῖτε   μετρηθήσεται   ὑμῖν

Here's κρινω and δικαιος combined into one word:

(Those who sin) are treasuring up wrath for the day of wrath and of the
revelation of the _____ of God (Rom. 2:5).
                  δικαιοκρισίας

__ _____ you know ____ ___ ____ ___ _____
Ἤ   οὐκ   ὅτι οἱ ἅγιοι τὸν κόσμον

will _____? ____ __ ___ _____ will be ____ -ed __
κρινοῦσιν;   Καὶ εἰ ἐν ὑμῖν κρίνεται   ὁ

_____, unworthy ____ ____ of lesser _____? (1 Cor. 6:2).
κόσμος   ἐστε   κριτηρίων

Exercise Two

English cognate of last word in the verse above: _____

Exercise Three

The word of God is alive and active . . . and _____ the thoughts and
intentions of the heart (Heb. 4:12).   κριτικὸς

English cognate of the word above: _____

Combining εκ with δικαιος yields the notion of "avenging":

   The widow said to the <u>unrighteous judge,</u> "_____ me from my
   opponent . . ."   ἀδικίας κριτὴς   Ἐκδίκησόν

   Jesus concluded "Won't God perform _____ for his chosen ones?"
   (Luke 18:3, 7).   ἐκδίκησιν

   Beloved, don't be _____-ing yourselves, but give place to wrath;
                        ἐκδικοῦντες

   for it is written, "Mine is _____, I will repay, saith the Lord" (Rom.
   12:19).   ἐκδίκησις

Combining δικαιος plus κατα = condemnation.
              (down)

The chief priests gave information against Paul, asking _____ against
him (Acts 25:15).   καταδίκην

Don't _____ and you won't be _____; don't _____ and
        κρίνετε   κριθῆτε   καταδικάζετε
you won't be _____ (Luke 6:37).
              καταδικασθῆτε

Lesson Thirty-Eight

Words about Sin

These are some of the New Testament words, each with a different shade of meaning, that illustrate the depth and meaning of sin.

First, words that have the letter α in front:

Root words: δικαιος—righteous   σεβασμα—object of worship

καθαρος—clean   νομος—law

πειθω—obey (be persuaded)   πιστις—faith

Resulting words (match to English descriptions):

____ 1. ασεβης   a. unrighteousness

____ 2. αδικια   b. uncleanness

____ 3. ακαθαρσια   c. law-breaker

____ 4. ανομος   d. disobey

____ 5. απειθεω   e. against what is worthy of worship

____ 6. απιστος   f. unbeliever

Some Scripture Quotes:

_____ ____ ____ _____ _____ __ greediness
Πορνεία   δὲ   καὶ   ἀκαθαρσία   πᾶσα   ἢ

_____ let be named ____ _____ _____ is fitting _____s
μηδὲ   ἐν   ὑμῖν   καθὼς   ἁγίοις

(Eph. 5:3).

_____ ὁ _____ _____ _____ , __ _____ _____ perdition, setting
...ὁ   ἄνθρωπος   τῆς   ἀνομίας   ὁ   υἱὸς   τῆς

himself up against _____ called _____ _____ _____ _____
                    πάντα   λεγόμενον   θεὸν   ἢ   σέβασμα   ὥστε

_____ _____ _____ _____ _____ _____ to sit, claiming
αὐτὸν   εἰς   τὸν   ναὸν   τοῦ   θεοῦ   καθίσαι

_____ ____ _____ _____ (2 Thess. 2:3–4).
ἑαυτὸν   ὅτι   ἐστὶν   θεός

Do not be unequally yoked together _____ _____ (2 Cor. 6:14).
                                    ἀπίστοις

The one _____ -ing _____ _____ _____ _____ _____ _____ eternal; __
ʹΟ   πιστεύων   εἰς   τὸν   υἱὸν   ἔχει   ζωὴν   αἰώνιον   ὁ

_____ _____ __ _____ _____ shall see _____ ... (John 3:36).
δὲ ἀπειθῶν   τῷ   υἱῷ   οὐκ   ζωήν

Exercise Two

The following word is the one usually translated by the word "sin" in the New
Testament. The general meaning has to do with "missing the mark." Here
are the forms used:

a. Verb: ἁμαρτάνω   "miss the mark"

b. Noun: ἁμαρτία   "a missing of the mark"

c. Noun: ἁμαρτωλός   "one who misses the mark"

On the blank at the end of each Scripture reference, write "a," "b," or "c," to
indicate which of the forms given above was used in that Scripture.

_____ we say _____ _____ _____ _____ , _____
ʹΕὰν   ὅτι   ἁμαρτίαν   οὐκ ἔχομεν   ἑαυτοὺς

we deceive _____ ___ _ truth _____ _____ ____ _____
πλανῶμεν   καὶ ἡ   οὐκ   ἔστιν   ἐν   ἡμῖν

(1 John 1:8).   (1) ____

_____ _____ _____ once _____ _____ _____ suffered— _____
Ὅτι   καὶ   Χριστὸς   περὶ   ἁμαρτιῶν   δίκαιος

_____ _____ (1 Peter 3:18).   (2) ____
ὑπὲρ   ἀδίκων

Through the disobedience ___ ___ ___ _____ ___ _____ were
               τοῦ ἑνὸς   ἀνθρώπου...οἱ   πολλοί

made _____ (Rom. 5:19).   (3) ____
      ἁμαρτωλοί

My children, _____ _____ _____ ____ _____ _____ye may ____
           ταῦτα   γράφω   ὑμῖν   ἵνα   μὴ ἁμάρτητε

(1 John 2:1).   (4) ____

Knowing _____, _____ _____ _____ _____ is laid down, _____
        τοῦτο   ὅτι   δικαίῳ   νόμος   οὐ   ἀνόμοις

___ _____unruly, _____ _____ _____ _____ _____(1 Tim. 1:9).   (5) ____
δὲ καὶ   ἀσεβέσι   καὶ   ἁμαρτωλοῖς

Sin-Words That Start with λαρα

λαρα (alongside) + λτωμα (fall) = λαραλτωμα (usually translated "trespass")

_____ _____being _____ (in regard) ____ ____ _____
καὶ   ὑμᾶς   νεκρούς   τοῖς   παραπτώμασιν

_____ _____ _____ _____ _____ (Eph. 2:1).   (6) ____
καὶ   ταῖς   ἁμαρτίαις   ὑμῶν

Note that by the choice of words, this sentence includes both aspects of the
nature of sin:

1. missing the mark—not doing what you should
   have done.
2. trespassing—doing what you were not supposed
   to do.

λαρα (alongside) + βαινω (go) = words about deviating, transgressing

    Verb: λαραβαινω (transgress)

    Noun: λαραβασις (transgression)

    Noun: λαραβατης (transgressor, violator)

_____those things I tore down, again ___ _____ _____
εἰ   γὰρ   οἰκοδομῶ,   παραβάτην

_____ I establish (Gal. 2:18).
ἐμαυτὸν

παρα (alongside) + ακουω (hear) = not hear, fail to listen, neglect to obey

Verb: παρακουω (disobey)
Noun: παρακοη (disobedience)

_____ _____ _____ _____ _____ received a just
καὶ   πᾶσα   παράβασις   καὶ   παρακοὴ

payment (Heb. 2:2).

οφειλω = owe, incur a debt

Used in a secular sense:

(The dishonest steward said to the first debtor:) "How much _____
_____?" (Luke 16:5).   ὀφείλεις
           τῷ κυρίῳ μου;

Verb: οφειλω (owe)
Noun: οφειλημα (debt)
Noun: οφειλητης (the one who owes a debt: the "debtor")

In the Lord's prayer: _____ forgive ____ ____ ____ _____ _____
                                          καὶ   ἡμῖν   τὰ   ὀφειλήματα   ἡμῶν,

_____ _____ _____ forgive _____ _____ ____ _____ (Matt.
ὡς   καὶ   ἡμεῖς   τοῖς   ὀφειλέταις   ἡμῶν

6:12).

κακος (evil) + ποιεω (do) = do evil

Verb: κακοποιεω (do evil)
Noun: κακοποιος (evil-doer)

_____ _____ _____ _____ let suffer _____ murderer __ _____
Μὴ   γάρ   τις   ὑμῶν   ὡς   ἢ   κλέπτης

____ _____ __ ____ mischief-maker (1 Pet. 4:15).
ἢ   κακοποιὸς   ἢ   ὡς

Finally, put the α in front of ἁμαρτωλός to get the opposite of sinner
(ν included for smoothness):

Let him who is _____ among you cast the first stone (John 8:7).
                      ἀναμάρτητος

Lesson Thirty-Nine

Confession and Repentance

Words based on ὁμος have to do with likeness, similarity:

I will tell you what the man _____-ing and _____-ing my words is
                        ἀκούων   ποιῶν

like: _____ _____ _____ _____ -ing _____
     ὅμοιός   ἐστιν   ἀνθοώπῳ   οἰκοδομοῦντι   οἰκίαν

____ dug and deepened and laid a foundation _____ _____ _____
ὅς   ἐπὶ   τὴν   πέτραν
(Luke 6:47–48).

The following word refers to the "communicating" that goes on among associates (those of *like* interests):

_____ _____ corrupt good morals (1 Cor. 15:33).
κακαί   ὁμιλίαι

Exercise One

English Derivative

The short talk given to a religious gathering is based on the word above.

Take off the ιαι and add y: _____

Combining ὁμο and λογος = "say the same," that is, profess something to be true which someone else has told you is true.

The Sadducees say there are no angels, resurrection, or spirit:

_____ ___ _____ both (Acts 23:8).
φαρισαῖοι δὲ ὁμολογοῦσιν

This word is often used in professing the truth of something God has said:

That if you <u>should</u> _____ with your _____ _____ (____)
       ὁμολογήσῃς   στόματί   κύριον

_____ <u>and should</u> _____ _____ _____ _____ _____ _____ _____ _____
Ἰησοῦν καὶ πιστεύσῃς   ἐν   τῇ   καρδίᾳ   σου ὅτι ὁ θεὸς

raised _____ _____ _____ _____, you shall be saved (Rom. 10:9).
       αὐτὸν   ἐκ   νεκρῶν

We have become accustomed to using the word mainly to profess something
negative:

_____ _____ _____ _____ _____ _____ _____ _____,
ἐὰν   ὁμολογῶμεν τὰς   ἁμαρτίας ἡμῶν   πιστός   ἐστιν

_____ _____ to forgive _____ _____ _____ and cleanse
καὶ   δίκαιος   ἡμῖν τὰς ἁμαρτίας

us _____ _____ _____ (1 John 1:9).
  ἀπὸ   πάσης   ἀδικίας

But in Scripture passages, it is usually used to profess something positive:

Whoever <u>should</u> _____ _____ _____ _____ _____ _____ _____
ὃς ἐὰν ὁμολογήσῃ   ὅτι Ἰησοῦς ἐστιν ὁ υἱὸς τοῦ

_____, _____ _____ _____ _____ _____ _____ _____ _____
θεοῦ   ὁ θεὸς   ἐν   αὐτῷ μένει καὶ αὐτὸς ἐν

_____ _____ (1 John 4:15).
τῷ   θεῷ

That's why the word "confess" is used not only about sin, but for claiming
the promises of God (confessing the truth), in talking about creeds ("let us
confess our faith"), and doctrinal writings (Augsburg Confession, Westmin-
ster Confession). If I say the same thing God says on a certain subject, I have
"confessed."

The word also appears with the prefix εξ: Every knee shall bow and every
tongue εξομολογησηται that Jesus Christ is Lord (Phil. 2:11).

You have used the preposition μετα to mean "with" and "after." In the following words, it is used as a prefix, with the idea of "change."

μετα + μορφη (form) = change form

Don't be conformed to this world, but <u>be ye</u> _____ by the renewing
of your minds (Rom. 12:2).   μεταμορφοῦσθε

Exercise Two

English Derivative

The process of a caterpillar changing into a butterfly: _____.

μετα + σχημα (form, plan) = English _____ (replace the final α with an e)

These are _____, evil workers, _____ _____
      ψευδαπόστολοι   μετασχηματιζόμενοι   εἰς

_____ _____. And no wonder: _____ _____ , _____
ἀποστόλους Χριστοῦ   αὐτὸς γὰρ ὁ Σατανᾶς

_____ _____ _____ _____ ᾽ ____ ____ ____
μετασχηματίζεται εἰς ἄγγελον φωτός οὐ μέγα οὖν

____ ____ ____ servants ____ ____ _____ ____ servants
εἰ καὶ οἱ διάκονοι αὐτοῦ μετασχηματίζονται ὡς διάκονοι

____ _____ ____ ____ ____ end shall be ____ ____ ____ _____
διακαιοσύνης, ὧν τὸ τέλος   κατὰ τὰ ἔργα

____ _____ (2 Cor. 11:13–15).
αὐτῶν

We return to our subject by introducing the word for "mind": νους.

Genitive example: I see another law striving against ____ _____ _____ (Rom. 7:23).
                                        τῳ   νόμῳ
τοῦ νοός μου

Dative example: With my _____ I am subject ____ ____ _____ ____ ____ . . .
(Rom. 7:25).   νοῒ'   τῷ νόμῳ θεοῦ

Combining μετα + νους = a change of mind

As a noun: μετανοια

I did not come to _____ _____ _____ _____ ____
          καλέσαι   δικαίους ἀλλὰ ἁμαρτωλοὺς εἰς
_____ (Luke 5:32).
μετάνοιαν

. . . not knowing that the kindness of God leads you to _____ (Rom. 2:4).
                                              μετάνοιαν

As a verb: μετανοεω

_____ _____ your brother <u>should</u>_____ seven times a day and
καὶ   ἐὰν   ἁμαρτήσῃ

should turn _____ ___ _____ ___ _____, forgive him (Luke 17:4).
              πρὸς   σὲ   λέγων,   μετανοῶ

Now God calls _____ _____ everywhere _____ (Acts 17:30).
               τοῖς   ἀνθρώποις   μετανοεῖν

___ ___ ____ there shall be more joy in heaven ____ _____
λέγω ὑμῖν ὅτι   ἐπὶ   ἑνὶ

_____ _____-ing __ _____ ninety-nine _____
ἁμαρτωλῷ   μετανοοῦντι   ἢ ἐπὶ   δικαίοις

_____ ___ need _____ ___ _____ (Luke 15:7).
οἵτινες   οὐ   ἔχουσιν   μετανοίας

I gave _____ _____ ___ ___ ___ <u>she might</u> _____, ____
         αὐτῇ   χρόνον   ἵνα   μετανοήσῃ   καὶ

_____ <u>to</u> _____ __ ____ _____ _____ (Rev. 2:21).
οὐ θέλει μετανοῆσαι ἐκ τῆς πορνείας αὐτῆς

Seeing repentance as a "change of mind" helps us avoid two extremes: If a person expresses sorrow, but is not yet willing to call what he's done a sin in God's sight, he hasn't really "changed his mind" about what he's done; on the other hand, if a person truly changes his attitude toward his sin, and hates it as God does, he has repented, even if later he should fall into the same sin again. The following word combines μετα and μελω (care about). It is translated with the word "repent" in the King James version, but it does not refer to repenting in the religious sense, but simply to a change of mind. Using the word "regret" to translate it is one way to bring out its difference from "repent":

If I grieved you in the letter, <u>I do not</u> _____, __ _____ I _____-ed
                                οὐ μεταμέλομαι   εἰ καὶ   μετεμελόμην
(for I see the letter brought you sorrow), I rejoice that you grieved ____
                                                                      εἰς

_____ . . . for grief towards God <u>works</u>_____ _____ _____
μετάνοιαν   ἐργάζεται   μετάνοιαν εἰς
salvation (which is) _____ (2 Cor. 7:8–10).
                      ἀμεταμέλητον

Words based on στρεφω (turn) are often found in conjunction with words about repenting. The following examples show that these words have both secular and sacred meanings:

Whoever hits you on the right cheek, _____ ____ _____ ____
$\quad$ στρέψον[1] $\qquad$ αὐτῷ $\quad$ καὶ

_____ _____ (Matt. 5:39).
τὴν $\quad$ ἄλλην

_____ ___ _____ ___ _____, except ye_____ _____ become ____
Ἀμὴν $\quad$ λέγω $\quad$ ὑμῖν, $\quad$ ἐὰν μὴ $\quad$ στραφῆτε[2] $\quad$ καὶ $\qquad$ ὡς

_____, you may not enter into the kingdom of heaven (Matt. 18:3).
τὰ παιδία

In the following examples the prefix επι is put in front of στρεφω, resulting in "turn upon" or "return."

Then (the demon) _____,___ _____ _____ ____ ____ I will _____
$\qquad$ λέγει $\;$ εἰς $\quad$ τὸν $\quad$ οἶκόν $\quad$ μου $\qquad$ ἐπιστρέψω[3]
whence I came (Matt. 12:44).

(Paul said he kept telling everyone, even Gentiles) . . . ____ _____ _____
$\qquad$ μετανοεῖν $\quad$ καὶ

____ _____ _____ _____, doing _____ worthy _____
ἐπιστρέφειν $\quad$ ἐπὶ $\quad$ τὸν θεόν $\qquad$ ἔργα $\qquad$ τῆς

_____ (Acts 26:20).
μετανοίας

_____ _____ ____ ____ ___ _____ _____ should wander
Ἀδελφοί $\quad$ μου, $\quad$ ἐάν $\quad$ τις $\quad$ ἐν $\quad$ ὑμῖν $\quad$ πλανηθῇ
from the truth, ____ _____ _____ _____, know _____
$\qquad$ καὶ $\quad$ ἐπιστρέψῃ $\quad$ τις $\quad$ αὐτόν $\quad$ γινωσκέτω ὅτι
the-one-_____ -ing _____ ____ wandering ____ _____
ὁ ἐπιστρέψας $\qquad$ ἁμαρτωλὸν $\quad$ ἐκ $\quad$ πλάνης $\quad$ ὁδοῦ $\quad$ αὐτοῦ
shall save _____ ____ ___ _____ ____ shall cover a mul-
σώσει $\quad$ ψυχὴν $\quad$ αὐτοῦ $\quad$ ἐκ $\quad$ θανάτου $\quad$ καὶ $\quad$ καλύψει
titude ___ _____ (James 5:19–20).
ἁμαρτιῶν

1. Spelling change, φ to ψ because it is a command
2. Spelling change, ε to η because it is conditional
3. Spelling change, φ to ψ because it is future

Exercise Three

Summary

On the long blanks, write the two Greek words each of the given words was constructed from. On the short blanks, write the letters of the two selections from the right-hand column that correspond to each word.

1. ____ ____   επιστρεφω _____ + _____   a. say the same thing
2. ____ ____   μετανοια   _____ + _____   b. repent
3. ____ ____   ομολογεω   _____ + _____   c. turn
                                                    d. confess
                                                    e. change of mind
                                                    f. be converted

Exercise Four

Review

Each Greek word below has related forms which correspond to the English meanings in the column at the right.

— — — 1. ἁγιος   a. justify   h. sin
— — — 2. πιστις   b. spirit   i. sanctify
— —   3. πνευμα   c. saint   j. faith
— —   4. οικος   d. belief   k. edify
— —   5. δικαιος   e. family   l. missing the mark
— —   6. ἁμαρτια   f. wind   m. righteousness
                           g. holy   n. being persuaded

Final example with α in front:

Because of your hardness and _____ _____, you're
                                 ἀμετανόητον   καρδίαν
storing up wrath for yourself (Rom. 2:5).

Lesson Forty

Blessing and Thanksgiving

Remember the word ευ (good) which we added to αγγελ (angel or messenger) to make words that had to do with evangelism—telling the good message?

It is important that you practice your pronunciation in these Scripture sections.

(Honor your father and mother) _____ _____ _____ _____ it may be . . . (Eph. 6:3).
ἵνα   εὖ   σοι

Behold, _____ _____ _____ _____ before your face . . .
ἐγὼ   ἀποστέλλω   τὸν   ἄγγελόν μου
(Matt. 11:10).

_____ _____ am I ashamed of _____ _____ . . . (Rom. 1:16).
Οὐ   γὰρ   τὸ   εὐαγγέλιον

Combining ευ with λογος = "good words."

1. As a verb: ευλογεω

_____ those who curse _____ (Luke 6:28).
εὐλογεῖτε   ὑμᾶς

_____ _____ _____ _____ _____ said
καὶ   εὐλόγησεν   αὐτοὺς   Συμεὼν   καὶ
_____ _____ _____ _____ . . . (Luke 2:34).
πρὸς   Μαριὰμ   τὴν   μητέρα αὐτοῦ

2. As a noun: ευλογια, ας f

_____ _____ _____ _____ _____ might come _____
ἵνα   ἡ   εὐλογία   τοῦ   Ἀβραὰμ   εἰς
_____ _____ (Gal. 3:14).
τὰ   ἔθνη

3. As an adjective: ευλογητος, η, ον

. . . the Creator, ____ _____ _____ forever. _____
(Rom. 1:25).   ὅς   ἐστιν   εὐλογητὸς   Ἀμήν

A sentence with all three uses:

_____ be _____ _____ _____ of our _____ _____ _____
Εὐλογητὸς   ὁ   θεὸς   καὶ   πατὴρ   κυρίου   Ἰησοῦ

_____, who has _____ us in every _____ _____
Χριστοῦ   εὐλογήσας   εὐλογίᾳ   πνευματικῇ

in the spiritual realm ____ _____ (Eph. 1:3).
                         ἐν   Χριστῷ

A form of the word "is" was added after the first word.

The word ευλογησας is a participle. Up to now, you have translated participles by adding "ing." This is a past participle, so translate "one having blessed," or "who has blessed."

Exercise One

What English word looks like ευλογια, and means the "good words" spoken about someone at his funeral? (Copy the word, changing the ending.)
_____

Combine ευ with χαρις.

One customary meaning of χαρις is "grace":

_____ _____ _____ _____ (Rom. 6:14).
. . . οὐ γάρ ἐστε ὑπὸ νόμον   ἀλλὰ   ὑπὸ   χάριν

Another common meaning of χαρις is "thanks."

_____, who always leads us in triumph in Christ (2 Cor. 2:14).
τῷ δὲ θεῷ χάρις

Adding ευ to this second meaning gives us the usual word for "thanksgiving."

1. As a noun: ευχαριστια, ας f

. . . foods, which God has created to be partaken of _____
                                                       μετὰ

_____ by believers and knowers of truth (1 Tim. 4:3).
εὐχαριστίας

2. As a verb:

__ _____, standing by himself, prayed these things: __
Ο   Φαρισαῖος   Ὁ

_____ ____ ____ _____ as others are . . . (Luke
θεός,   εὐχαριστῶ   σοι   ὅτι   οὐκ εἰμὶ

18:11).

While they were eating, Jesus took bread, _____ _____
                                                                    καὶ   εὐλογήσας[1]

broke and gave ____ ____ _____, saying, "Take,   eat;   ___
                          τοῖς   μαθηταῖς   Λάβετε   φάγετε,

_____ _____ _____." And taking the cup
τοῦτό   ἐστιν   τὸ σῶμά μου

_____ _____, he gave _____ _____, _____,
καὶ   εὐχαριστήσας[2]   αὐτοῖς   λεγῶν

"Drink ____ _____ _____, _____ _____
            ἐξ   αὐτοῦ   πάντες   τοῦτο γάρ   ἐστιν

_____ of the covenant . . ." (Matt. 26:26–28).
τὸ αἷμά μου

1. These are both "past participles." Translate: "having . . . ed."
2. English word. Take the ending off ευχαριστια, spell it in English letters, and you get another name for the Lord's Supper: _____.

Four Word Families That Mean "Speak"

Exercise Two

Match the Greek word with its English translation.

A. λογος, "word"

____ 1. λογος (noun)

____ 2. λεγει (verb)

____ 3. απο (from) + λογια

____ 4. ευ (good) + λογος

____ 5. θεος (God) + λογος

____ 6. λογικος

____ 7. ὁμο (same) + λογεω

a. Logical, reasonable. Based on thinking about words, not based on feelings or physical actions.

b. "word"

c. To say the same thing about yourself that God does: to "confess."

d. "says"

e. *Words from* a person who has been criticized: his "explanation." Theological explanations are called "apologies"; the study of how to stand up for your faith is called "apologetics."

f. *A good word*, blessing, eulogy.

g. The study of God; (theology).

Scriptures Based on the Previous Words

1. ____ beginning was __ _____ _____ _ _____ was with ____
   Ἐν   ἀρχῇ   ἦν   ὁ   λόγος,   καὶ   ὁ   λόγος   ἦν   πρὸς   τὸν

   _____ ___ _____ ___ __ _____ (John 1:1).
   θεόν,   καὶ   θεὸς   ἦν   ὁ   λόγος

   ____ _ _____ flesh became, and lived among us . . . (John 1:14).
   καὶ   ὁ   λόγος   σὰρξ

   Who is the λογος mentioned in this passage?
   _____

   (The same thought is in Hebrews 1:1—"God has spoken to us in his
   Son.")

2. _____ ___ __ _ _____ _____ _____ _____ _____
   Εὐλογητὸς   ὁ   θεὸς   καὶ   πατὴρ   τοῦ   κυρίου

   _____ _____ _____ _ _____ _____ ___
   ἡμῶν   Ἰησοῦ   Χριστοῦ,   ὁ   εὐλογήσας   ἡμᾶς   ἐν

   _____ _____ _____ in the heavenlies ____
   πάσῃ   εὐλογίᾳ   πνευματικῇ   ἐν

   _____ (Eph. 1:3).
   Χριστῷ

3. I beseech you, _____, by the mercies ____ ____, to present your
                    ἀδελφοί   θεοῦ
   bodies as a living sacrifice, well pleasing ____ ____, which is your
                                                  θεῷ
   _____ service (Rom. 12:1).
   λογικὴν

4. If we say we have no _____, we are lying to ourselves and the
                          ἁμαρτίαν
   truth is not in us. If we _____ our _____, (God)
                              ὁμολογῶμεν   ἁμαρτίας
   is faithful _____ righteous to forgive us our _____ _____
   πιστός   καὶ   δίκαιος   ἁμαρτίας   καὶ
   make us clean from all _____ (1 John 1:8–9).
                           ἀδικίας

Exercise Three

Match the Greek word with its English meaning.

B. φη, "speak"

_____ 1. φημι (verb)

_____ 2. φημη (noun)

_____ 3. βλασφημεω

_____ 4. προ (forth) + φη + της = προφητης (one who)

_____ 5. προφητικος

_____ 6. προφητεια

a. a speech or a report. Notice how the Greek word sounds like the English word "fame."

b. speak

c. one who speaks out about something God has told him; prophet.

d. prophetic

e. something a prophet would say; a prophecy

f. speak against (blaspheme)

Famous Scripture Quotes

5. (After one of Jesus's miracles): And the _____ of it went out unto all that land (Matt. 9:26).
   φήμη

6. We have _____ _____ made more sure . . . because
   προφητικὸν   λόγον

   no _____ of <u>scripture</u> is a matter of one's own interpreta-
   προφητεία   γραφῆς

   tion; because no _____ was ever made by an act of human
   προφητεία

   will; but _____ moved by the _____ _____ spoke
   ἄνθρωποι   ἁγίου   πνεύματος

   from _____ (2 Pet. 1:19–21).
   θεοῦ

C. λαλεω, "speak"; noun: λαλια

7. ____ ____ ____ ____ fullness ____ ____ ____ ____ ____
   'Εκ   γὰρ   τοῦ   τῆς   καρδίας   τὸ   στόμα

   _____ (Matt. 12:34).
   λαλεῖ

8. ____ _____ _____ ____ ____ ____ ____ more than
   Εὐχαριστῶ   τῷ θεῷ   λαλῶ   γλώσσαις

   _____ _____ (1 Cor. 14:18).
   πάντων   ὑμῶν

D. ῥημα, ατος n, "word"

(All flesh is as) the flower of grass, _____ ___ _____ _____ _____
                                        τὸ   δὲ   ῥῆμα κυρίου   μένει

forever; _____ ____ _____ ____ having been _____ -ed ____
         τοῦτο   δέ ἐστιν τὸ ῥῆμα τὸ εὐαγγελισθέν   εἰς

_____ (1 Pet. 1:25).
ὑμᾶς

_____ __ _____ ____ ____ kept _____ ___ _____ ___ ___
καὶ   ἡ μήτηρ   αὐτοῦ   πάντα τὰ   ῥήματα ἐν τῇ

_____ _____ (Luke 2:51).
καρδίᾳ   αὐτῆς

Lesson Forty-One

Salvation Words

Remember that σωτηρ means "savior." The other related words are:

verb: σωζω, save; εσωθην,* was saved; σωσω, shall save
*means aorist (a type of past) passive: "was saved"

noun: σωτηρια, ας f, "salvation"
also found as σωτηριος m and σωτηριον n

"Save" implies there is something to be saved from. The following Scripture quotes are classified according to what the problem is:

A flood. By _____ _____ prepared . . . an ark for the _____
πίστει Νῶε   σωτηρίαν

____ ____ _____ _____ (Heb. 11:7).
τοῦ   οἴκου   αὐτοῦ

A storm. They awoke him, saying, "_____, _____, or we
perish" (Matt. 8:25).   Κύριε,   σῶσον,

Sickness. The prayer ____ _____ shall _____ the sick, and will raise
τῆς   πίστεως   σώσει

_____ __ _____ (James 5:15).
αὐτὸν   ὁ   κύριος

(The woman said to herself) "_____ _____ I touch his gar-
Ἐὰν   μόνον

ment I shall be _____-ed." . . . Jesus said, "Courage, daughter,
σωθήσομαι

__ _____ ___ has _____ -ed ___. _____ __ woman
ἡ   πίστις   σου   σέσωκέν   σε   Καὶ   ἡ   γυνὴ

was _____ _____ ____ ____ _____ _____" (Matt. 9:21–22).
ἐσώθη   ἀπὸ   τῆς   ὥρας   εκείνης

217

Death. Know that <u>the one</u>   -ing   _____ ____ ____
        ὁ ἐπιστρέψας   ἁμαρτωλὸν ἐκ   πλάνης

____ ____ ____ <u>will</u>   ____ ____ ____ ____
 ὁδοῦ   αὐτοῦ   σώσει   ψυχὴν   αὐτοῦ ἐκ

____ ____ ____ <u>multitude</u> ____ ____ (James 5:20).
 θανάτου καὶ καλύψει πλῆθος ἁμαρτιῶν

Sins. You shall call his name _____, _____ ____ ____
          Ἰησοῦν,   αὐτὸς γὰρ σώσει

the people _____ _____ _____ ____ ____ (Matt 1:21).
        ἀπὸ   τῶν   ἁμαρτιῶν   αὐτῶν

Many passages speak in a general way, where "save" seems to cover the entire area of freedom from sin and the gaining of an eternal relationship with God:

____ ____ <u>sent</u> ____ ____ ____ ____ ____ ____
οὐ γὰρ ἀπέστειλεν* ὁ θεὸς τὸν υἱὸν εἰς τὸν κόσμον

____ <u>he might</u> ____ ____ ____ ____ <u>he might</u>____
 ἵνα   κρίνῃ   τὸν κόσμον, ἀλλ᾽ ἵνα   σωθῇ

__ _____ ____ _____ (John 3:17).
 ὁ κόσμος δι αὐτοῦ

____ ____ _____ _____ have seen ____ _____ ____ ____ (Luke 2:30).
οἱ ὀφθαλμοί μου   τὸ σωτήριόν σου

* past tense of αποστελλω, which is related to αποστολος.

Exercise One:

More uses for the word σωζω. Match each passage to the letter of the concept found on the next page.

____ 1. <u>To all</u> I have become <u>all things</u> _____ <u>by all ways</u> <u>some</u> <u>I</u> _____
    τοῖς πᾶσιν   πάντα   ἵνα   πάντως τινὰς σώσω
(1 Cor. 9:22b).

____ 2. Will rescue ____ __ _____ _____ _____ _____ evil _____ ____
          μ ὁ κύριος ἀπὸ παντὸς ἔργου   καὶ σώσει
me into his heavenly kingdom (2 Tim. 4:18).

____ 3. The one remaining unto the end <u>shall be</u>_____ (Matt. 24:13).
                                   σωθήσεται

____ 4. _____ _____ _____ trembling _____ _____ _____ work
     μετὰ   φόβου   καὶ   τὴν   ἑαυτῶν   σωτηρίαν

out (Phil. 2:12).

____ 5. ____ _____ _____ of the cross to those perishing <u>foolishness</u> _____
    ὁ   λόγος   γὰρ   μωρία   ἐστίν,

_____ ____ <u>being</u> _____ ____ ____ _____ _____
   τοῖς   δὲ   σῳζομένοις   ἡμῖν   δύναμις   θεοῦ

____ ____ (1 Cor. 1:18).
  ἐστιν

____ 6. And cried (in a) _____ _____, saying, "_____ ____
               φωνῇ   μεγάλῃ   ἡ σωτηρία   τῷ

_____ _____ seated _____ ___ _____ _____ to the
  θεῷ   ἡμῶν   ἐπὶ   τῷ   θρόνῳ   καὶ

Lamb" (Rev. 7:10).

a. Something to be worked into your present experience
b. As a worship-word
c. Referring to conversion
d. It will take endurance
e. Referring to believers in general
f. Looking ahead to eternal life

Exercise Two

Remember αλλος, "other?" A related word is αλλασσω, "to make other," "to change, transform."

I wish I were present with you now _____ _____ ____ _____
                              καὶ   ἀλλάξαι   τὴν   φωνήν

___ ___, for I am perplexed (Gal. 4:20).
 μου

Combine κατα + αλλασσω for the idea of "exchange," used often for changing enemies into friends (reconciling).

verb: καταλλασσω

noun: καταλλαγη

All these things are from God, the <u>one</u> _____ -ing ____ ____ ____
                                   καταλλάξαντος   ἡμᾶς   ἑαυτῷ   διὰ

_____ and giving ___ ___ the ministry _____ _____, for God
Χριστοῦ   ἡμῖν   τῆς   καταλλαγῆς

was ___ _____ _____ -ing _____ ___ ___, ____ <u>reckoning</u>
   ἐν   Χριστῷ   καταλλάσσων   κόσμον   ἑαυτῷ   μὴ   λογιζόμενος

____ ____ τὰ _____ ____ ____, _____ giving us _____
αὐτοῖς   τὰ   παραπτώματα   αὐτῶν,   καὶ   τὸν

_____ _____ _____ (2 Cor. 5:18–19).
λόγον   τῆς   καταλλαγῆς

Combine απο + κατα + αλλασσω. The meaning is roughly the same as κατα + αλλασσω.

In Him all the fullness "<u>indwells</u>," _____ ____ _____ to_____
                                      κατοικῆσαι,* καὶ   δἰ   αὐτοῦ   ἀποκαταλλάξαι

_____ ____ _____, making peace _____ _____ _____ of his
τὰ   πάντα   εἰς   αὐτόν   διὰ   τοῦ   αἵματος

cross (Col. 1:19–20).

* This was one of the words from the οικος study.

Lesson Forty-Two

Salvation Words (continued)

λυω = loosen

Jesus said, "_____! Each of you on the _____ _____ his ox
         ὑποκριταί   σαββάτῳ   οὐ λύει
and donkey from the manger?" (Luke 13:15).

_____ _____ _____ _____ _____, whatever you shall bind on earth shall be what
Ἀμὴν   λέγω   ὑμῖν
is bound in heaven, and whatever _____ _____ _____ _____ shall
                                      λύσητε   ἐπὶ   τῆς   γῆς
be what is loosed in heaven (Matt. 18:18).

λυτρον = the price paid for release

___ _____ _____ _____ _____ came to be served but to serve, and
Ὁ   υἱὸς   τοῦ   ἀνθρώπου   οὐκ
give _____ _____ _____ _____ _____ _____ (Matt. 20:28).
       τὴν   ψυχὴν   αὐτοῦ   λύτρον   ἀντὶ   πολλῶν

λυτροω = release, ransom

Who gave himself for us _____ _____ _____ _____ _____
                              ἵνα   λυτρώσηται   ἡμᾶς   ἀπὸ   πάσης
_____ _____ <u>cleanse</u> _____ _____ a people for his own possession,
ἀνομίας   καὶ   καθαρίσῃ*   ἑαυτῷ
_____ _____ _____ (Titus 2:14).
ζηλωτὴν   καλῶν   ἔργων

* cognate with English _____, a physical cleansing in medicine, an emotional cleansing in drama.

λυτρωσις = liberation

Not through the blood of bulls and calves, _____ ____ _____ _____
                                           διὰ   δὲ   τοῦ   ἰδίου

_____ he entered once into the _____, having earned eternal _____
αἵματος   ἅγια   αἰωνίαν λύτρωσιν

(Heb. 9:12).

απο + λυω is not used about eternal redemption, but about letting people go . . . *physically*:

Then _____ _____ _____ _____ _____ (Matt. 27:26).
     ἀπέλυσεν   αὐτοῖς τὸν   Βαραββᾶν

. . . and *spiritually*:

Don't _____ and you won't be judged; don't _____, and
      κρίνετε   καταδικάζετε

you won't be condemned; _____ ____ you shall be _____ -en
                        ἀπολύετε,   καὶ ἀπολυθήσεσθε

(Luke 6:37).

But the other form of this word, the noun ἀπολυτρωσις, is used entirely in the New Testament to refer to eternal redemption:

All have sinned and fall short of the glory of God, but are justified freely
by his grace _____ _____ _____ _____ ____
             δὶα   τῆς   ἀπολυτρώσεως   τῆς   ἐν

_____ _____ (Rom. 3:23–24).
Χριστῷ   Ἰησοῦ

Exercise One

A Word that Is Difficult to Translate

Above the ark of the covenant were cherubim of glory, with their wings covering ____ _____ (Heb. 9:5).
      τὸ   ἱλαστήριον

This referred to the place of payment for sins in the Old Testament temple. Blood was sprinkled here, and the end results were that God's people had forgiveness.

In the New Testament, the location for payment of sins is a person:

Jesus, whom God set forth as a _____ through faith in his
blood (Rom. 3:25).   ἱλαστήριον

The word could be translated "means by which sins are forgiven."
Related word: ἱλασμος (noun)

And He is the _____ for our sins . . . (1 John 2:2).
                    ἱλασμός

Related verb: ἱλασκομαι

(The publican said,) "__ _____ _____ _____, a sinner" (Luke
18:13).   ὁ   θεός   ἱλάσθητί   μου

The more common verb for "have mercy" is ελεεω.

Two blind men followed Jesus, crying and saying, "_____ _____,
_____ _____" (Matt. 9:27).   ἐλέησον   ἡμᾶς,
   υἱὸς   Δαυίδ

And in the Beatitudes:

Blessed are the _____, for they _____ (Matt. 5:7).
                    ἐλεήμονες   ἐλεηθήσονται

The corresponding noun is ελεος.

_____ ____ _____ which we have done ____ _____ _____
 οὐκ   ἐξ   ἔργων   ἐν   δικαιοσύνη   ἀλλὰ
____ ____ ____ _____ he saved _____ (Titus 3:5).
 κατὰ   τὸ   αὐτοῦ   ἔλεος   ἔσωσεν   ἡμᾶς

The following words are based on αγω (lead). Remember συν + αγω gave us
συναγωγη, the place where the Jews came together.

αγορα = a secular place where people come together: the marketplace.

And going out about the _____ _____ he saw _____ standing ____
                         τρίτην   ὥραν   ἄλλους   ἐν
____ _____ idle (Matt. 20:3).
 τῆ   ἀγορᾷ

αγοραζω = do a transaction that would take place in a market; acquire by paying a price (the past tense of this word starts with η).

(When the man finds the treasure he hides it,) and out of his joy he goes and sells all ___ ___ _____ ____ _____ _____ (Matt. 13:44).
  ἔχει   καὶ   ἀγοράζει   τὸν   ἀγρὸν   ἐκεῖνον

Ye are not your own; <u>ye were</u>_____ with a <u>price</u>; therefore glorify God
              ἠγοράσθητε   τιμῆς
in your body (1 Cor. 6:20).

Worthy are you . . . for you were slain, _____ _____ ____ _____
                                          καὶ   ἠγόρασας   τῷ   θεῷ

____ ___ _____ _____ from every <u>tribe</u>_____ _____ and people
 ἐν   τῷ   αἵματι   σου   φυλῆς καὶ   γλώσσης
and _____ (Rev. 5:9).
     ἔθνους

Exercise Two

Words based on ιημι. This word ἱ, which basically means "go," is not found itself in the New Testament, but is found in combination with απο. When απο is put in front of ιημί, it is written in the form it takes before vowels: αφ.

Verb: αφιημι
Noun: αφεσις

This word has many meanings. Can you guess from context? Match each passage to the letter of one of the suggestions given here:

a. send away, dismiss
b. leave, go away from
c. forgive

____ 1. Then ____ _____ _____ _____ _____ _____
            οἱ   μαθηταὶ   πάντες   ἀφέντες   αὐτὸν
        and fled (Matt. 26:56).

____ 2. I came from the Father and have come _____ _____
                                               εἰς   τὸν

_____; again _____ _____ _____ and go
  κόσμον   ἀφίημι   τὸν   κόσμον
_____ _____ _____ (John 16:28).
 πρὸς   τὸν   πατέρα

_____ 3. Jesus, crying again with a _____ _____,
                                         φωνῇ   μεγάλῃ
_____ ____ _____ (Matt. 27:50).
   ἀφῆκεν   τὸ   πνεῦμα

_____ 4. If we confess our sins, he is faithful and righteous so that he _____
our sins . . . (1 John 1:9).   ἀφῇ

From the Lord's Prayer and following verses:

Give us this day our daily bread, _____ _____ ____ ____ ___
                                      καὶ   ἄφες   ἡμῖν   τὰ

_____ _____ ____ ____ _____ _____
  ὀφειλήματα   ἡμῶν   ὡς   καὶ   ἡμεῖς   ἀφήκαμεν
_____ (Matt. 6:11–12).
τοῖς ὀφειλέταις ἡμῶν

At the institution of the Lord's Supper:

_____ _____ _____ ____ _____ ___ ___ of the covenant shed
 τοῦτο   γάρ   ἐστιν   τὸ   αἷμα   μου   τῆς
for many for _____ _____ _____ (Matt. 26:28).
              ἄφεσιν   ἁμαρτιῶν

Lesson Forty-Three

People

The family (οικειοι or πατρια)

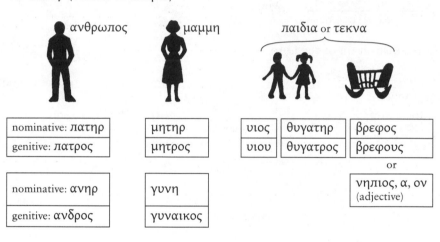

α–νθρωπος   μαμμη   παιδια or τεκνα

nominative: πατηρ	μητηρ	υιος	θυγατηρ	βρεφος
genitive: πατρος	μητρος	υιου	θυγατρος	βρεφους

or

nominative: ανηρ	γυνη
genitive: ανδρος	γυναικος

νηπιος, α, ον (adjective)

Cognates

Write corresponding Greek word after each description:

    a. Mammary. Pertaining to a woman's breasts. _____

    b. Repatriate. Return to fatherland. _____

    c. Gynecologist. Doctor specializing in care of women. _____

    d. Nepotism. Granting favors to your relatives. _____

    e. Matriarchy. Rule by mothers. Adds αρχια to the word above.

    _____

    f. Android. A man-like robot. _____

Scriptures

Since _____ ____ _____ share _____ _____ _____, also
Ἐπεὶ   οὖν   τὰ   παιδία   κεκοινώηκεν   αἵματος   καὶ   σαρκός καὶ
_____ partook of the same . . . (Heb. 2:14).
αὐτὸς

A certain _____ named _____ served him (Luke 10:38).
τις   γυνὴ   Μάρθα

(After the resurrection:) __ _____ said ___ ____ _____, " _____ "
(Matt. 28:5).   ὁ   ἄγγελος   ταῖς   γυναιξίν   μὴ φοβεῖσθε

(From Peter's Pentecost sermon:) "_____ __ _____, _____ _____
Ἄνδρες   Ἰσραηλῖται,   ἀκούσατε   τοὺς
_____ _____. _____ ____ _____ ____ ____ approved
λόγους   τούτους   Ἰησοῦν   τὸν   Ναζωραῖον,   ἄνδρα
by God . . ." (Acts 2:22).

__ _____ submit _____ _____ ____ ____ ____ _____,
Αἱ   γυναῖκες   τοῖς   ἰδίοις   ἀνδράσιν   ὡς   τῷ   κυρίῳ,
_____ _____ _____ _____ ____ _____ ____ καὶ ὁ
ὅτι   ἀνήρ   ἐστιν   κεφαλὴ   τῆς   γυναικὸς   ὡς   καὶ ὁ
_____ _____ ____ _____, _____ _____
Χριστὸς   κεφαλὴ   τῆς   ἐκκλησίας,   αὐτὸς   σωτὴρ
___ ___ _____ (Eph. 5:22–23).
τοῦ   σώματος

Words about Slaves and Servants

δουλος
διακονος
λειτουργος
ὑπηρετης
θεραπων
οικετης

παιδισκη

__ _____, _____ _____ ____ _____ _____
οἱ   δοῦλοι,   ὑπακούετε   τοῖς κατὰ σάρκα[1] κυρίοις   μετὰ
_____ _____ trembling, not as menpleasers but ____ _____
φόβου   καὶ   ὡς   δοῦλοι

1. According to the flesh, i.e., here on this earth

_____ -ing ____ will _____
Χριστοῦ   ποιοῦντες   τὸ   θέλημα   τοῦ   θεοῦ   ἐκ ψυχῆς²
(Eph. 6:5).

2. From the soul, or from the heart; heartily, with all your might.

Jesus answered, "_____ _____ _____ _____ _____ _____
                  Ἀμὴν   Ἀμὴν   λέγω   ὑμῖν   ὅτι   πᾶς
                                                                          "
___ _____ ___ _____ _____ _____ ____ _____
ὁ   ποιῶν τὴν ἁμαρτίαν   δοῦλός   ἐστιν   τῆς   ἁμαρτίας
(John 8:34).

James ____ ___ _____ _____ _____ _____ _____ ___ ___
Ἰάκωβος θεοῦ   καὶ   κυρίου Ἰησοῦ Χριστοῦ δοῦλος ταῖς
_____ greetings (James 1:1)
δώδεκα   φυλαῖς   ταῖς   ἐν   τῇ   διασπορᾷ,   χαίρειν

In the following example, the δουλος has a position of authority over the rest
of the household staff:

_____ _____ _____ __ _____ and wise _____, ____ sets up
τίς   ἄρα   ἐστὶν   ὁ   πιστὸς   δοῦλος   ὅν
__ _____ ___ ____ _____ _____ _____ to give them their
ὁ   κύριος   ἐπὶ   τῆς   οἰκετείας   αὐτοῦ
food at the right time? (Matt. 24:45).

Other forms related to δουλος:

  Noun: δουλεια (bondage)
  Verb: δουλευω (serve)
  Verb: δουλοω (be in bondage)

Not-one _____ is able _____ _____ _____ _____, either _____
Οὐδεὶς   οἰκέτης   δύναται   δυσὶ   κυρίοις δουλεύειν   ἢ   γὰρ
___ ___ _____ ___ ___ _____ _____ ... _____ ye are able
τὸν   ἕνα   μισήσει   καὶ   τὸν   ἕτερον ἀγαπήσει ...   οὐ   δύνασθε
_____ ___ _____ ___ _____ (Luke 16:13).
θεῷ   δουλεύειν   καὶ   μαμωνᾷ

The last word above is a spelling in Greek letters of an Aramaic word. (Aramaic, related to Hebrew, was the language spoken in Palestine in the time of Jesus.) The meaning of the word: wealth, riches.

Words related to παις (child)—genitive is παιδος:

Nouns: παιδιον (child)

παιδεια (nurture of children, education)

παιδευτης and παιδαγωγος (both mean "instructor")

παιδισκης (female slave)

Verb: παιδευω (instruct, chastise)

My son, do not despise the _____ _____ _____ or faint when
                                          παιδείας   κυρίου

you're reproved; _____ _____ _____ _____ _____, and
                        ὃν   γὰρ   ἀγαπᾷ   κύριος   παιδεύει

scourges _____ _____ _____ he receives. _____ _____ ye en-
              πάντα   υἱὸν   ὃν   Εἰς   παιδείαν   ὑπομένετε

dure; ____ _____ _____ is treating _____; _____ ____ ____
          ὡς   υἱοῖς   ὑμῖν   ὁ   θεός   τίς   γὰρ   υἱὸς

____ _____ _____ _____? (Heb. 12:5–7).
  ὃν   οὐ   παιδεύει   πατήρ

διακονος and related words:

(At the wedding of Cana:) Λέγει ἡ μήτηρ αυτοῦ τοῖς διακόνοις, "Whatever he says to you, do!" (John 2:5).

Other related words:

Verb: διακονεω (serve)

Noun: διακονια (serving, service)

Both are used in the following sentence:

_____ was distracted _____ _____ _____; she approached
ἡ   Μάρθα   περὶ   πολλὴν   διακονίαν

and said, "_____, doesn't it matter ___ ___ __ _____ ___ ___
              Κύριε,   οὐ μέλει   σοι   ὅτι   ἡ   ἀδελφή   μου

_____ _____ has left ___ _____ ?"(Luke 10:40).
  μόνην   με   διακονεῖν;

These words are often used to refer to Christian work:

... and he gave some _____, some _____, some
                          ἀποστόλους   προφήτας

_____, some pastors and teachers, for building up ____ ____
    εὐαγγελιστάς   τῶν

_____ ____ _____ _____ ____ _____ ____ ___
  ἁγίων   εἰς   ἔργον   διακονίας,   εἰς   οἰκοδομὴν   τοῦ

_____ ____ _____ (Eph. 4:11–12).
  σώματος   τοῦ   Χριστοῦ

The English words "minister," "ministry" are often used to translate these words. Apparently certain people in the early churches were singled out for service, and received a title:

_____ ____ _____ _____ _____ _____
  Παῦλος   καὶ   Τιμόθεος,   δοῦλοι   Χριστοῦ   Ἰησοῦ

___ _____ _____ ___ _____ _____ who are in Philippi
  πᾶσιν   τοῖς   ἁγίοις   ἐν   Χριστῷ   Ἰησοῦ

_____ _____ ____ _____ (Phil. 1:1).
  σὺν   ἐπισκόποις[1]   καὶ   διακόνοις

The last word above is spelled in English as _____.

1. translated as "overseer." This word is explained in Lesson Forty-Four.

Lesson Forty-Four

Combine λειτος (public) + εργον, and you get λειτουργος. This word is sometimes used to apply to the government, the "public servant":

For this reason you must pay taxes, _____ ____ ____ ____
                                         λειτουργοὶ   γὰρ   θεοῦ

_____ for this very thing (Rom. 13:6).
εἰσιν

Related words:

> Verb: Λειτουργεω (serve, minister)
>
> Noun: Λειτουργια (service, ministration)
>
> Adjective: λειτουργικος (serving, ministering)

Here it is applied to angels:

<u>Are they not all</u> _____ _____, <u>sent out</u> _____
Οὐχὶ πάντες εἰσὶν   λειτουργικὰ   πνεύματα,   ἀποστελλόμενα   εἰς

_____ (Heb. 1:14).
διακονίαν . . .

About believers "serving" God through worship:

(Paul and others gathered at Antioch:) <u>As they were</u> _____-ing ____ ____
                                              λειτουργούντων   τῷ

_____ _____ fasting, _____ said . . . (Acts 13:2).
κυρίῳ   καὶ   τὸ πνεῦμα τὸ ἅγιον

Referring to artifacts used in the worship of God:

And in the same way he sprinkled with blood both the tabernacle and all
the vessels ____ ____ _____ (Heb. 9:21).
            τῆς   λειτουργίας

English spelling of the last word (remove the αις and add y) _____:
It is used to name the order of service in Christian worship, and thus brings
out the "corporate, public" character of worship.

Combine ὑπερ (under) + ερετης (a rower), and you get a word that was first used to describe a member of a ship's crew.

> Noun: ὑπηρετης (servant, assistant)
>
> Verb: ὑπηρετεω (serve)

You know that these hands _____-ed to my needs and the needs
                              ὑπηρέτησαν
of those with me (Acts 20:34).

Peter followed afar, and sat with the _____and warmed himself
_____ ____ _____ (Mark 14:54).   ὑπηρετῶν
  πρὸς   τὸ   φῶς

Then the <u>captain</u> _____ _____ _____ went and brought them,
              στρατηγὸς σὺν   τοῖς   ὑπηρέταις
without violence . . . (Acts 5:26).

English cognate of the word used above for "captain": _____.
We use it to refer to military plans.

Apparently ὑπηρετης was used to indicate an official in the synagogue:

> (Jesus read from Isaiah), and closing the _____ he gave it ___ ___
>   βιβλίον   τῷ
> _____ and sat down; ____ _____ ___ _____ __ ___
> ὑπηρέτη   καὶ πάντων οἱ ὀφθαλμοὶ ἐν τῆ
> _____ were fixed ____ _____ (Luke 4:20).
> συναγωγῆ   αὐτῷ

θεραπων and related forms:

___	_____	____	_____	__	___	___	____	_____
Καὶ	Μωϋσῆς	μὲν[1]	πιστὸς	ἐν	ὅλω	τῷ	οἴκῳ	αὐτοῦ

____ _____ _____ _____ of things spoken later; _____
 ὡς   θεράπων   εἰς   μαρτύριον   Χριστὸς

___ ___ _____ ___ ___ _____ _____ (Heb. 3:5–6).
 δὲ ὡς υἱὸς ἐπὶ τὸν οἶκον αὐτοῦ

1. When μεν and δε are in the same sentence, they can be translated "on the one hand . . . on the other hand . . ."

Related words:

Noun: Θεραπεια (service, including physical help, healing)

Verb: θεραπευω (serve, also offer divine service [worship] and physical help [heal])

_____ _____ _____ __ _____ _____ and wise _____, ___ sets up __
Τίς   ἄρα   ἐστὶν   ὁ   πιστὸς   οἰκονόμος   ὃν   ὁ

_____ ___ ___ _____ to give them food in time (Luke 12:42).
κύριος ἐπὶ τῆς θεραπείας

And calling to himself _____ _____ _____ ____ _____, he
                        τοὺς   δώδεκα   μαθητὰς   αὐτοῦ

gave authority _____ _____ _____ _____ ____
                ὥστε   ἐκβάλλειν πνευμάτων ἀκαθάρτων καὶ

____ _____ _____ illness and malady (Matt. 10:1).
θεραπεύειν πᾶσαν

He spoke to them about the kingdom of God, and healed those having need
_____ _____ (Luke 9:11).
θεραπείας

The English spelling of this last word, _____, we use to refer to healing activities.

Some Titles of Officials

ἱέρευς = priest
ἱέρον = temple

Exercise Five

Match the English derivatives:

____ 1. hieroglyphics (with γλυφω, "carve")

____ 2. hierarchy (with αρχη, "chief")

____ 3. hieratic

a. The organizational pattern of religious officials

b. Pertaining to priests

c. Those Egyptian symbols known only to the priests

Combine επι (on, over) and σκολεω (look, see).

As a verb:

1. The general _____ his army.
   επισκολεῖ

As a noun:

2. Titus appointed an _____ to watch over the Christians
   ἐπίσκολον

   in Crete—he had to be blameless (Titus 1:7).

3. An _____ is one who _____ large numbers of
   επίσκολος   επισκολεῖ

   Christians.

What happened to the word επισκολος when Christianity reached England? (simplified explanation:)

<u>επισκολος</u> 4. Write the Greek word for one who supervises Christians.

_____ 5. The English took off the ending and first letter, leaving:

_____ 6. The English softened the sk sound to an sh sound:

_____ 7. They softened the opening p sound to a b sound:

_____ 8. Write the result in English letters:

_____ 9. After the church of England withdrew from the Catholic Church in the 1500's, it still wanted to keep these overseers or supervisors over groups of Christians and it still wanted to call them bishops. To describe the kind of church system they now had, they coined a word by taking the original Greek term for overseer and changing the ending. A method of church government that makes use of bishops is called an (fill in answer by 9) system.

People

Summary

. . . of religious titles, including some new ones.

Exercise Six

Match the descriptions in the right-hand column to the two small blanks to the left of each Greek word. Then match the English translation from below the Greek words to the small blank at the right of each Greek word.

___ ___ 1. πρεσβυτερος ____

___ ___ 2. αποστολος ____

___ ___ 3. διακονος ____

___ ___ 4. προφητης ____

___ ___ 5. μαθητης ____

___ ___ 6. επισκολος ____

___ ___ 7. ευαγγελιστας ____

___ ___ 8. ποιμην ____

___ ___ 9. κατηχουμενος ____

Match to these customary English translations:

A. Prophet

B. Evangelist

C. Deacon or Minister

D. Catechumen

E. Elder

F. Bishop

G. Apostle

H. Disciple

G. Pastor

a. one who serves under others

b. supervisor, overseer

c. one who tends a flock; related to ποιμνη, which means "a flock"

d. older person

e. one who speaks forth a message from God

f. one who is sent out on a mission

g. one who is under discipline; a follower, learner

h. one who is taught; from κατα + ηχεω, which means "to sound in the ears." (cf. Eng. echo)

i one who tells a good message; from ευ "good" + αγγελος "messenger"

j. presbyter

k. related to: αποστελλω—send forth
      αποστολη—expedition, mission

l. related to "catechesis," an English word which means "the religious instruction program of the church." A "catechism" is a religious instruction book based on the question/answer method.

m. related to: διακονεω—attend upon
      διακονια—aid, ministering

n. shepherd

o made by combining φημι "speak" with προ "forth"

p. related to: ευαγγελιον—good news
      ευαγγελιζω—to proclaim good news

q. related to: μανθανω—learn
      μαθητευω—follow as a disciple

r. related to: επισκοπεω—look over
      επισκοπη—oversight, supervision

Scriptures

This man (had been) _____ _____ _____ (Acts 18:25).
         κατηχημένος   τὴν   ὁδὸν   τοῦ   κυρίου

All power is given unto me in heaven _____ _____ _____. Going _____
                              καὶ   ἐπὶ   τῆς   γῆς   οὖν

_____ _____ ___ _____ , _____ _____ ___ ___
μαθητεύσατε   πάντα   τὰ   ἔθνη,   βαπτίζοντες   αὐτοὺς   εἰς   τὸ

_____ ___ _____ ___ ___ _____ ___ ___ _____
ὄνομα   τοῦ   πατρὸς   καὶ   τοῦ   υἱοῦ   καὶ   τοῦ   ἁγίου

_____ (Matt. 28:18–19).
πνεύματος . . .

You May Ask

Why didn't you say anything about the qualities of the different servants—which one is considered a "bond-servant," etc.?

> The answer is that this workbook is not a Bible dictionary or a theological dictionary, but only an introduction to New Testament words. There were no Bible quotes I could find that brought out the differences between types of slaves. This matter depends on information gathered from outside the Bible. At this point, you are able to use some of the more advanced theological dictionaries and get *something* out of them.

Why didn't you devote a page to the three types of love, αγαπη, φιλια and ερος?

> 1. Ερος is not even found in the New Testament.
> 2. Again, I could find no passages that clearly showed or contrasted the shades of difference between the two. In many instances, they mean about the same thing. This is a matter for theological dictionaries.
> 3. Incidentally, there is a fourth word for love, στοργη, which refers to natural family-type affection. It is not found in the New Testament, but its opposite is the last word in the following quote.

> > For men shall be lovers-of-self, lovers of money, proud, arrogant, _____ ,
> >   φίλαυτοι   φιλάργυροι   βλάσφημοι
> > to parents _____ , unthankful, unholy, _____ . . . (2 Tim. 3:2–3).
> >   ἀπειθεῖς   ἀχάριστοι   ἄστοργοι . . .

Cognate Origins

Why are some English words like Greek words?

1. Sometimes it is because both the Greek and English words came from their common ancestor.

2. Sometimes it is because Latin borrowed from Greek, and then the languages that are descendants of Latin, like French, came into the English language when French-speaking invaders conquered England in 1066.

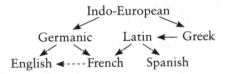

3. Sometimes it reflects the fact that Latin borrowings from Greek were used to coin words needed for intellectual purposes.

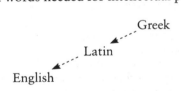

4. Most recently, scientific words have been coined by taking roots directly from Greek and formulating new English words:

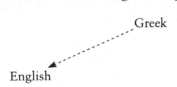

5. There are also technical terms which came from Greek, but which underwent a lot of change and development as the English language itself changed over the years. Examples given in this workbook have been "bishop" and "church."

$$\text{Old English} \longleftarrow \text{-----------------} \text{Greek}$$
$$\downarrow$$
$$\text{English}$$

Part V

VERBS

You will:

1. Survey the shades of meanings of verbs.

2. Use charts to learn how to put the endings on verbs that express these shades of meaning.

3. Learn how to use an analytical lexicon.

Lesson Forty-Five

Verbs

In Part II, you learned the six "personal endings" which are added to verbs:

	singular		plural	
1st person	I	−ω	we	−ομεν
2nd person	you	−εις	ye	−ετε
3rd person	he	-ει	they	−ουσι (ν)

Example: λεγω = I speak   λεγουσι = they speak

These endings are for "present" tense. On the following pages, you will be introduced to different endings used for the other tenses (past, future, etc.). In Part II, you were introduced to the infinitive (the basic sense of the verb without any personal ending), which we show in English by the use of the word "to": λεγειν = to speak. On the coming pages you will find additional infinitive endings and uses.

In Part II, you were told about participles, and you have been using the participle ending -ων: λεγων = speaking. You will learn more endings for participles and more uses for them here in Part V.

Other information about verbs you will learn includes:

1. Mood—shades of meaning indicated by different verb-endings.
2. Voice—such as "active," when the subject is doing the acting (I throw), and "passive," when the subject is receiving the action (I am being thrown).

Verb Tenses

The following chart lists six Greek verb tenses and their English meaning.

Tense	Description	Identifying Marks Include	Example
Present	continuous action	The word in simple form, or with "-ing" on the end and preceded by a form of "be" (such as "am," "is," "are").	I throw, or, more characteristically, I am throwing
Future	Action in future time, either continuous or a single act	"will" or "shall"	I will throw
Imperfect[3]	continuous action in past time	"was" plus "-ing"	I was throwing
Aorist[1]	an act	past form, or use of "did"[3]	I threw, or
Perfect[2]	a completed act with emphasis on existing present results		I did throw
Pluperfect	a completed act which had continuing results in the past	had	I had thrown

1. In theory, aorist is used for a single act, whenever it happened. In actual use, aorist is the most common form used to describe single events in the past.

2. It is hard to differentiate aorist from perfect in English—both of them sound like our "past tense."

3. The word "perfect" means completed. Imperfect tense then gets its name from the fact that it describes a continuous action, one that was not completed.

The following diagram illustrates the characteristics of the tenses:

Remember that each of the six tenses listed has six possible endings which stand for the six persons, making a total of 36 ways a verb can end. The following pages will add additional ways.

There is also a tense called "future perfect," which is translated "will have." Example: "I will have thrown."

Exercise One

Matching

Match the underlined English phrase to the Greek tense it would translate; in the other blank, match to the "person" used in the example:

—— ——   1. He will give at the office.

—— ——   2. Ye were taking candy each time ye walked past the counter.

—— ——   3. I wrote the letter you are now reading

—— ——   4. We are being good.

—— ——   5. They will have arrived home by then.

—— ——   6. You gave a good speech.

—— ——   7. He had eaten the cake before I arrived.

—— ——   8. Ye shall see a light in the heavens.

—— ——   9. I was taking a shower.

—— —— 10. We built that house you're looking at.

a. Present
b. Future
c. Future Perfect
d. Imperfect
e. Aorist
f. Perfect
g. Pluperfect

Persons

1s (1st singular)
2s
3s
1p (1st plural)
2p
3p

Each underlined phrase above can be written as a single Greek word.

Exercise Two

Match the tense name to the kind of action it describes:

Tense Name	Kinds of Action
____ 1. Present	a. Completed
____ or ____ 2. Future	b. Single act
____ 3. Imperfect	c. Continuing action
____ and ____ 4. Aorist	
____ 5. Perfect	
____ 6. Pluperfect	

Note: The perfect tense indicates continuing results, but not continuing action.

Moods of Verbs

The verb endings you learned in Part II were for the "indicative" mood—they "indicate" what is going on: "I tell a story."

There are four additional moods, each with a different set of endings:

A. **Imperative** mood—used to give a command: "Tell a story":

Scripture examples:

Ephesians 4:30. λυπεω means "grieve." ". . . and <u>do not λυπεῖτε</u> the Holy Spirit."

Ephesians 4:28. κλεπτω means "steal." "The one who stole, no longer κλεπτέτω" ("let him steal").

B. **Subjunctive** mood—used after the word "if": "If <u>I should tell</u> you what I did, would you punish me?"

Here are eight examples of uses of the subjunctive. Remember that the underlined portions can be said with a single word in Greek:

1. To exhort: "<u>Let us believe</u>"; "I command that <u>you love</u> one another."
2. To express purpose: "We came in order that <u>we might see</u> him."
3. Possibility: "If <u>we go</u> into the house, we will see him."
4. After "until" (when it hasn't happened yet): "Remain until <u>I come</u>."
5. Concerning fear: "I fear that <u>he would come</u>."
6. Warnings: "Do this lest <u>you come</u> into judgment."
7. Sentences using "whoever": "Whoever <u>would want</u> to save his life shall lose it."
8. Certain questions: "<u>Shall I come?</u>"

Scriptural examples:

Ephesians 4:28b. εχω means "have." "Let him no longer steal, in order that <u>he may have</u> to give to the one in need."
ἔχη

Ephesians 4:14. The word used in this sentence is a form of "be." ". . . in order that we no longer <u>might be</u> infants."
ὦμεν

C. **Optative** mood—for wishing: "If only <u>I could tell</u> a joke." Also used for wondering, and when the second part of a sentence depends on a first part which is in the past: "I had gone, so that <u>I might see</u> him leave."

Scriptural example:

Ephesians 1:17, using a form of the word that means "give." "In order that God <u>would give</u> you a spirit of wisdom . . ."
δώη

D. **Infinitive** mood—in Part II, you used it as a verb which comes after the word "to": "I want <u>to tell</u> a story."

In Greek, it is often used after the word "the," and acts like a noun. This is tricky to translate:

Romans 7:18. "The <u>to wish</u> is present to me."
θέλειν

See how various Bible translations try to deal with this sentence. RSV paraphrases it, "I can will what is right."

Exercise Three

Summary

Here is an English sentence using all five moods. Place the letter from the list below in each set of parentheses.

If any <u>should call</u> (   ), <u>tell</u> (   ) them <u>I had decided</u> (   ) <u>to leave</u> (   ), so I <u>could arrive</u> (   ) on time.

<u>Matching</u>:
   a. indicative
   b. imperative
   c. subjunctive
   d. optative
   e. infinitive

Note: Concepts of "past" and "present" are only clearly expressed in the indicative mood; the other moods bring out the character ("kind of action"—single act, continuing, or completed) but not necessarily any time element.

Exercise Four

Indentifying Mood and Tense

Match the underlined part of each sentence to the correct term from each of the two lists on the next page:

_____ _____ 1. It's been worthwhile <u>to have been giving</u> to charities all year.

_____ _____ 2. If he <u>should fall</u> to the ground, he would get up again.

_____ _____ 3. She <u>might have made</u> the cake we see before us now.

_____ _____   4. The editor <u>had sent</u> the letter before I arrived.

_____ _____   5. We must preserve our resources, or else <u>we will have given</u> them all away by the time we need them.

_____ _____   6. They <u>are to send</u> their friends away immediately!

_____ _____   7. I wonder if he <u>would make</u> a fool of himself if he showed up next.

_____ _____   8. You must like <u>to be writing</u> letters all the time.

_____ _____   9. I wish God <u>would have been giving</u> me that kind of comfort all along.

_____ _____   10. They <u>should have moved</u> in long ago.

_____ _____   11. <u>Give</u> me a piece of pie, Mom.

Tenses	Moods
a. present	A. indicative
b. future	B. imperative
c. imperfect	C. subjunctive
d. aorist	D. optative
e. perfect	E. infinitive
f. pluperfect	
g. future perfect	

Voice of Verbs

The examples described so far have been in "active" voice—which means the subject is doing the acting. Before we move on to "passive" voice, let's take a minute to summarize all the possible endings in "active" voice.

Active Voice: The numbers indicate the number of endings in each category to match the six "persons."

Tenses	Moods				
	Indicative	Imperative	Subjunctive	Optative	Infinitive
Present	6	4	6	6	1
Future	6		6	6	1
Imperfect	6				
Aorist	6	4	6	6	1
Perfect	6	4	6	6	1
Pluperfect	6				

A blank space on the chart means that particular possibility was not actually used in Greek.

Note that imperative only needs four personal endings; "I" and "we" are not used. There is only one infinitive for each tense.

If you add together all the possibilities, you will find that there are 100 different ways to write a Greek verb.

Passive Voice

All 100 of these possibilities appear, with 100 different forms, in "passive" voice (in which the subject is being acted upon). There is also something called "middle" voice, which is used when the subject acts upon himself. Fortunately, middle voice does not add another 100 endings, because "passive" and "middle" are formed identically in some tenses. The passive voice has one tense that the active voice does not have, the "future perfect."

The three voices then are:

Active   **Passive**   **Middle**

I <u>threw</u> the ball.   I <u>was thrown</u> for a loop.   I <u>threw myself</u> at his feet.

Examples of passive voice from Scripture:

Present, indicative: In Christ you <u>are being built</u> together into a dwelling of God in the Spirit (Eph. 2:22).

Aorist, indicative: . . . which now <u>has been revealed</u> to the apostles and prophets . . . (Eph. 3:5).

Aorist, imperative: . . . all bitterness <u>let be gone</u> from you (Eph. 4:31).

Aorist, subjunctive: . . . so that ye <u>might be filled</u> with all the fullness of God (Eph. 3:19).

Example of middle voice:

I do not <u>cease</u> to give thanks concerning you (Eph. 1:16).

Exercise Five

Identifying Voice

A.

    ____ 1. I <u>washed</u> the dishes.

    ____ 2. I've <u>been washed</u> in the blood.

    ____ 3. I <u>washed myself</u>.

A. Active

M. Middle

P. Passive

B.

    ____ 1. He <u>is washing</u> himself.

    ____ 2. We <u>will be clothed</u> in His righteousness.

    ____ 3. Ye <u>have fed</u> my lambs.

    ____ 4. They <u>will be washed</u> by His word.

    ____ 5. I <u>am dressing</u> myself.

    ____ 6. You <u>were being fed</u> intravenously.

    ____ 7. He <u>washed</u> your sins away.

    ____ 8. We <u>are being dressed</u> because we can't do it ourselves.

    ____ 9. They <u>will feed themselves</u> when they are able.

Exercise Six

Identifying Verb Characteristics

Match the underlined phrase from each sentence to the correct term from each of the three lists below.

——— —— —— 1. When ye <u>had given</u> the money, were ye still ashamed?

——— —— —— 2. If you <u>would be built up</u> in faith, read His word.

——— —— —— 3. I <u>will have made</u> four trips to the dentist by the time it's over.

——— —— —— 4. Was it worth it <u>to have washed yourself</u> before eating?

——— —— —— 5. They <u>would have been thrown</u> from their saddles if they hadn't hung on.

——— —— —— 6. <u>Write</u> what I tell you to the seven churches.

——— —— —— 7. If only I <u>could pass</u> that test tomorrow!

——— —— —— 8. He <u>would have been rescued</u> if he had shouted for help.

——— —— —— 9. You must have been patient <u>to have been building</u> that wall for so long.

——— —— —— 10. We <u>might have been declared</u> innocent had it not been for that witness.

Mood	Tense	Voice
A. Indicative	a. present	X. Active
B. Imperative	b. future	Y. Middle
C. Subjunctive	c. imperfect	Z. Passive
D. Optative	d. aorist	
E. Infinitive	e. perfect	
	f. pluperfect	
	g. future perfect	

The following material summarizes all the possibilities for a Greek verb; the examples are all given in "first person," so each example given stands for six possibilities (except imperative, which has four; and infinitive, which has one).

Summary of Verb Possibilities

X = does not occur in Greek

	Indicative	Imperative	Subjunctive	Optative	Infinitive
Active					
Present	I throw.	Throw!	I should throw.	I would throw.	To throw.
	I am throwing.	Be throwing!	I should be throwing.	I would be throwing.	To be throwing.
Future	I will throw.	X	X	I might throw.	To be going to throw.
Imperfect	I was throwing.	X	X	X	X
Aorist	I threw.	Throw!	I should have thrown.	I would have thrown.	To have thrown.
Perfect	I did throw.	X	I should have thrown.	I would have thrown.	To have thrown.
Pluperfect	I had thrown.	X	X	X	X
Middle					
Present	I throw myself.	Throw yourself!	I should throw myself.	I would throw myself.	To throw myself.
Future	I will throw myself.	X	X	I might throw myself.	To be going to throw myself.
Imperfect	I was throwing myself.	X	X	X	X
Aorist	I threw myself.	Throw yourself!	I should have thrown myself.	I would have thrown myself.	To have thrown myself.
Perfect	I have thrown myself.	X	I should have thrown myself.	I would have thrown myself.	To have thrown myself.
Pluperfect	I had thrown myself.	X	X	X	X
Passive					
Present	I am being thrown.	Be thrown!	I should be thrown.	I would be thrown.	To be thrown.
Future	I will be thrown.	X	X	I might be thrown.	To be going to be thrown.
Imperfect	I was being thrown.	X	X	X	X
Aorist	I was thrown!	Be thrown!	I should have been thrown.	I would have been thrown.	To have been thrown.
Perfect	I have been thrown.	X	I should have been thrown.	I would have been thrown.	To have been thrown.
Pluperfect	I had been thrown.	X	X	X	X
Future Perfect	I will have been thrown.	X	X	I will have been thrown.	Shall have to be thrown.

Using an Analytical Lexicon

An analytical lexicon lists each word used in the New Testament separately—
every time it appears with a different ending, it receives a different listing. You
do not need to know all the details of forming Greek words in order to look
them up in such a book. Let's go through the procedure together of tracking
down the meaning of a word through the use of this type of lexicon.

Ephesians 1:11 includes the word ἐκληρώθημεν.

If we look up the word, we find this entry:

ἐκληρώθημεν 1 pers. pl. aor. 1 ind. pass. καλεω

We see at the far right that the word is a form of the word καλεω, which
means "call." The last abbreviation stands for "passive," so use the last third
of the chart on the previous pages. "Ind." stands for "indicative," so use
the first column. "Aor." stands for "aorist." When looking for the English
meaning, you do not need to be concerned with the number found after the
word "aorist." At the aorist location in the first column, the English example
given is "I was thrown." Since the word we are concerned with means "call,"
simply substitute the word "call" for the word "throw," and you get "I was
called." It states at the beginning of the lexicon entry that the word is "first
person plural"—that is, the subject is "we." By substituting "we" for "I" in
our translation, we arrive at the final translation: "we were called."

Summary of Abbreviations Used in an Analytical Lexicon

There are a few abbreviations in the book you don't have to use. After some
words, you will see something like (§ 7 rem 1) or (tab B). This refers to "sections" (§) in the front of the book, which include "remarks" (rem.) and "tables"
(tab.). This is only meaningful to the intermediate Greek student. Other places
in the book refer to certain scholars and books to back up the information
being given. You will find a list of these at the bottom right of the abbreviation page which comes right after the table of contents.

Following are abbreviations for the terms used in this book, which are the
basic ones you will need to know:

abl.	ablative (shows separation)
acc.	accusative (direct object)
act.	active voice

aor.	aorist, a type of past tense
compar.	comparative, used with adjectives to indicate "more"
dat.	dative (indirect object)
fem.	feminine
fut.	future tense
gen.	genitive (possessive)
indic.	indicative (statement of fact)
inf.	infinitive (verb form that we translate using "to": "to write")
imp. or imper. or imperat.	imperative (giving a command)
imperf.	imperfect tense (a type of past tense)
inst.	instrumental (expresses the means by which the action is accomplished)
loc.	locative (indicates the location or position of the noun it describes)
masc.	masculine
mid.	middle voice
neut.	neuter
nom.	nominative (subject of sentence)
part.	participle
pass.	passive voice
pers.	person (such as 2nd person = you, 3rd person = he)
perf.	perfect (a type of past tense)
pl. or plur.	plural
pluperf.	pluperfect (a type of past tense)
sing.	singular
subj.	subjunctive
superl.	superlative (used with adjectives to mean "most")
voc.	vocative (an ending put on a noun when you are speaking directly to that noun)

Lesson Forty-Six

Constructing Greek Verbs

The chart on pages 253–254 shows how to make common verb forms in the indicative mood. Part II of the chart lists various sets of endings, labeled (a), (b), and so on. These endings are in sets of six, representing the six "persons," first person singular "I," second person singular "you," and so on. Using this chart is only possible if you have information provided by a Greek lexicon (= Greek/English dictionary).

In the lexicon, you will notice that each verb is listed with six forms.[1] These are called the "six principal parts." They give you the information you need to construct the various forms of the verb. To see how these are used, here are the principal parts for the verb λυω (loose).

λυω   λυσω   ελυσα   λελυκα   λελυμαι   ελυθην

The first principal part tells you what you need to know to construct present and imperfect tenses; the second, to construct future tenses; the third, aorist; the fourth and fifth, perfect; and the sixth, passive in aorist and future. These principal parts all have the first person ending attached. When you remove the ending, you are left with the "stem." You can then add whatever ending you need to the stem in order to construct the verb form that you want.

The right-hand half of the chart shows how to follow the instructions using λυω as an example. The third person singular is worked out for each tense and voice, as follows: The ending is removed from the principal part, and the third person ending is attached.

1. Sometimes only the forms actually used in the New Testament are listed.

Exercise One

Matching from the verb construction chart. (These are all found in the sixth column of the chart.)

In the first blank, write the tense (present, future, etc.);

in the second blank, write the voice (active, passive, etc.);

in the third blank, write the letter of the English translation from the list at the right.

Tense   Voice

_____ _____ ___   1. ελυσατο   a. He was loosening himself

_____ _____ ___   2. λελυται   b. He loosened himself (simple act)

_____ _____ ___   3. λυει   c. He had loosened

_____ _____ ___   4. ελυετο   d. He has been loosened

_____ _____ ___   5. ελελυκει   e. He will be loosened

_____ _____ ___   6. λυεται   f. He is loosening

_____ _____ ___   7. λυθησεται   g. He is being loosened

The instructions for imperfect, in the fourth column of the chart, include the term "aug." For now, when you see this term, place an ε in front of the principal part, as you see has been done in the sixth column example for imperfect.

Verb Construction Chart for Indicative

I. Instructions

If you want to make: Example using λυω (= loosens)

Tense	Voice	Principal Part to Use	Add Endings from Column	Principal Part Looks Like	Third Person Singular Would Be	Which Means
Present	Active	1	a	λυω	λυει	he loosens, or he is loosening
Present	Middle	1	a	λυω	λυεται	he loosens himself
Present	Passive	1	a	λυω	λυεται	he is being loosened
Imperfect	Active	1	aug b	λυω	ελυε	he was loosening
Imperfect	Middle	1	aug b	λυω	ελυετο	he was loosening himself
Imperfect	Passive	1	aug b	λυω	ελυετο	he was being loosened
Future	Active	2	a	λυσω	λυσει	he will loosen
Future	Middle	2	a	λυσω	λυσεται	he will loosen himself
Aorist	Active	3	c	ελυσα	ελυσε	he loosened
Aorist	Middle	3	c	ελυσα	ελυσατο	he loosened himself
Perfect	Active	4	d	λελυκα	λελυκε	he has loosened

Tense	Voice	Principal Part to Use	Add Endings from Column	Principal Part Looks Like	Third Person Singular Would Be	Which Means
Pluperfect	Active	4	aug f	λελυκα	ελελυκει	he had loosened
Perfect	Middle	5	d	λελυμαι	λελυται	he has loosed himself
Perfect	Passive	5	d	λελυμαι	λελυται	he has been loosened
Aorist	Passive	6	e	ελυθην	ελυθη	he was loosened
Future	Passive	6	remove aug, add "σ," and use endings from col. (a)	ελυθην	λυθησεται	he will be loosened

II. Endings

	Person	(a) For Present & Future	(b) For Imperfect & Second Aorist	(c) For Aorist	(d) For Perfect	(e) For Aorist Passive	(f) For Pluperfect
ACTIVE	I 1	ω	ον	α	α		ειν
	you 2	εις	ες	ας	ας		εις
	he 3	ει	ε	ε (ν)	ε		ει
	we 1	ομεν	ομεν	αμεν	αμεν		ειμεν
	you 2	ετε	ετε	ατε	ατε		ειτε
	they 3	ουσι (ν)*	ον	αν	ασι (ν) or αν		εισαν
MIDDLE & PASSIVE	I 1	ομαι	ομην	αμην	μαι	ην	
	you 2	η	ου or σο	ω	σαι	ης	
	he 3	εται	ετο	ατο	ται	η	
	we 1	ομεθα	ομεθα	αμεθα	μεθα	ημεν	
	you 2	εσθε	εσθε	ασθε	σθε	ητε	
	they 3	ονται	οντο	αντο	νται	ησαν	

* The "ν" is sometimes added for a smooth connection to the next word.

Exercise Two

Drill in Adding Endings to λυω

Step-by-step procedure:

1. Decide which tense and voice the example is in.
2. Select the correct principal part and remove the ending (unless the subject of your sentence is "I"; in that case, the correct ending is already on the principal part in most "active" examples).
3. Decide which "person" the example calls for, and select the correct ending from the right column of endings.

As an example, let's construct the future middle form for the word λυω, and let's select "you" as the subject. We want to construct a form that will mean "you will loosen yourself." Future middle is the eighth row on the chart; we are told to use second principal part, and endings from column (a). After we remove the ending from the second principal part we are left with λυσ. Now we go to the endings columns; since we are making a "middle" form, we need an ending from the lower half of the column. The second person ending there is η; adding that to λυσ, λυση, "you will loosen yourself."

Construct the form of λυω required to translate each phrase:

	Form of λυω	Tense	Voice	
1.	_____	_____	_____	– You were loosening
2.	_____	_____	_____	– She will loosen herself
3.	_____	_____	_____	– We have loosened
4.	_____	_____	_____	– Ye were loosened
5.	_____	_____	_____	– They are loosening themselves
6.	_____	_____	_____	– You will loosen
7.	_____	_____	_____	– It had loosened
8.	_____	_____	_____	– I am being loosened
9.	_____	_____	_____	– We loosened
10.	_____	_____	_____	– They have been loosened

More about "Aug"

The abbreviation stands for "augment," an addition or change at the beginning of the verb.

1. If the principal part starts with a consonant, place an ε at the beginning.
2. If the principal part starts with a vowel, it is changed to what is called a "long vowel." Here are some of the changes:

   α or ε to η; ι to ει; o to ω.

   Example: εγειρω means "I rise." To make imperfect, change ε to η, and add an ending from column (b); ηγειρον means "I was rising." In other cases, you can find out the correct way to make the augment by looking at the third and sixth principal parts as listed in the lexicon, because those principal parts already have the augment attached.

   Example: οικοδομεω means "build." The third principal part is ῳκοδομησα, which shows us that adding the ε changed οι to ῳ. Put that ῳ at the beginning to construct your imperfect, add an ending from column (b), and the result is ῳκοδομουν, "I was building."

3. Another complication arises if your verb is a compound word. For example, απαγω, "lead away," is made of the word απο, "away," and αγω, "lead." The letter to be changed is the α on αγω, not the α on απο. The augment for α is η; the imperfect of απαγω then is απηγον. Again, in more complicated cases, the third or sixth principal part will show you how to augment the verb in question.

Examples with Other Verbs

Let's construct "he wrote," the aorist of γραφω (write). We will need the third principal part, which according to the lexicon turns out to be εγραψα. Our chart tells us that we need the endings from column (c). The first person ending is α. If we remove that from the principal part, the stem turns out to be εγραψ. Now, from column (c), find and add the third person ending, ε, and the result is εγραψε, "he wrote."

Second Aorist

Some verbs form certain tenses in a different way. The same thing occurs in English. We have "regular" verbs, that form the past tense by adding –ed. Example: "love," "loved." We have other verbs that change within themselves to form the past. Example: "throw," "threw." When a Greek aorist is formed in a different way than the regular way, the formation is called "second aorist."

The meaning is still the same; only the method of formation is different. If the formation is "second aorist," you will use endings from column (b) instead of column (c), (p. 254 How will you know when to do this? If your third principal part ends with ον, you will know that you are to use the endings from the column that is headed up that way, which is column (b). Another giveaway is that regular (also called "first") aorists always have an σ before the ending (the aorist of λυω, for example, was ελυσα); second aorists never have this σ.

Example: You decide to construct the form that means "we threw." You know that "throw" is βαλλω, so you look up βαλλω in the lexicon. The third principal part is εβαλον. You notice that it doesn't have an σ, and it ends with the ον, which shows you it is taking its endings from column (b). You remove the ending, obtaining the stem εβαλ; you add the ending for "we," ομεν, and construct εβαλομεν, "we threw." For second aorist passive, use the same column as for first aorist passive. Forms called second future and second perfect also exist; and even some "third" forms.

Exercise Three

Drill with Various Verbs

Here are the principal parts:

write	γραφω	γραψω	εγραψα	γεγραφα	γεγραμμαι	εγραφην
call	καλεω	καλεσω	εκαλεσα	κεκληκα	κεκλημαι	εκληθην
drink	πινω	πιομαι	επιον	πεπωκα	πεπομαι	εποθην

    1. He will write _____

    2. They have been called (summoned) _____

    3. He drank _____

    4. We had drunk _____

    5. He was called _____

    6. We have written _____

"Deponent"

A verb is called "deponent" when it has a middle or passive form but an active meaning. The second principal part of "drink," above, is deponent. It looks like it has a passive ending, but it will be translated "I will drink." More about deponents later.

Connecting Vowels

Sometimes you will notice a change in the vowels where the endings connect with the principal part. Here is an example:

The lexicon entry for "love" is αγαπαω, so the stem is αγαπα. To say "he loves," you would add ει. But that ει interacts with the α, and the result is that the α cancels out the ε and the ι becomes miniaturized; the result is αγαπᾳ, "he loves."

This chart shows what happens when vowels interact with one another:

ε + diphthong = ε disappears.   ε + o = ου   ε + ε = ει

α + o = ω   α + ω = ω   α + ε = α   α + ει = ᾳ

o + ε or o or ου = ου   o + α or ω = ω   o + ι = οι

This workbook over-simplifies when explaining that endings can be connected to principal parts. In actual fact, there is a connecting vowel between the stem and the ending. A comprehensive, 40-page explanation of this matter can be found in *Handbook of New Testament Greek*, © 1973 by William Sanford LaSor, Eerdmans, in volume 2, starting on page B-85.

Since this matter will not be taken up in this workbook, simply realize that some of the following examples will show slight variations from the endings given in the tables due to the connecting vowels.

Lesson Forty-Seven

Forming Principal Parts

If the verb follows regular patterns, your lexicon might not list the principal parts. Here is how they are constructed (basic concept):

Principal Part	Tense It Consists Of	How It Is Formed	Example with λυω
1.	Present	Stem + ending	λυω
2.	Future	Stem + σ + ending[1]	λυσω
3.	Aorist	Augment + stem + σ + ending	ελυσα
4.	Perfect	Reduplication[2] + aug. = stem + κ = ending	λελυκα
5.	Perfect passive	Red. + aug. + stem + ending	Λελυμαι λελυμαι
6.	Aorist passive	Aug. + stem + θ[3] + ending	ελυθην

1. When certain letters occur with σ, something happens. Sometimes this is common sense: If you take βλεπ, add σ and then the ending ω, you get βλεπσω. Obviously you can "save ink" by writing that πσ sound as ψ, and write βλεψω.

Here are some of the possibilities:

π, β, or φ + σ + ψ   κ, γ, or χ + σ = ξ
τ, δ, or θ simply disappears when σ is added

Since your interest is in reading Scriptures, your usual approach will be not to create a Greek word, but to work backward from a form so you can look it up in a dictionary. For example, let's say you find a word, γραψω, but cannot find it in a dictionary. You surmise that the ψ might be there because an σ was added to a π, β, or φ to form a future tense. You try looking up γραπ, γραβ, and γραφ—and sure enough, you find there is a word γραφω.

When you come across the future of a verb whose stem ends in λ, ρ, μ, or ν, it will look something like present tense! The reason is that when these consonants interact with the σ used for future, they eliminate it. There is a change in accent, however. The first two principal parts of κρινω (judge) are κρίνω and κρινῶ.

2. Reduplication is formed either by:
   a. repeating the first letter of the stem in front of the augment. Example: since λυω starts with λ, we simply put another λ at the beginning.
   b. If the stem starts with certain sounds that we form in English by using "h" with a letter (ph, th, ch), the reduplication is the sound without the "h": The reduplication of φ is π; θ becomes τ; χ becomes κ.

For example, the fourth principal part of φιλεω is πεφιληκα.

3. Certain stem letters change before θ. If the stem ends in ζ, it is pretty hard to say ζθ, so the Greeks simply replaced that combination with an σ. Here are some of the possibilities:

κ or γ + θ = χ   π or β + θ = φ   ζ, τ, δ, or θ + θ = σ

Exercise One

The explanation above enables you to make the principal parts of some of the easier verbs.

Make the six parts of πιστευω (believe).

Now try πεμπω (send), referring to footnotes 1 and 3. (Skip fourth and fifth parts, which are unusual.)

Exercise Two

Verbs in Sentences

Generally you will not know the principal part of a verb before you look it up. The Word List on the next page contains only the present tense forms, which are the lexicon entries, so it is important to practice guessing at the present tense form when you see a word.

Each sentence is preceded by two blanks. Find the verb in the sentence, and match it both to the Word List and to the list of Tenses.

___ ___ 1. That which we beheld, _____ ___ _____ ___ ____
                                          καὶ   αἱ   χεῖρες   ἡμῶν

   _____ concerning _____ _____ _____
   ἐψηλάφησαν   τοῦ   λόγου   τῆς

   _____ . . . (1 John 1:1).
   ζωῆς

___ ___ 2. The prayer of faith _____ the sick (James 5:15).
            τῆς πίστεως σώσει

___ ___ 3. As the bridegroom was delayed, they all slumbered _____
   _____ (Matt. 25:5).   καὶ
   ἐκάθευδον

___ ___ 4. We have fellowship _____ _____ _____ ____ _____
                                        μετ'   ἀλλήλων   καὶ   τὸ   αἷμα

   ____ _____ ____ _____ _____ _____
   Ἰησοῦ   τοῦ   υἱοῦ   αὐτοῦ   καθαρίζει   ἡμᾶς

   _____ _____ _____ (1 John 1:7).
   ἀπὸ   πάσης   ἁμαρτίας

___ ___ 5. Courage, daughter, __ _____ ___ ___ _____ ____ (Matt.
   9:22).   ἡ   πίστις   σου   σέσωκέν   σε

Word List

A. σωζω—save

B. ψηλαφαω—touch

C. καθαριζω—cleanse

D. καθευδω—sleep

Tenses

a. present

b. future

c. imperfect

d. aorist

e. perfect

f. pluperfect

Exercise Three

Some Varieties of Aorist Forms

Match the verb from the Bible verse with its present tense form from the Word List and with the best description from the Word Forms List (both on next page):

____ ____ 1. For no one ever _____ his own flesh . . . (Eph. 5:29).

ἐμίσησεν

____ ____ 2. For God so _____ _____ _____ (John 3:16).

ἠγάπησεν   τὸν   κόσμον

____ ____ 3. _____ _____ already _____ or already have been made

οὐχ   ὅτι   ἔλαβον

complete (Phil. 3:12).

____ ____ 4. _____ _____ _____ and fall short of the glory

πάντες   γὰρ   ἥμαρτον

of God (Rom. 3:23).

____ ____ 5. Then _____ ____ _____ _____ (Matt. 27:26).

ἀπέλυσεν   αὐτοῖς   τὸν   βαρραβᾶν

____ ____ 6. As the Father has sent me into the world, ____ _____

κἀγὼ

_____ _____ ____ _____ _____ (John 17:18).

ἀπέστειλα   αὐτοὺς   εἰς   τὸν   κόσμον

Word List

A. αποστελλω—send
B. απολυω—release
C. αγαπαω—love
D. αμαρτανω—sin
E. μισεω—hate
F. λαμβανω—take, obtain

Word Forms List

a. It has a prefix, so the ε (the augment) is found after the prefix rather than at the beginning of the word.
b. A "second aorist"—same meaning as any other aorist, but with no σ and using endings from column (b) on page 254. Also illustrates a letter removed from the stem of the present.
c. A word that started with a vowel, so adding the augment changed the vowel.
d. Second aorist, in a word with a prefix.
e. Second aorist, in a word that started with a vowel.
f. Ordinary aorist; regular augment at the beginning, with σ and endings from (c) on page 254.

Exercise Four

Three Very Common but Unusual Verbs

You will see these often in the New Testament.
Learn by guessing:

Answer choices:
a. he saw
b. knows
c. said
d. we saw
e. we know

_____ 1. He answered and εἶπεν to them (John 6:29).
_____ 2. They answered and ειπαν to him (Matt. 21:27).
_____ 3. Walking along the sea, εἶδεν two brothers (Matt. 4:18).
_____ 4. Where is he born King of the Jews? εἴδομεν his star in the East . . . (Matt. 2:2).

The next word is aorist in form, but present in meaning:

_____ 5. Your Father οἶδεν what you need before you ask (Matt. 6:8).
_____ 6. . . . came to him by night and said, "ῥαββί, οἴδαμεν you are a teacher sent from God (John 3:2).

Comments

1. ειπον (I said) is a second aorist form; it is the third principal part of λεγω. Not that one can form ειπον from λεγω, but rather, the Greeks simply used a different word in order to express the aorist of "speak." We do the same type of thing in English. Our present tense words about "being" are: "is," "are"; past tense words are: "was," "were." These were originally from two different word families. There is a present tense form of the "was" word family, but it has fallen into disuse.

2. ειδον (I saw) is second aorist, the third principal part of οραω, see.

3. οιδα has a different background. It is in perfect tense, but it is translated as though it were present.
   The subjunctive first person singular is ειδω (I would or should know).
   The imperative second person singular is ισθι (Know thou).
   The pluperfect forms are translated as though they were imperfect: ηδειν is translated, "I was knowing."

Exercise Five

Middles and Passives—Examples

Match the verbs with their present tense forms from the Word List and their tense and voice from the Word Use List (both on next page).

____ ____ 1. We are more than conquerors through him who loved us.

_____ _____ _____ _____ _____ _____
πέπεισμαι   γὰρ   ὅτι   οὔτε   θάνατος   οὔτε

_____ . . . will separate us from the love of God . . . (Rom.
ζωὴ
8:38).

____ ____ 2. (Since I heard of your faith and love,) ____ _____ giving
οὐ   παύομαι

thanks _____ _____ (Eph. 1:16).
ὑπὲρ   ὑμῶν

____ ____ 3. She said to herself, "If only I touch his garment, _____ "
ἐν ἑαυτῇ   σωθήσομαι

(Matt. 9:21).

____ ____ 4. . . . and the woman _____ ___ ___ _____ _____
ἐσώθη   ἀπὸ   τῆς   ὥρας

_____ (Matt. 9:22).
ἐκείνης

_____ _____ 5. I bow my knee _____ _____ _____ from whom
                          πρὸς   τὸν   πατέρα

every fatherhood _____ (Eph. 3:14–15).
                        ὀνομάζεται

Word List

A. ονομαζω—name
   cognate to English onomatopoeia
   (words that imitate natural sounds)

B. πειθω—persuade

C. παυω—cease

D. σωζω—save

Word Uses List

a. present middle
b. present passive
c. future passive
d. aorist passive
e. perfect passive

Deponent Verbs

By this term, lexicon entries will point out that certain verbs receive middle
or passive endings but are translated as though they were active. A give-away
is that the lexicon entry itself will show the verb with a passive ending:

These things therefore I say and _____ in the Lord . . . (Eph. 4:17).
                                      μαρτύρομαι

θεαομαι = behold (related word θεατρον, cognate to English "theater")

This one could also be explained as a "middle" form, since you see "for
yourself." The point is it is called "deponent" because its lexicon entry is
not in "active" form.

Example (in imperfect tense):

That which was from the beginning, which we have heard, which our
eyes have seen, which we have_____ and our hands have
touched . . . (1 John 1:1).   ἐθεασάμεθα

ψευδομαι = lie

_____ we say _____ fellowship _____ _____ and walk in the
   ἐὰν   ἔχομεν   μετ᾽   αὐτοῦ

darkness, ____ _____ and do not do the truth (1 John 1:6).
              ψευδόμεθα

Here is the same verb in another tense. The form is aorist middle, the translation is active:

Why did you plan this in your heart? _____ _____ _____
οὐκ   ἐψεύσω   ἀνθρώποις

_____ _____ _____ (Acts 5:4).
ἀλλὰ   τῷ   θεῷ

Some verbs are deponent in one tense, but not in another.

Lesson Forty-Eight

Verb Examples: Mixed Tenses and Voices

Match the verbs from these sentences with their present tense form from the Word List and its tense and voice from the Form List (on the next page).

___ ___ 1. You did not so learn Christ, ____ _____ _____ and in
εἴ γε αὐτὸν ἠκούσατε

him were taught (Eph. 4:20–21.)

___ ___ 2. When he had received the vinegar, _____ _____,
"_____" (John 19:30). ὁ Ἰησοῦς εἶπεν
Τετέλεσται

___ ___ 3. Knowing that ____ _____ _____ ___ _____
οὐ δικαιοῦται ἄνθρωπος ἐξ ἔργων

____ ____ but through faith . . . (Gal. 2:16).
νόμου

___ ___ 4. Then the righteous _____ ___ ____, saying, "Lord,
ἀποκριθήσονται αὐτῷ

when did we see you hungry?" (Matt. 25:37).

___ ___ 5. _____ _____ ___,___ _____ _____
Ἐπίστευσεν δὲ Ἀβραὰμ τῷ θεῷ καὶ ἐλογίσθη

_____ _____ _____ (Rom. 4:3).
αὐτῷ εἰς δικαιοσύνην

___ ___ 6. Having heard the king, _____ and the star went before them (Matt. 2:9). ἐπορεύθησαν

___ ___ 7. If they don't hear Moses and the prophets, not _____ _____
ἐάν τις

should rise ____ _____ _____ (Luke 16:31).
Ἐκ νεκρῶν πεισθήσονται

___ ___ 8. (He'll be born) ____ _____ _____ _____; _____
ἐν βηθλεὲμ τῆς Ἰουδαίας οὕτως

_____ _____ by the prophet (Matt. 2:5).
γὰρ γέγραπται

___ ___ 9. . . . did not deem it robbery to be equal with God, _____
                                                          ἀλλὰ

_____ _____, taking the form of a servant (Phil. 2:6–7).
   ἑαυτὸν   ἐκένωσεν

___ ___ 10. That which was from the beginning, __ _____ __
                                               ὅ   ἀκηκόαμεν,   ὅ

_____ ___ ____ _____ ___ ____ (1 John 1:1).
   ἑωράκαμεν   τοῖς   ὀφθαλμοῖς   ἡμῶν

___ ___ 11. No man can serve two masters; the one _____ and the
            other _____ (Luke 16:13).   μισήσει
                  ἀγαπήσει

___ ___ 12. Beware of _____ which _____ _____ ___ __
                        ψευδοπροφητῶν   ἔρχονται   πρὸς   ὑμᾶς

            in sheep's clothing (Matt. 7:15).

___ ___ 13. Ye are not your own, for _____ _____. Therefore
                                      ἠγοράσθητε   τιμῆς

            glorify God . . . (1 Cor. 6:19–20).

___ ___ 14. He who endures to the end _____ (Matt. 24:13).
                                       σωθήσεται

Word List

A. απокρινομαι = answer
B. σωζω = save
C. μισεω = hate
D. αγαπαω = love
E. πειθω = persuade
F. πιστευω = believe
G. λογιζω = reckon
H. αγοραζω = buy
I. ακουω = hear
J. κενοω = deprive of power, empty; source of
   theological term "kenosis," Christ's emptying
   of power as he became man
K. ὁραω = see
L. γραφω = write
M. τελεω finish
N. δικαιοω = make right
O. πορευομαι = go
P. ερχομαι = come

Form List

a. present,
   deponent
b. present, passive
c. future
d. future,
   deponent
e. future, passive
f. aorist
g. aorist,
   deponent
h. aorist, passive
i. perfect

Exercise Two

Infinitives

You have learned the ending ειν. λεγειν = to speak. Another infinitive ending is αι. The following chart shows examples of infinitive endings added to principal parts:

A List of Infinitives of the Verb λυω

	Active	Middle	Passive
Present	λυειν	λυεσθαι	λυεσθαι
Future	λυσειν	λυσεσθαι	λυθησεσθαι
Aorist	λυσαι	λυσασθαι	λυθηναι
Perfect	λελυκεναι	λελυσθαι	λελυσθαι

Matching

_____ 1. λελυσθαι   a. to have loosed

_____ 2. λελυκεναι   b. to be about to loose

_____ 3. λυσαι   c. to be loosing one's self

_____ 4. λυθησεσθαι   d. to have been loosed

_____ 5. λυσειν   e. to be being loosed

_____ 6. λυεσθαι   f. to be about to be loosed

                               g. to loose

An example of the passive infinitive (based on δικαιοω, make "right"):

For we reckon man _____ by faith without deeds of the law (Rom. 3:28).   δικαιουσθαι

Translation: "To have been made right."

The infinitive can be used as a noun; in such cases the word for "the" can be placed in front of it, as in το ποιειν. "The to-make" (from the phrase "το ποιειν") is obviously not smooth English; your paraphrase might end up something like "the act of making" or "the making process."

Example

For God is the one working in you, both (in regards to) ____ _____ _____
____ _____ for His good pleasure (Phil. 2:13).   τὸ   θέλειν   καὶ
τὸ   ἐνεργεῖν

Since the infinitive has past and future forms, as well as present, it can express when something takes place, compared to when the main action of the sentence takes place. Prepositions may be added to make these relationships even more clear. The following list is excerpted from *New Testament Greek Made Functional*, © 1972 by Fred Nofer, pages 132–33. Used by permission.

Preposition and "the" Placed before Infinitive	Possible English Translation
μετα το	after
εν το	as or while
πριν or προ + "the"	before
Other relationships that can be shown:	
εις το	in order to (shows purpose)
ωστε	so that (shows result)
δια το	because (shows cause)

Exercise Three

Infinitive Examples

You are not expected to understand why the stem changes developed, but only to recognize the words as infinitives. Try to match them to the chart. (Forms List and Word List on p. 270.) You will see it is not always obvious to English speakers why the writers chose the tense they did. Remember that present is usually chosen for "continuation," aorist for speaking of an event without regard to time, and perfect for an event with a definite start and repercussions in the future.

Start by trying to work the word "to" into your translation; after you have said it somewhat literally, you can paraphrase into more acceptable English if needed:

____ ___ 1. Christ came into the world ____ ____ sinners (1 Tim. 1:15).
σῶσαι

____ ___ 2. That he may give you the ability _____ through
κραταιωθῆναι

___ ___ his Spirit in your inner man, _____ _____

$$\overline{\text{κατοικῆσαι}} \quad \overline{\text{τὸν}} \quad \overline{\text{Χριστὸν}}$$

$$\overline{\text{διὰ}} \quad \overline{\text{τῆς}} \quad \overline{\text{πίστεως}} \quad \overline{\text{ἐν}} \quad \overline{\text{ταῖς}} \quad \overline{\text{καρδίαις}} \quad \overline{\text{ὑμῶν}}$$

(Eph. 3:16–17).

___ ___ 3. Unless you remain on the ship, you will not be able

___ ___ _____ (Acts 27:31).

$$\overline{\text{σωθῆναι}}$$

___ ___ 4. Put off the old man corrupted by deceit, _____ in the

spirit of your mind (Eph. 4:22–23). $\quad$ ἀνανεοῦσθαι

___ ___ 5. I beseech you worthily _____ of the calling with which

$$\overline{\text{περιπατῆσαι}}$$

you are called (Eph. 4:1).

Examples with the word "the" before the infinitive:

___ ___ 6. _____ _____ _____ the working-one ____ _____

$$\overline{\text{θεὸς}} \quad \overline{\text{γάρ}} \quad \overline{\text{ἐστιν}} \quad \overline{\text{ὁ ἐνεργῶν}} \quad \overline{\text{ἐν}} \quad \overline{\text{ὑμῖν}}$$

___ ___ _____ ____ _____ ____ ____ _____ _____

$$\overline{\text{καὶ}} \quad \overline{\text{τὸ}} \quad \overline{\text{θέλειν}} \quad \overline{\text{καὶ}} \quad \overline{\text{τὸ}} \quad \overline{\text{ἐνεργεῖν}} \quad \overline{\text{ὑπὲρ}}$$

his good pleasure (Phil. 2:13).

___ ___ 7. The eyes of your heart being enlightened _____

$$\overline{\text{εἰς τὸ εἰδέναι}}$$

_____ what is the hope of his calling (Eph. 1:18).

$$\overline{\text{ὑμᾶς}}$$

Word List

a. περιπατεω = walk
b. οιδα = know; the form used is based on ειδω
c. ανανεοω = transform (see the word νεος in it?)
d. κραταιοω = strengthen
e. σωζω = save
f. κατοικεω = dwell within
g. ενεργεω = work, do
h. θελω = will, want

Forms List

A. present
B. present passive
C. aorist
D. aorist passive
E. perfect

Lesson Forty-Nine

Forming the Imperative

I. Instructions

This is the way the endings work out with the word λυω. There will be vowel changes with other verbs.

To Form		Use				
	Voice	Principal Part	Plus Ending	Principal Part Is	Second Person	Example (a command to you)
Present	Active	1	g	λυω	λυε	Loosen!
continuity	Middle	1	g	λυω	λυου	Loose yourself!
	Passive	1	g	λυω	λυου	Be loosened!
Aorist	Active	3	h	ελυσα	λυσον	
simple	Middle	3	h	ελυσα	λυσαι	The English language does not have simple equivalents for these; translate the same as you would for present.
event	Passive	6	j	ελυθην	λυθη	
Perfect	Active	4	i	λελυκα	λελυκε	
effect	Middle	5	i	λελυμαι	λελυσο	
continues	Passive	5	i	λελυμαι	λελυσο	

II. Ending to Use

Only four endings are needed in each category, since there are no first person forms. Note that the augment is removed from the aorist.

	Person		(g)	(h)	(i)	(j)
ACTIVE	Singular	2	ε	ον	ε	
		3	ετω	ατω	ετω	
	Plural	2	ετε	ατε	ετε	
		3	ωσαν	ωσαν	ωσαν	

271

	Person	(g)	(h)	(i)	(j)
MIDDLE & PASSIVE — Singular	2	ου	αι	σο	ητι
	3	εσθω	ασθω	σθω	ητω
Plural	2	εσθε	ασθε	σθε	ητε
	3	εσθωσαν	ασθωσαν	σθωσαν	ητωσαν

A Scripture example: λυπεω = grieve:

> . . . and μὴ λυπεῖτε the Holy Spirit . . . (Eph. 4:30; second person plural)

Note vowel change. According to the vowel change chart on page 258 ε + ε = ει.

Exercise One

Imperative Examples

Match the Greek verb from each sentence with its present tense from the Word List and its tense and voice from the Form List (both on the next page).

___ ___ 1. Going, therefore, _____ _____ _____, baptizing them in the name of . . . (Matt. 28:19).
                   μαθητεύσατε   πάντα τὰ ἔθνη

___ ___ 2. Wherefore _____ _____ you were then without
          μνημονεύετε   ὅτι
Christ (Eph. 2:11).

___ ___ 3. Don't fear when people harm you for doing right; rather,
_____ Christ in your hearts (1 Pet. 3:14–15).
  ἁγιάσατε

___ ___ 4. Our Father who art in heaven, _____ thy name (Matt. 6:9).
          ἁγιασθήτω

___ ___ 5. All bitterness . . . _____ from you . . . (Eph. 4:31).
    ἀρθήτω

___ ___ 6. __ _____ said to the women, "_____!" (Matt.
  28:5) ἄγγελος   Μὴ φοβεῖσθε

Word List

A. αιρω = remove

B. ἁγιαζω = related to ἁγιος—make holy, sanctify, regard with reverence

C. μνημονευω = remember, cognate to English "mnemonics" (a system of memorizing) and "anamnesis," the remembering part of a communion prayer

D. μαθητευω = instruct, disciple; related to μαθητης

E. φοβεω = fear

Form List

a. present active

b. aorist active (aorist used for emphasis)

c. aorist passive

d. present middle

An Example of a Passive Imperative

This example also demonstrates the idea of the present tense as giving the idea of continuous action.

Do not be drunk with wine . . . but _____ with the Spirit (Eph. 5:18).
                                          πληροῦσθε

The dictionary entry is πληροω, "fill." Since the form is passive, that means it is not something you do, but something that someone else does to you. However, since it is imperative (command), that means you must have the ability to either allow or prohibit the process from happening—you are commanded to let it happen. And since it is present, it suggests the idea of a continuous process, as a way of life. The passage could be translated, "And be ye continually being filled . . ."

While on the subject of imperatives, I would like to mention something else about nouns. There is an ending we haven't talked about yet, used when you are talking directly to someone. It is called the vocative case. It often ends with the letter ε: If talking to Paul, you would call him Παυλε. In other instances, the vowel of the nominative is changed: Jesus addressed the Father in John 17:25 as πάτερ δίκαιε (righteous father).

The disciples woke him saying, "_____ _____ or we perish" (Matt. 8:25).
                                  Κύριε   σῶσον

Forming the Subjunctive

Remember that the endings may differ as they interact with the vowels in a particular verb-stem. These endings will fit with the word λυω. Remove the augment from the aorist indicative.

Person		(k)	(l)
Singular	1	ω	ωμαι
	2	ης	η
	3	η	ηται
Plural	1	ωμεν	ωμεθα
	2	ητε	ησθε
	3	ωσι	ωνται

		Use Principal Part	Plus Ending	Principal Part Is	Example with λυω	
To Form	Voice				Third Person Singular	Which Means
Present	Active	1	k	λυω	λυη	he might loosen
	Middle	1	l	λυω	λυηται	he might loosen himself
	Passive	1	l	λυω	λυηται	he might be loosened
Aorist	Active	3	k	ελυσα	λυση	he might have loosened
	Middle	3	l	ελυσα	λυσηται	he might have loosened himself
	Passive	6	k	ελυθην	λυθη	he might have been loosened
Perfect	Active	4	k	λελυκα	λελυκη	he might have loosened
	Middle	5	*	λελυμαι	λελυμενος η	he might have loosened himself
	Passive	5	*	λελυμαι	λελυμενος η	he might have been loosened

* This form is expressed with two words: the participle (in this case λελυμενος) plus the ending from column (k) as a separate word.

A Scripture Example: πληροω = fill

. . . in order that _____ all things (Eph. 4:10).
                              πληρώση

It is aorist, which indicates a one-time filling. (The idea of pastness is not necessarily implied in any but the indicative mood forms.)

Optative

Because it is seldom used, a chart will not be given. Many of the forms stand out because of οι or αι as the connecting vowels between stem and ending, as in this example:

Μὴ γένοιτο, "may it never be" (Rom. 6:2).

Here is an optative based on the word "give." Translate as "would give":

ἵνα ὁ θεὸς . . . δώη ὑμῖν πνεῦμα σοφίας . . . (Eph. 1:17).

Exercise Two

Practice with Subjunctive Endings

Match the correct Greek verb with each of these English sentences:

_____ 1. You might have loosened yourself. (completed action)

_____ 2. He might have been loosened. (simple action)

_____ 3. We might loosen.

_____ 4. They might have loosened themselves. (simple action)

_____ 5. I might have been loosened. (completed action)

_____ 6. You might be loosened. (or, might be being loosened).

_____ 7. We might have loosened ourselves. (simple action)

_____ 8. they might have loosened. (completed action)

a. λυσωμεθα
b. λυσωνται
c. λελυμενος ης
d. λελυκωσι
e. λελυμενος ω
f. λυθη
g. λυη
h. λυωμεν

Exercise Three

Subjunctive Examples

Translate using words like "might," "may," "should" using the lists on 277.

___ ___ 1. My children, _____ ____ _____ ____ ___
             ταῦτα   γράφω   ὑμῖν   ἵνα   μὴ

_____ (1 John 2:1).
ἁμάρτητε

___ ___ 2. . . . who gave himself for us _____ _____ _____
                                          ἵνα   λυτρώσηται   ἡμᾶς

___ ___ from lawlessness and _____ ___ _____ a people for his
                                 καθαρίσῃ   ἑαυτῷ

own possession (Titus 2:14).

___ ___ 3. What we have heard and seen we announce to you _____
                                                           ἵνα

_____ you fellowship _____ _____ _____ (1 John 1:3).
  καὶ   ἔχητε   μεθ'   ἡμῶν

___ ___ 4. ____ _____ ___ _____ ____ _____ ,
            Ἐὰν   εἴπωμεν   ὅτι   ἁμαρτίαν   οὐκ   ἔχομεν

we deceive ourselves and the truth is not in us (1 John 1:8).

___ ___ 5. We have believed in Jesus _____ _____ _____
                                       ἵνα   δικαιωθῶμεν   ἐκ

_____ _____ ____ ____ __ _____
  πίστεως   Χριστοῦ   καὶ   οὐκ   ἐξ   ἔργων

_____ (Gal. 2:16).
  νόμου

___ ___ 6. . . . that whosoever believes in him _____ _____ ____
                                                  μὴ   ἀπόληται   ἀλλ'

___ _____ _____ _____ (John 3:16).
   ἔχῃ   ζωὴν   αἰώνιον

The little word αν is sometimes used in connection with statements that are "iffy." You don't necessarily have to translate the word itself, but make sure the character of the entire sentence is affected by it.

___ ___ 7. . . . and whoever _____ against the Son of Man, it will be
εἴπῃ

forgiven him; _____ ___ _____ against the Spirit, it
ὃς   δ'   ἂν εἴπῃ

will not be forgiven (Matt. 12:32).

___ ___ 8. Whoever _____ ____ _____ his life shall lose it (Matt. 16:25).
θέλῃ   σῶσαι

___ ___ 9. To all people I have become _____ _____ _____
πάντα   ἵνα   πάντως

_____ _____ (1 Cor. 9:22).
τινὰς   σώσω

___ ___ 10. _____ _____ ____ _____ and my words remain in you,
Ἐὰν   μείνητε   ἐν   ἐμοὶ

ask whatever _____ and it shall be done for you (John
θέλητε

15:7).

Word List

A. ειπον = say

B. εχω = have

C. δικαιοω = make right

D. απολλυμι = perish

E. ἁμαρτανω = sin

F. μενω = remain

G. σωζω = save

H. θελω = want

I. λυτροω = release

J. καθαριζω = cleanse

Form List

a. Present; therefore stress on the continuing action of the verb.

b. Aorist, illustrating that in the subjunctive mood aorist does not indicate past, but a simple reference to an event.

c. Second aorist. If it were a present, more of the present stem would remain.

d. Aorist middle. Looks like a passive ending, but there's no sense of passive in the meaning of the sentence.

e. The θ is a give-away that it is aorist passive.

Lesson Fifty

There is a completely different set of endings for a group of verbs called -μι verbs. Some of these verbs are unusual in that they have reduplication in the present tense, as well as in the perfect tense.

Example: The word for "give" has the stem δο.

Placing the reduplication at the front makes it into διδο.

The endings are:

Person	Singular	Plural
1	μι	μεν
2	ς	τι
3	σι	ασι

Adding the endings, with allowance for interaction of connecting vowels:

1	διδωμι	διδομεν
2	διδως	διδοτε
3	διδωσι	διδοασι

Other common -μι verbs are:

τιθημι = put
αφιημι = let go (this is the usual word for "forgive")
ἱστημι = cause to stand

Can you match these despite variations in connecting vowels? (Watch out for a final ν added to one example.)

___ 1. διδωσι   a. they forgive

___ 2. ισταμεν   b. you cause to stand

___ 3. αφιεισι   c. he gives

___ 4. τιθεμεν   d. we place

___ 5. τιθησιν   e. you forgive

___ 6. ιστης   f. we cause to stand

___ 7. διδοασι   g. she places

___ 8. αφιης   h. they give

Principal parts of διδωμι are (Note some do not have reduplication):

διδωμι   δωσω   εδωκα[1]   δεδωκα   διδομαι   εδοθην

This chart is a selection of some -μι verb endings, using διδωμι as an example:

Tense	Voice	Mood	Principal Part to Use	Reduplication?	Augment?	Ending from Column	Example
Present	Active	Ind	1	yes	no	above	διδωμι
Present	Active	Imper	1	yes	no	o	διδου
Present	Active	Subj	1	yes	no	p	διδω
Present	Passive	Ind	1	yes	no	d	διδομαι
Present	Passive	Imper	1	yes	no	r	διδοσο
Present	Passive	Subj	1	yes	no	l	διδωμαι
Imperfect	Active	Ind	1	yes	yes	n	εδιδουν
Imperfect	Passive	Ind	1	yes	yes	b	εδιδομην
Aorist	Active	Ind	3	no	yes	d	εδωκα
Aorist	Middle	Ind	3	no	yes	b	εδομην
Aorist	Passive	Ind	6	no	yes	c	εδοθην
Second Aorist	Active	Ind	stem	no	yes	n	εδων
Second Aorist	Active	Imper	stem	no	yes	s	δος
Second Aorist	Active	Subj	stem	no	yes	p	δω

Some infinitives:

present—διδοναι "to be giving" (continuous)
aorist—δουναι "to give" (simple statement)

1. Note that κ is used instead of σ.

New Columns of Endings

Voice	Person		(n)	(o)	(p)	(s)
ACTIVE	Singular	1	οων		ω	
		2	οως	ου or θι	ως	ς
		3	οω	οτω	ω	τω
	Plural	1	ομεν		ωμεν	
		2	οτε	οτε	ωτε	τε
		3	οσαν	οτωσαν	ωσι	τωσαν

Voice	Person		(d)	(r)	(l)
MIDDLE & PASSIVE	Singular	1	μαι		ωμαι
		2	σαι	σο	ω
		3	ται	σθω	ωται
	Plural	1	μεθα		ωμεθα
		2	σθε	σθε	ωσθε
		3	νται	σθωσαν	ωνται

Examples with -μι Verbs

If you, being evil, know how _____ _____ good gifts . . . (Matt. 7:11).
        διδόναι

(from the Lord's Prayer) _____ us this day our daily bread (Matt. 6:11).
        Δὸς

God so loved the world that _____ his only Son . . . (John 3:16).
        ἔδωκεν

____ ____, the least _____ _____ ___ ____, _____ _____
 Ἐμοὶ   πάντων   ἁγίων   ἐδόθη   ἡ   χάρις
_____ . . . (Eph. 3:8).
  αὕτη

Son of man came to serve and ____ _____ _____ _____ as a ransom
for many (Matt. 20:28).   δοῦναι   τὴν   ψυχὴν   αὐτοῦ

The following examples use the word αφιημι, "let go." Expect some vowel changes.

I came from the Father and come _____ _____ _____ ; again _____ _____

εἰς   τὸν   κόσμον   ἀφίημι

_____ _____ and go to the father (John 16:28).

τὸν   κόσμον

Aorists

Jesus, crying with a _____ _____ _____ _____ _____ (Matt. 27:50).

φωνῇ   μεγάλῃ,   ἀφῆκεν   τὸ   πνεῦμα

He is _____ _____ _____ _____ _____ our sins (1 John 1:9).

πιστός   καὶ   δίκαιος   ἵνα   ἀφῇ

(column [p] with a different vowel)

(from the Lord's Prayer) _____ _____ us our debts, as we _____

καὶ   ἄφες   ἀφήκαμεν

our debtors (Matt. 6:12).

(column [s] with a connecting vowel, p. 280)

All the Forms of "To Be"

Present	Indicative	Imperative	Subjunctive	Optative	Infinitive
	I am, etc.	Be!	That I might be	That I would be	"to be"
I am	εἰμί		ὦ	εἴην	εἶναι
you are	εἶς or εἶ	ἴσθι	ᾖς	εἴης	
he is	ἐστί	ἔστω	ᾖ	εἴη	
we are	ἐσμέν		ὦμεν	εἴημεν	
ye are	ἐστέ	ἔστε	ἦτε	εἴητε	
they are	εἰσί	ἔστωσαν	ὦσι	εἴησαν or εἶεν	

Future	Indicative	Optative	Infinitive
	I will be	That I may be about to be	be about to be
I will be	ἔσομαι	ἐσοίμην	
you will be	ἔσῃ	ἔσοιο	ἔσεσθαι
he will be	ἔσται	ἔσοιτο	
we will be	ἐσόμεθα	ἐσοίμεθα	
ye will be	ἔσεσθε	ἔσοισθε	
they will be	ἔσονται	ἔσοιντο	

Imperfect	Indicative Only	
I was	ἤμην or ἦν	
you were	ἦσθα	
he was	ἦν	Differentiate these forms from the feminine forms of "the" by the fact that the word "the" does not have an accent mark; only the "breathing" mark.
we were	ἤμεθα or ἦμεν	
ye were	ἦτε	
they were	ἦσαν	

No Perfect, Aorist, or Pluperfect

Exercise Two

Matching with Meanings of "To Be"

____ 1. εστε	a. you will be
____ 2. εστωσαν	b. you were
____ 3. ειην	c. we might be
____ 4. εση	d. they are to be!
____ 5. εσοιο	e. be about to be
____ 6. ἦςθα	f. ye are
____ 7. ισθι	g. ye would be
____ 8. ὦμεν	h. Be!
____ 9. ειητε	i. I would be
____ 10. εσεσθαι	j. you may be about to be

Exercise Three

Examples of "To Be" in Various Tenses

Match the tenses below to these two possibilities:

a. present subjunctive   b. imperfect

____ 1. _____ _____ ____ __ _____ (John 1:1).
      Ἐν   ἀρχῇ   ἦν   ὁ   λόγος

____ 2. . . . in order that, no longer _____ infants, tossed to
                                          ὦμευ

    and fro . . . (Eph. 4:14).

___ 3. ____ ____ ____ ____ ____, but you were washed . . . (1 Cor. 6:11).
         καὶ   ταῦτά   τινες   ἦτε

___ 4. I sanctify myself, _____ _____ sanctified in truth (John 17:19).
                          ἵνα   ὦσιν

___ 5. Doing the will of the flesh and understanding, _____ _____ by
                                                       καὶ   ἤμεθα

   nature _____ of wrath (Eph. 2:3).
          τέκνα

___ 6. _____ _____ _____ _____ ____ our joy __ full (1 John 4:14).
        καὶ   ταῦτα   γράφομεν   ἡμεῖς   ἵνα   ᾖ

A Very Common Deponent Verb

It means about the same as "is" (matching possibilities found below):

γινομαι = become, be

___ 7. And _____ in those days . . . (Luke 2:1).
           ἐγένετο

___ 8. After two days _____ the Passover . . . (Matt. 26:2).
                       γίνεται

___ 9. _____ therefore imitators of God . . . (Eph. 5:1).
        Γίνεσθε

___ 10. _____ _____ _____ _____ __ _____ _____
         τοῖς   πᾶσιν   γέγονα   πάντα   ἵνα   πάντως

   _____ _____ (1 Cor. 9:22).
    τινὰς   σώσω

___ 11. _____ _____ ____ _____ ____ τά _____ _____
         Ἐὰν   μείνητε   ἐν   ἐμοὶ   καὶ τά ῥήματά   μου

   ____ _____ _____, ask whatever ____ _____
    ἐν   ὑμῖν   μείνῃ,   θέλητε   καὶ

   _____ ____ ____ (John 15:7).
    γενήσεται   ὑμῖν

Match examples 7 through 11 to:

   c. present
   d. imperative
   e. aorist (it's second aorist: there is an augment, but no σ.)
   f. perfect. It is a second perfect because while there is reduplication, there
      is no letter κ.
   g. future

Lesson Fifty-One

Participles

So far you have learned the ending ων, as in λεγων, "saying." There are many more endings used to make participles.

1. Participles are made from the principal parts of verbs.
2. Like verbs, they appear in various tenses (present, perfect, etc.) and voices (active, passive, etc.). They do not appear in imperfect and pluperfect.
3. The participle receives endings from the noun chart to indicate whether it is nominative, genitive, etc., and whether it is singular or plural. The ων ending you have used happens to be nominative, and you have seen it used when it happens to be the subject of the sentence, or to describe the subject.

The man <u>loosening</u> the ropes is my friend.
      λυων

If the word which the participle is describing is plural, the participle uses one of the plural endings from the chart of noun endings in Part II (p. 124). In our example, the ending will be from the third column (third declension) and will be from the fifth row (nominative plural):

The men <u>loosening</u> the ropes were my friends.
      λυοντες

If the word which the participle is describing is not the subject of the sentence but has some other function, the participle ending will again change, using the appropriate ending from column three of the noun chart.

Exercise One

Matching (refer to noun-ending chart on p. 124, column III).

___ 1. I sold the slave loosening the ropes to a new master.

___ 2. I have the lunch of the man loosening the ropes.

___ 3. I spoke to the man loosening the ropes.

___ 4. I spoke to the men loosening the ropes.

a. λυοντι (dative singular)

b. λυοντα (accusative singular)

c. λυουσι (dative plural)

d. λυοντος (genitive singular)

Chart of Participle Endings

The masculine and neuter endings are from third declension, the feminine from first:

Singular	Masculine	Feminine	Neuter
Nominative	ων	ουσα	ον
Genitive	οντος	ουσης	οντος
Dative	οντι	ουση	οντι
Accusative	οντα	ουσαν	ον

Plural			
Nominative	οντες	ουσαι	οντα
Genitive	οντων	ουσων	οντων
Dative	ουσι	ουσαις	ουσι
Accusative	οντας	ουσας	οντα

(The endings above are also the exact forms of the present participle of εἰμι, "I am," so they can all be translated "being.")

Exercise Two

Constructing the participles based on the word λυω, "Loosen."

Fill in the blanks.

Present stem is λυ. Adding singular masculine endings, the result is:

_____ 1. Nominative

_____ 2. Genitive

_____ 3. Dative, etc. (The approach given continues through the accusative and the plurals.)

For singular feminine, the result is:

_____ 4. nominative

_____ 5. genitive

_____ 6. dative, etc.

Examples 1 through 6 would be translated "loosing" (or "loosening"). To make future, the stem (from the second principal part) is λυσ.

Singular masculine:

_____ 7. nominative

_____ 8. genitive

_____ 9. dative, etc.

There is no single word in English that can be used to translate a Greek future participle. One way to express the thought is to use the phrase "about to": λυσων = about to loosen.

In Greek, participles are not formed in the imperfect tense.

Exercise Three

Present Tense Examples

The following sentences make use of four different verbs (use the endings just as they are): "be," "loose," "believe," and "speak."

To work these out, first write the stem of the underlined word. Then decide if it is masculine, feminine, or neuter, singular or plural, and go to the corresponding column of the endings-chart. Then decide if it is subject, genitive, dative, etc., and select the ending from the correct row. All these are in present tense.

___ 1. This is the house of the man <u>loosening</u> that screw.

___ 2. I wrote a letter to the girls <u>being</u> at college.

___ 3. I spoke to the men, <u>believing</u> they were the winners.

___ 4. The car, <u>being</u> by the hydrant, received a ticket.

___ 5. I appreciate the words of the man <u>speaking</u> to us now.

___ 6. I sent roses to her, the girl <u>believing</u> I had overlooked her birthday.

___ 7. I removed the doorknob of the door, the one <u>being</u> open.

___ 8. The men <u>loosing</u> the rope fell overboard.

a. λεγοντος
b. λυοντες
c. λυοντος
d. ὦον
e. ουσαις
f. ονσης
g. πιστευουσι
h. πιστευουση

Exercise Four

To Form Aorist

1. Use the third principal part as listed on page 252 but remove the augment.
   ελυσα less ε = λυσα; stem then is λυσ
2. Use the endings from page 285 but use the letter α instead of the connecting vowels used on the chart. For example, write οντα as αντα; write ουσαν as ασαν.
3. Change the masculine nominative singular ending from ν to ς.

Masculine: _____ 1. nominative

_____ 2. genitive

_____ 3. dative, etc.

Feminine: _____ 4. nominative

_____ 5. genitive

_____ 6. dative, etc.

To Form Perfect

1. Do not use the letter ν. (Write οντος as οτος.)
2. Use ς instead of ν in masculine nominative singular. Otherwise, use the endings as they are.
3. Use fourth principal part (λελυκ-).

Masculine: _____ 7. nominative

_____ 8. genitive

_____ 9. dative, etc.

For feminine, use υι as the connector, and take the endings not from the participle chart but from the noun chart on page 124, first column of declension.

Feminine: _____ 10. nominative

_____ 11. genitive

_____ 12. dative, etc.

Both the aorist and perfect participles are translated "having loosed." The difference in shade of meaning does not appear in English; you are to keep in mind that perfect refers to completed actions with continuing results, while aorist is a simple statement.

Exercise Five

Matching

___ 1. The girls <u>having loosed</u> each others hair went to bed. (completed)

___ 2. I spoke to the man <u>about to loose</u> the rope.

___ 3. I spoke to the man <u>having loosed</u> his grip for a moment. (simple)

___ 4. I have the address of the girl who <u>loosed</u> the dog. (completed)

a. λυσοντι

b. λελυκυιας

c. λυσαντι

d. λελυκυιαι

Lesson Fifty-Two

Forming Passive Participles

To make aorist passive, the connecting vowel is ε or ει, and the nominative ending is εις. To form examples which mean "was loosened," use the sixth principal part of λυω, ελυθην, whose stem is: λυθ.

Aorist Passive

Masculine _____ 1. nominative

_____ 2. genitive

_____ 3. dative, etc.

For the other passive forms and for the middle forms, take the ending off the indicative form and add a connecting vowel, the syllable μεν, and endings from this pattern:

Singular	Masculine	Feminine	Neuter
Nominative	ος	η	ον
Genitive	ου	ης	ου

. . . and so on, using second declension for masculine and neuter and using the second column of first declension endings for feminine, as shown on the chart from page 124.

Present Passive

Masculine _____ 4. nominative

_____ 5. genitive

_____ 6. dative, etc.

Feminine   _____   7. nominative

                _____   8. genitive

                _____   9. dative, etc.

Present passive would be translated "being loosed."

    Aorist and perfect passive would be translated "having been loosed."

The middle voices would be translated "loosing one's self," etc.

Exercise Two

Participles in Various Tenses, Voices, "Cases," and Genders

Match the Greek participles from the Word List below with their English equivalent.

Word List

____ 1. I wrote to the ones <u>about to be believing</u>.

____ 2. I helped the girl <u>being spoken to</u>.

____ 3. The bone, <u>having been</u> in the dog's mouth, was crushed.

____ 4. The dentist inspected the status of the teeth <u>having been loosened</u>.

____ 5. I spoke to the girls (the ones <u>having been</u> in Europe).

____ 6. I fired him (the man <u>having been written</u> on the report).

____ 7. I spoke to my wife, who <u>had been loosed</u> from her chores.

____ 8. This is the gathering of them, the ones <u>having believed</u> in God.

a. ον

b. γραφεντα

c. πιστευσαντων

d. πιστευσουσι

e. ουσαις

f. λεγομενην

g. λυθειση

h. λυθεντας

Obviously, the sentences above are not written in usual English style. We would rephrase them in translating:

    1. I wrote to the ones who would believe.

    2. I helped the girl who was being addressed.

    3. The bone which had been in the dog's mouth was crushed.

    etc.

This is the kind of rephrasing you will do when you translate a Greek participle into acceptable English.

Here are some of the participle uses you will see in the upcoming Scripture examples.

1. When the participle is used as an adjective, it has to match the ending on the noun it is describing. If I want to say "of the living God," I take the verb for live (ζαω). With nominative ending it would be ζων, which I could use with the subject of a sentence. With the genitive ending (see p. 285), it would be ζωντος, so ζωντος θεου would be "of living God." Adding the word for "the" = ζωντος θεου, "of the living God."

   The participle, like an adjective, can be placed after the noun, with each word having its own word "the":

   του θεου του ζωντος = of the living God.
   τω ζωντι θεω or τω θεω τω ζωντι = to the living God.

2. When there is no noun provided, then the participle acts as a noun, and I add the word "one" or "thing" as I translate.

   ὁ ζων = the living one
   του ζωντος = of the living one
   τοις ζωσι = to the living ones
   των αγαπαντων = of the loving ones

3. In both cases described above, there can be added words that go with the participle.

   A prepositional phrase can be added (underlined below):

   του <u>εν ναον</u> ζωντος θεου or ⎫
   του θεου του ζωντος <u>εν ναον</u> ⎬ = of the living-in-the-temple God.
   　　　　　　　　　　　　　　　　⎭

   A direct object can be added (underlined below).

   του αγαπαντος <u>παντα</u> θεου or ⎫
   του θεου του αγαπαντος <u>παντα</u> ⎬ = of the loving-<u>everyone</u> God.
   　　　　　　　　　　　　　　　　 ⎭

4. Sometimes a participle with the other words in its portion of the sentence is put in the genitive case as a way of setting off that part from the rest of the sentence.

   λεγοντος θεου, ακουω = God speaking, I listen. (literal)
   　　　　　　　　　　 = While God is speaking, I listen.
   　　　　　　　　　　　(smooth English)

As you look at the participle examples coming up, don't be discouraged if you are not able to explain why every single letter is the way it is; you simply have not been given that much instruction on these matters. You can be proud of yourself if

1. you can figure out which words are the participles; and
2. you can match them to the words at the bottom of the page.

Give yourself an extra pat on the back if you can guess the tense. Proceed like this:

1. If it has the endings on the chart on page 285, it has to be active, so that rules out middle and passive (except that it could be aorist passive).
2. If its letters are like the spelling in the Word List, it is probably present. The only other possibilities I have given examples for are aorist and perfect.
3. If the beginning of the word is tampered with, it is probably perfect (since there are no augments or reduplications anywhere outside indicative mood, except for perfects).
4. I did not give you the principal parts, which will slow you down; you might remember that aorists have an σ added to the stem (if it is a second aorist, you are sunk). Aorist passives include a θ. Expect vowel changes after these letters.
5. You can't tell middles from passives anyway; they look the same (except for aorists, which do look different). So if you see a word with μεν in it, and the sense of the sentence does not indicate anyone doing anything to the subject, it is probably middle.

Exercise Three

Participle Examples from Scripture

Match to Word List and Tense List on page 294.

___ ___ 1. _____ ____ ____ _____   _____ ___
       Παῦλος   τοῖς   ἁγίοις   τοῖς   οὖσιν   ἐν

_____ (Eph. 1:1).
Ἐφέσῳ

The participle is dative because it is being used to describe the word "saints," which is dative. Word for word: "Paul to the saints, the ones being in Ephesus."

Could you find the ending? Remember that ν can be added to endings for smoothness.

___ ___ 2. Whatever you ask in prayer _____ you shall
receive (Matt. 21:22).   πιστεύοντες

> The participle is nominative plural because the subject is you—plural.

___ ___ 3. According to the ruler of the authority of the air, ___ ___
                                                                  τοῦ

_____ _____ _____ _____ in the sons of dis-
πνεύματος   τοῦ   νῦν   ἐνεργοῦντος

obedience (Eph. 2:2).

> The participle is genitive to match "spirit" which is genitive. Word for
> word: "of the spirit, the one now working . . ." It is common to trans-
> late a participle into English by making up a phrase that starts with
> "who": the spirit who is now working. This is not a word-for-word
> translation, but it does bring out the meaning.

___ ___ 4. For all have sinned and fall short of the glory of God,
_____ freely by his grace (Rom. 3:24).
δικαιούμενοι

> (Passive participle of "make right" = being made right)

___ ___ 5. . . . to do all we ask or think according to _____ _____
                                                         τὴν   δύναμιν   τὴν

_____ ___ _____ . . . (Eph. 3:20).
ἐνεργουμένην   ἐν   ὑμῖν

___ ___ 6. You, _____ _____ _____ of truth, were sealed by
                ἀκούσαντες   τὸν   λόγον
the Spirit (Eph. 1:13).

___ ___ 7. (We are those) serving the Spirit of God, boasting in Christ,
_____ _____ ___ _____ _____ (Phil. 3:3).
καὶ   οὐκ   ἐν   σαρκὶ πεποιθότες

___ ___ 8. _____ _____ these things so our joy might be _____
           Γράφομεν   πεπληρωμένη
(1 John 1:4).

Word List

A. ακουω   = hear
B. ενεργεω   = work
C. ειμι   = be
D. δικαιοω   = make right
E. πειθω   = convince (put confidence)
F. πληροω   = fill
G. πιστευω   = believe

Tense List

a. present
b. present middle
c. present passive
d. aorist
e. aorist passive
f. perfect
g. perfect passive

More Practical Examples

In the next example, the first word "the" goes with the participle, and they are both in the genitive; the second word "the" goes with "all things," and is the plural direct object of the participle. Use the lists on p. 295.

___ ___ 9. According to the purpose _____
        (Eph. 1:11).   τοῦ τὰ πάντα ἐνεργοῦντος

___ ___10. You are the _____ _____ _____, _____ on
               οἰκεῖοι   του θεοῦ   ἐποικοδομηθέντες
       the foundation of the apostles . . . (Eph. 2:19–20).

___ ___11. Paul to the church in Corinth, _____ ___
                           ἡγιασμένοις   ἐν
       _____ _____ called saints . . . (1 Cor. 1:2).
         Χριστῷ   Ἰησοῦ,

___ ___12. . . . that he sent his only-begotten Son, _____ _____.
                                   ἵνα   πᾶς ὁ
       _____ _____ _____ might not perish but have
         πιστεύων   εἰς   αὐτὸν
       eternal life (John 3:16).

___ ___13. I do not cease giving thanks _____ _____, remem-
                              ὑπὲρ   ὑμῶν
       brance _____ in my prayers . . . (Eph. 1:16).
         ποιούμενος

        (In genitive because it is a sentence portion of its own, set off from the
        main sentence.)

____ ____14. Are they not all ministering _____, _____
for serving? (Heb. 1:14).   πνεύματα,   ἀποστελλόμενα

____ ____15. _____ _____ _____ _____ _____ _____ _____
Εὐλογητὸς   ὁ   θεὸς   καὶ   πατὴρ   τοῦ   κυρίου

_____ _____ _____, | ο εὐλογήσας | _____
ἡμῶν   Ἰησοῦ   Χριστοῦ   ὁ εὐλογήσας   ἡμᾶς

_____ _____ _____ _____ . . . (Eph. 1:3).
ἐν   πάσῃ   εὐλογίᾳ   πνευματικῇ

About the bracketed part: The participle has its own word "the" since it is
acting like an adjective would act to describe the subject of the sentence.
Word for word: the having-blessed-(us with every spiritual blessing)-one.

____ ____16. (The word) is foolishness to those perishing, ___ _____ _____
τοῖς   δὲ

_____ it is the _____ ____ ____ (1 Cor. 1:18).
σωζομένοις   δύναμις   θεοῦ

____ ____17. _____ _____ _____ for my followers ___ also they
Ἐγὼ   ἁγιάζω   ἐμαυτόν   ἵνα

might be _____ in truth (John 17:19).
ἡγιασμένοι

Word List

A. ἁγιαζω   = make holy, sanctify
B. ελοικοδομεω = build upon
C. σωζω   = save
D. ενεργεω   = work
E. πιστευω   = believe
F. ευλογεω   = bless
G. αποστελλω   = send
H. ποιεω   = do

Tense List

a. present
b. present middle
c. present passive
d. aorist
e. aorist passive
f. perfect
g. perfect passive

Comparing Participle and Main Verb of the Sentence

The participle can express action occurring during, before, or after the event
expressed by the main verb of the sentence.

A present participle expresses action during the main verb.

Example: λυων το τεκνον, εβλεψα τον ανθρωπον.
is translated with sentence (b) below

The three possible translations:

a. After loosing the child, I saw the man.
b. While loosing the child, I saw the man.
c. Before loosing the child, I saw the man.

An aorist participle indicates action before the main verb.

Example: λυσας το τεκνον, εβλεψα τον ανθρωπον.
is translated with sentence (a) above

A perfect participle would always express completed action before the main verb.

Example: λελυκως το τεκνον, εβλεψα τον ανθρωπον.
corresponds to sentence (a) above

The future participle would always express action after the main verb.

Example: λυσων το τεκνον, εβλεψα τον ανθρωπον.
corresponds to sentence (c) above

Information from *New Testament Greek Made Functional*, © 1972 by H. Fred Nofer, page 88.

Participles with "Be"

When a participle is used, plus some form of "to be," ειναι, (or similarly-used words such as γινομαι, "to become"), the result can be translated using English helping-verbs:

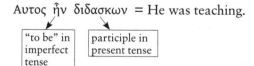

Αυτος ἦν διδασκων = He was teaching.

| "to be" in imperfect tense | participle in present tense |

Here is a more complete chart of the possibilities, taken from the book by Nofer, page 92.

Form of Participle	Form of "to be"	Resulting Translation Will Sound Like
Present	Present	Present
Present	Imperfect	Imperfect
Present	Future	Future
Perfect	Present	Perfect
Perfect	Imperfect	Pluperfect
Perfect	Future	Future perfect

An example: Εγω εσομαι λελυκως

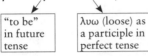

| "to be" in future tense | λυω (loose) as a participle in perfect tense |

This sentence corresponds to the last option on the chart above, and the translation would therefore sound like a future perfect:

"I shall have loosed."

Exercise Four

Example with four different uses of the word ἔχω "have"

After translating, match each form of εχω with the best description from the list following the Scripture passage.

Jesus, looking at him, loved him, and said to him, "You lack one thing; go, sell

what ____ ____ ( ) and give to the poor, and ____ ____ ____ ( ) riches
        ἔχεις   ἔξεις

in heaven, and come follow me." But he, saddened by these words, went away

grieving, for ____ ____ ____ ( ) many possessions. And looking around,
              ἦν   ἔχων

Jesus said to his disciples, "How hard it is for those ____ ____ ( ) riches to
                                                        ἔχοντες

enter into the kingdom of heaven" (Mark 10:21–23).

a. participle

b. participle + form of "be"

c. future ($\chi + \sigma = \xi$)

d. present

Exercise Five

The Verb Forms of 1 John 1

Meanings for words you do not know—look up in your English Bible.

That which ____ from the beginning, which _____, which our eyes
     ἦν   ἀκηκόαμεν

_____ which _____ and our hands _____
ἑωράκαμεν   ἐθεασάμεθα   ἐψηλάφησαν

concerning the word of life . . . and the life _____, and
                             ἐφανερώθη

_____ and _____ and _____ to you the eternal
ἑωράκαμεν   μαρτυροῦμεν   ἀπαγγέλομεν

life which ____ with the father and _____ to you . . . that which
     ἦν   ἐφανερώθη

_____ and _____ _____ also to you, in order that
ἑωράκαμεν   ἀκηκόαμεν   ἀπαγγέλλομεν

you also _____ fellowship with us. And our fellowship ____ with the Father
    ἔχητε   (no "is": it must be added)

and with his Son Jesus Christ. And _____ these things in order that our
                                γράφομεν

joy ____ _____. And this is the message which _____
  ᾖ   πεπληρωμένη   ἀκηκόαμεν

from him and _____ to you, that God _____ light, and dark-
          ἀναγγέλλομεν   ἐστιν

ness _____ not in him at all. If _____ that _____ fellowship
   ἐστιν   εἴπωμεν   ἔχομεν

with him and _____ in darkness, _____, and _____
        περιπατῶμεν   ψευδόμεθα   ποιοῦμεν

not the truth. But if _____ in the light, as he _____ in the
           περιπατῶμεν   ἐστιν

light, _____ fellowship with one another and the blood of Jesus his Son
ἔχομεν

_____ us from all sin. If _____ that _____ no sin, _____
καθαρίζει   εἴπωμεν   ἔχομεν   πλανῶμεν

ourselves and the truth _____ not in us; if _____ our sins, _____
          ἐστιν   ὁμολογῶμεν   ἐστιν

faithful and righteous in order that _____ our sins and _____ us from
          ἀφῇ   καθαρίσῃ

all unrighteousness. If _____ that not _____, _____
      εἴπωμεν   ἡμαρτήκαμεν, ποιοῦμεν

him a liar, and his word _____ not in us.
            ἐστιν

List the words that are

    a. subjunctive, present tense (translate with "might," etc.)

    b. deponent (looks like passive, but translated as if it were active)

    c. aorist

    d. perfect (shown by κ)

    e. participle

A College Course

It is the writer's hope that you will now be interested enough, and self-confident enough, to continue in Greek by taking an academic course or by working through a standard Greek textbook. What will you learn in such a course that you do not already know?

    1. Rules about accents.

    2. Rules about the changes that occur when various letters come together.

    3. Grammatical terms.

    4. More detailed rules of usage for words.

    5. Vocabulary. Your vocabulary so far is almost entirely limited to cognates; but you do not know hundreds of words that are not cognates.

    6. Memorization of endings.

Topical Index

(In Order of Appearance)

A Word to the Greek Specialist

Here are some of the principles used in this workbook:

1. The vocabulary is based on cognates, so that the student does not have to consciously memorize meanings. I have tried to avoid false etymologies in setting forth these cognates. The few words I have used which are not cognates were chosen because they helped me use pictures (οικος) or to lay the groundwork for word studies in Part IV (χαρις). While virtually all the commonly used cognates (for example, those listed in the frequency lists of Bruce Metzger) are used, I also had to use many words which occur but seldom in the New Testament in order to keep to the ideal of using cognates. The vocabulary is also strictly limited to words actually used in the New Testament. The only exceptions are in some compound words used as illustrations to bring out the meaning of a New Testament word (στέλλω, ἱστημι).

2. The approach to grammar: second declension masculine endings are used to introduce case meanings, adjectives, the article, pronouns, and prepositional phrases; and all this is done using the minimum vocabulary (second declension cognates). Then a chart is used to introduce the fact that there are other endings, but there is little drill or exercise on these endings. Accent rules are conspicuously absent from this workbook. Contraction rules and vowel and stem changes are given only passing reference.

The assumption is that the person using this book will either go on to an academic course, or will learn to make use of an analytical lexicon. Regarding verbs, only present tense is used until Part V. However, the notion that there is such a thing as a participle is introduced early, and the masculine singular participle is used often in the scriptural examples.

I'm sure my decision to minimize grammatical terminology will at times seem to cause more difficulties than it is avoiding, particularly as one struggles through my circumlocutions. Typical of these decisions is postponing the use of the correct names for the cases. After much consideration, I decided not even to use a common word like "appositive." The guiding principle was: if something is self-evident, don't bother to give it a name. The same decision was made in regard to usage and word-order rules. Scriptures are simply quoted and the student is able to see for himself that the writers put the words in a different order from the customary English order. The overriding consideration was: avoid getting bogged down; the goal is that the student will want to study further in other, more academic works.

I am aware that languages today are taught without word-for-word translation to English, and that the approach used in the scriptural examples will seem far from modern teaching practice. The excitement of the non-scholar when he begins to grasp the meaning of portions of sentences has confirmed for me the approach I have taken here, for the purposes of this volume.

However, I have made much use of the idea of having the student grasp the overall meaning of sentences simply by recognizing the vocabulary, without stopping to analyze the endings.

Answers—Part I

Exercise One	Exercise Two		Exercise Three	
The words sound like	The words sound like		The words sound like	
bed	pet	rope	lips	log
dotted	pot	road	lap	ring
bet	top	robe	pill	gear
dad	pit	crib	call	map
bat	tip	drip	land	lamp
tab	dip	dart	plan	rim
cat	pop	cart	sell	men
kit	pope	cork	sink	milk
cot	boat	parrot	star	mask
kid	toad	pin	pencil	grass
bit	code	can	spot	most
cab	coat	pan	sled	leg
boss	rat	bone	gas	goal
cost	rabbit	coat	glas	man
dot	bred	cone	pig	mar

304

Exercise Four

I.	c	II.	h	III.	d	IV.	i
	e		j		a		j
	f		l		c		g
	a		g		e		h
	b		k		b		f
	d		i				k

Lesson Two

Exercise One	*Exercise Two*		*Exercise Three*	
1–a	I. 1–b	II. 5–h, k	I. 1–c	II. 5–g
2–a	2–c	6–e, l	2–b	6–f
3–a	3–a	7–i, o	3–d	7–h
4–b	4–d	8–g, m	4–a	8–i
5–b		9–f, n		9–j
		10–j, p		10–e
				11–k

Exercise Four

1–b (ι as in "pin" or "machine," never as in "like")
2–a (α is short, as in "father")
3–a
4–b (ε is short, as in "let")
5–a (each α has to be pronounced separately)
6–b (αυ as in "cow," never as "awe")
7–b (αι as in "aisle")
8–a

Six Greek Words—	house	=	οικος	rock	=	πετρα
	scorpion	=	σκορπιος	lamp	=	λαμπας
	book	=	βιβλος	lion	=	λεων

9–b
10–b
11–a
12–a
13–a
14–b

Exercise Five

1–a	6–b
2–b	7–a
3–b	8–b
4–a	9–a
5–a	10–b

Lesson Three

Exercise One	Exercise Two	Exercise Three		
1–c	1–c	phone	phonograph	phantom
2–e	2–d	photograph	Philadelphia	Phil
3–b	3–b			
4–f	4–e			
5–a	5–f			
6–d	6–a			

Exercise Four

English words—thumb   thorn   thread
Bible names—Martha   Nathan   Bethlehem (no "h" in Greek)

Exercise Five			Exercise Six	Exercise Seven		
1–c	5–f	9–c	1–c	1–b	6–a	
2–a	6–h	10–d	2–b	2–b	7–b	
3–g	7–d	11–b	3–a	3–a	8–a	
4–e	8–b	12–a	4–e	4–a	9–a	
		13–e	5–f	5–a	10–no	
			6–d		(man and orphan in house)	
				11–no		
				(rock and stone on house)		

Exercise Eight

1–a	12–f
2–b	13–a
3–a	14–g
4–a	15–d
5–a	16–h
6–b	17–b
7–b	18–e
8–a	19–c
9–b	20–k
10–a	21–i
11–b	22–j

Lesson Four

Exercise One

1–e	μικρος + σκολος	10–g	εν + εργον	A–4
2–g	μικρος + μετρον	11–d	μονος + λιθος	B–13
3–f	σοφος + μωρος	12–j	μονος + λογος	C–10
4–a	τιμιος + θεος	13–h	φιλος + σοφια	D–14
5–i	μικρος + κοσμος	14–a	φιλος + ανθρωπος	
6–c	θεος + σοφος	15–c	φωτος + γραφω	
7–b	μακρος + σκολος	16–e	ανθρωπος + λογος	
8–h	κοσμος + λογος	17–i	βιος + λογος	
9–d	μακρος + κοσμος	18–b	μεγα + λιθος	
		19–f	λιθος + γραφω	

Lesson Five

Exercise One		Exercise Two
1–b	10–d	1–a
2–c	11–g	2–b
3–a	12–b	3–b
	13–e	4–a
4–b	14–a	5–a
5–c	15–f	6–b
6–a	16–c	7–b
	17–j	8–b
7–c	18–m	
8–a	19–h	
9–b	20–o	
	21–k	
	22–n	
	23–l	
	24–i	

Lesson Six

Exercise One

1–f	φωνη	9–n	πλαστος	17–x	θανατος
2–c	γαλακτος	10–l	ανθρακος	18–q	λευκος
3–h	φως	11–i	νεκρος	19–u	γερων
4–a	σκληρος	12–p	κλεπτω	20–w	ιδιος
5–d	τοπος	13–m	δενδρον	21–s	εσωτερος
6–g	νεος	14–o	ακουω	22–v	μελας
7–b	φοβος	15–k	γραμμα	23–r	μεγας
8–e	σκολιος	16–j	ορθος	24–t	κρανιον
				25–y	τραυμα

Lesson Seven

Exercise One

1–k	9–b
2–m	10–p
3–n	11–d
4–i	12–e
5–j	13–c
6–o	14–f
7–a	15–g
8–h	16–l

Exercise Two

1–b	4–f	10–i	16–b
2–c	5–a	11–k	17–d
3-a	6–d	12–j	18–a
	7–c	13–m	19–e
	8–b	14–h	20–f
	9–e	15–g	21–c

Exercise Three

1–b	15–e
2–b	16–d
3–a	17–c
4–b	18–b
5–b	19–a
6–a	20–k
7–b	21–f
8–b	22–i
9–a	23–g
10–b	24–h
11–a	25–j
12–b	26–o
13–b	27–m
14–a	28–n
	29–l

Lesson Eight

Exercise One

1–c	a. ελι
2–a	b. παρα
3–i	c. εν
4–h	d. αɩo
5–g	e. δια
6–e	f. εκ
7–b	g. προς
8–f	h. αντι
9–d	i. εις

Exercise Two

1–d	9–f
2–e	10–b
3–n	11–k
4–m	12–i
5–j	13–c
6–l	14–h
7–a	15–o
8–g	

Lesson Nine

Exercise One

1–d	7–j	13–o	17–v	23–t
2–e	8–k	14–l	18–s	24–u
3–a	9–g	15–p	19–r	25–x
4–c	10–i	16–m	20–y	
5–b	11–h		21–q	
6–f	12–n		22–w	

Exercise Two

man – ανθρωπος	law – νομος	see – σκοπεω
write – γραφω	treasure – θησαυρος	shining – φανερος
skin – δερμα	seed – σπορα	throne – θρονος
grave – ταφος	earth – γη or κοσμος	

Exercise Three

1–g	7–h	11–l	18–v
2–j	8–c	12–n	19–u
3–e	9–f	13-t	20–y
4–d	10–a	14–s	21–x
5–i		15–r	22–w
6–b		16–m	23–k
		17–o	24–z

Lesson Ten

Exercise One	Exercise Two		Exercise Three
paradox	1–c	5–i	1–anoints
exodus	2–h	6–h	2–anointed
	3–a	7–e	3–anoint
	4–d	8–g	4–anoint
		9–f	Christ

Exercise Four	Exercise Five	Exercise Six	
Charismatic	psychic, psychology	1–b	4–f
	pseudonym, pseudo	2–a	5–g
		3–c	6–d
			7–e
			8–h

Lesson Eleven

Exercise One

see – σκοπεω	stomach – στομαχος	skull – κρανιον
body – σωμα	hear – ακουω	stomach area – γαστηρ, γαστρος
white – λευκος	head – κεφαλη	rip or tear – σχιζω
bone – οστεον	brain – φρην	eye – οφθαλμος
mouth – στομα	chest – στηθος	heart – καρδια
skin – δερμα, δερματος	hand – χειρ	chair – καθεδρα
foot – πους, ποδος		

1–e	ποδος	6–g	οστεον
2–c	φρην	7–j	καθεδρα
3–i	οφθαλμος	8–f	γαστρος
4–k	δερματος	9–a	χειρ
5–b	δερμα	10–h	σχιζω + φρην
		11–d	στηθος + σκοπεω

Exercise Two	Exercise Three	Exercise Four
1–c	1–c ὁλος	type
2–a	2–a ὁμος	hymn
3–d	3–b εσχατος	myths
4–b	4–f ἡγεμον	Greek υ became English "y"
	5–e Μιχαηλ	but for "David," υ became "v"
	6–g σχολη	
	7–h ἑτερος	
	8–d ὁμος	

Exercise Five		Exercise Six	
1–f	9–i	1–f	6–e
2–n	10–k	2–a	7–c
3–c	11–j	3–h	8–d
4–a	12–e	4–g	9–j
5–d	13–l	5–b	10–i
6–b	14–m		
7–h	15–o		
8–g			

Lesson Twelve

Exercise One

1–βοτανη	13–θερμη + μετρος
2–ιρις	14–ανεμος + μετρος
3–χρυσος	15– ἱππος + ποταμος
4–αστηρ	16–αστηρ + λογος
5–ἡλιος	17–αστηρ + νομος
6–σπερμα, σπορος	18–πετρα + λογος
7–κρυσταλλος	19–λιθος + γραφω
8–ποταμος	20–ιχθυς + λογος
9–πετρα	21–χλορος + φυλλα
10–πνευμα	22–αγρος + νομος
11–ἱππος, ποταμος	23–δενδρον + λογος
12–αγρος	24–ξυλος + φωνη

Exercise Two

Word for word — Jesus
Christ
of God
Son
Savior

In usual English word order — Jesus Christ, Son of God, Savior

Exercise Three		Exercise Four	
1–c	δεκα	1–d	8–k
2–f	πρωτος	2–f	9–l
3–i	ἑξ	3–b	10–p
4–a	πρωτος	4–g	11–o
5–h	μυριαι	5–e	12–j
6–d	χιλιοι	6–c	13–h
7–g	δεκα	7–a	14–i
8–b	πεντε		15–n
9–e	δευτερος		16–m
			17–t
			18–s
			19–r
			20–q

Lesson Thirteen

Exercise One	Exercise Two		Exercise Three
angel	1–b 3–b		evangelist
	2–a 4–c		evangelize
	5–a		

Exercise Four	Exercise Five	Exercise Six	Exercise Seven		
1–b	1–d	1–angel	1–c	5–g	9–j
2–c	2–c	2–anchor	2–d	6–h	10–l
3–d	3–a	3–larynx	3–a	7–e	11–i
4–a	4–e		4–b	8–f	12–k
	5–b				
	6–f				
	7–g				

Lesson Fourteen

Exercise One

I.		II.			III.		
1–5		1–4	7–6		1–7	6–2	
2–1		2–12	8–9		2–4	7–6	
3–3		3–7	9–11		3–1	8–3	
4–2		4–2	10–10		4–9	9–5	
5–4		5–1	11–8		5–8		
		6–13	12–5				
			13–3				

Answers—Part II

Lesson Fifteen

Exercise One	Exercise Two	Exercise Three
1–a b a	1–say	1–call
2–f a b c a d e a	2–word	2–calls
rocks	3–says	
man head	4–say	
3–a, d b a, f c a, e	5–saying	
past	words	
4–e d f c g		
a h		
b		

Exercise Four

I.	1–b	II.	4–b	III.	8–d
	2–a		5–b		9–i
	3–c		6–a		10–a
			7–a		11–k
					12–f
					13–h
					14–b
					15–l
					16–j
					17–c
					18–g
					19–e

Exercise Five

1–a	7–d
2–b	8–f
3–a	9–c
4–a	10–g
5–b	11–i
6–b	12–e
	13–h
	14–j
	15–k

Lesson Seventeen

Exercise One

1–c
2–f
3–a g h
4–e
5–d
6–b
7–g

Lesson Eighteen

Exercise One

I.	1–c	II.	4–c	III.	7–c	IV.	10–c	V.	13–c
	2–a		5–b		8–a		11–a		14–b
	3–b		6–a		9–b		12–b		15–a

Exercise Two

1–b
2–e
3–f
4–d
5–h
6–a
7–c
8–g

Exercise Three

1–b	9–b	21–o
2–a	10–f	22–p
3–a	11–a	23–n
4–b	12–d	24–m
5–b	13–h	25–t
6–b	14–e	26–s
7–b	15–c	27–q
8–b	16–g	28–r
	17–l	
	18–k	
	19–i	
	20–j	

Exercise Four

1–Pp
2–Ds
3–Os Ss
4–Os Ps
5–Ds
6–Os Os Ps
7–Sp Ps
8–Op Op
9–Op
10–Op
11–Os Pp Os Ps
12–Op
13–Ps
14–Ps

Lesson Nineteen

Exercise One

1–Men throw stones
2–Brother writes words
3–God speaks to Philip
4–Brothers speak to lepers
5–I write to Mark
6–He writes to Paul
7–I throw stone
8–You write words
9–Brothers write law of God
10–Mark speaks word of men
11–Slave writes to men of God
12–Lepers speak to slaves of Paul
13–We speak words of God to men
14–They speak word of law to Philip
15–I want to speak words
16–He teaches to write words
17–Cornelius writes book in house
18–God loves men in world
19–Slaves speak to scorpion on house
20–Nicodemus writes to brother on stone

21–Men of God write words of book to brothers of Paul in house of prophets
22–Brothers of lepers speak words of God to men of God in house of God

Lesson Twenty

Exercise One	Exercise Two	Exercise Three		
1–τιμιους	1–f C	1–d	9– ὁ	m
2–μονω σοφω	2–e F	2–h	10–του	l
3– πρωτοι εσχατοι	3–d A	3–g	11–τω	j
4–ἑτέρω	4–c D	4–e	12–τον	o
5–αλλος δευτερος	5–b E	5–f	13–οἱ	p
6–νεκρων	6–a B	6–c	14–των	k
7–ομοιον	7–g C	7–a	15–τοις	i
		8–b	16–τους	n

Lesson Twenty-One

Exercise One

first – πρωτος	large – μεγας	temple – (n) ναος
second – δευτερος	small – μικρος	grave – (n) ταφος
third – τριτος	other – αλλος	dead – νεκρος

full – πληρης	numbers – (n) αριθμοι
medium – μεσος	
empty – κενος	

Exercise Two

1–d	5–h	9–k	13–n	17–y
2–f	6–e	10–j	14–p	18–z
3–a	7–b	11–l	15–i	19–w
4–g	8–c	12–o	16–m	20–x
				21–v
				22–t
				23–u
				24–q
				25–s
				26–r

Exercise Three

1–The first man, in the house, speaks a word
2–The second man writes words in the temple
3–The third man sees the dead man
4–The first man throws the small stone in the house
5–The second man hears the word of the first man
6–The other man sees the empty tomb
7–The men throw hard stones
8–The brother writes a crooked word
9–Mark says a hard word of the law to the holy brothers
10–We speak good words of the holy God to the apostles
11–They speak a new word of God to the wise men

Exercise Four

ολον   αγιοις   αγιων   μονος   νεον

Lesson Twenty-Two

Exercise One		Exercise Two	Exercise Three	Exercise Four
I. 1–e	II. 7–c	1–b	A–with	1–b
2–c	8–f	2–a	B–after	2–e
3–f	9–a	3–e		3–a
4–d	10–e	4–d		4–d
5–a	11–d	5–c		5–f
6–b	12–b	6–g		6–c
		7–f		

Lesson Twenty-Six

Exercise One	Exercise Two	
1–b	1–d	8–d
2–d	2–b	9–a
3–a	3–d	10–d
4–c	4–d	11–d
	5–b	12–a
	6–d	13–c
	7–a	14–e

Lesson Twenty-Seven

Exercise One

1–b	5–g
2–d	6–i
3–a	7–h
4–c	8–e
	9–f

Answers—Part III

Lesson Twenty-Eight

Exercise One

1–e
2–a
3–f
4–c
5–b
6–d

Lesson Thirty

Exercise One	Exercise Two	
1–e	1–b	5–b
2–c	2–b	6–b
3–h	3–a	7–a
4–a	4–a	8–a
5–d		
6–g		
7–f		
8–b		

Lesson Thirty-Two

Exercise One

I. 1–b
    2–c
    3–a
    4–d

II. 4–f
    5–g
    6–e

Answers—Part IV

Lesson Thirty-Three

Exercise One	Exercise Two	Exercise Three	Exercise Four	Exercise Five
1–call	1–c	A–call out	Kyrie	1–kuriak
2–calls	2–a	B–calls out		2–kurk
3–called	3–b	ecclesiastical		–kirk
4–called				3–church
5–calling				
6–called one				

Lesson Thirty-Four

Exercise One	Exercise Two	
adjective	Cross out	-love
		-peace
		-faith
		-word
		-apostle
		-Lord

Lesson Thirty-Five

Exercise One

economy
ecumenical

Lesson Thirty-Six

Exercise One

I.	1–B	II.	5–H	III.	9–K	IV.	13–N	V.	17–S	VI.	21–W	VII.	25–Y
	2–C		6–F		10–J		14–P		18–T		22–V		26–AA
	3–A		7–E		11–L		15–O		19–R		23–U		27–Z
	4–D		8–G		12–I		16–M		20-Q		24–X		28–DD
													29–BB
													30–CC

Exercise Two	Exercise Three
1–c	apothecary
2–a	pyromaniac
3–d	
4–b	
5–e	
Anamnesis	

Lesson Thirty-Seven

Exercise One		Exercise Two	Exercise Three
Cross out	-holy	criterion	critic
	-love		
	-faith		
	-saint		
	-lordship		
	-believe		

Lesson Thirty-Eight

Exercise One		Exercise Two	
1–e	4–c	1–b	4–a
2–a	5–d	2–b	5–c
3–b	6–f	3–c	6–b

Lesson Thirty-Nine

Exercise One	Exercise Two	Exercise Three		
homily	metamorphosis	1-b f	επ + στρεφω	
	scheme	2–b e	μετα + νους	
		3-a d	όμο + λογος·	

Exercise Four

1–c g i
2–d j n
3–b f
4–e k
5–a m
6–h l

Lesson Forty

Exercise One	Exercise Two	Exercise Three
eulogy	1–b	1–b
eucharist	2–d	2–a
	3–e	3–f
	4–f	4–c
	5–g	5–d
	6–a	6–e
	7–c	

Lesson Forty-One

Exercise One

1–c
2–f
3–d
4–a
5–e
6–b

Lesson Forty-Two

Exercise One	Exercise Two
catharsis	1–b
	2–b
	3–a
	4–c

Lesson Forty-Three

Exercise One	Exercise Two
a–μαμμη	deacon
b– ιατρος	
c–γυναικος	
d–νηπιος	
e–μητρος	
f–ανδρος	

Lesson Forty-Four

Exercise One	Exercise Two	Exercise Three	Exercise Four
liturgy	strategy	therapy	1–c 2–a 3–b

Exercise Five	Exercise Six		
1–oversees or looks over, etc.	1–d	j	E
2–overseer or supervisor	2–f	k	G
3–overseer . . . oversees, or any other words	3–a	m	C
with similar meaning	4–e	o	A
	5–g	q	H
5–piskop	6–b	r	F
6–pishop	7–i	p	B
7–bishop	8–c	n	G
8–bishop	9–h	l	D
9–episcopal			

Answers—Part 5

Lesson Forty-Five

Exercise One		Exercise Two	Exercise Three	Exercise Four		Exercise Five	Exercise Six		
1–b	3s	1–c	c	1–e	E	A. 1–A	1–A	f	X
2–d	2p	2–b or c	b	2–d	C	2–P	2–D	a	Z
3–f	1s	3–c	a (pluperfect)	3–e	D	3–M	3–A	g	X
4–a	1p	4–a and b	e	4–f	A		4–E	e	Y
5–c	3p	5–a	d	5–g	A	B. 1–M	5–C	d	Z
6–e	2s	6–a		6–a	E	2–P	6–B	a	X
7–g	3s			7–b	D	3–A	7–D	b	X
8–b	2p			8–a	E	4–P	8–C	d	Z
9–d	1s			9–c	D	5–M	9–E	c	X
10–f	1p			10–e	C	6–P	10–C	e	Z
				11–a	B	7–A			
						8–P			
						9–M			

Lesson Forty-Six

Exercise One

1–aorist	middle	b
2–perfect	passive	d
3–present	active	f
4–imperfect	middle	a
5–pluperfect	active	c
6–present	passive	g
7–future	passive	e

Exercise Two

1– ελυες	imperfect	active
2– λυσεται	future	middle ("she" is 3rd person)
3– λελυκαμεν	perfect	active
4– ελυθητε	aorist	passive
5– λυονται	present	middle
6– λυσεις	future	active
7– ελελυκει	pluperfect	active
8– λυομαι	present	passive
9– ελυσαμεν	aorist	active
10– λελυνται	perfect	passive

Exercise Three

1–γραψει	(future active)
2–κεκληνται	(perfect passive)
3–επιε	(aorist active)
4–ελελωκειμεν	(pluperfect active)
5–εκληθη	(aorist passive)
6–γεγραφαμεν	(perfect active)

Lesson Forty-Seven

Exercise One

πιστευω	λεμλω
πιστευσω	λεμψω (from λεμλσω)
επιστευσα	ελεμψα
λελιστευκα	————
λελιστευμαι	ελεμφθην
επιστευθην	(π changes to φ before θ)

Exercise Two		Exercise Three		Exercise Four	Exercise Five	
1–B	d	1–f	E	1-c	1–B	e
2–A	b	2–c	C	2–c	2–C	a
3–D	c	3–b	F	3–a	3–D	c
4–C	a	4–e	D	4–d	4–D	d
5–A	e	5–a	B	5–b	5–A	a or b both pos-
		6–d	A	6–e		sible: "is named" or
						"names itself"

Lesson Forty-Eight

Exercise One				Exercise Two	Exercise Three	
1–I	f	9–J	f	1–d	1–e	C
2–M	i	10–I	i	2–a	2–d	D
3–N	b	K	i	3–g	f	C
4–A	d	11–C	c	4–f	3–e	D
5–F	f	D	c	5–b	4–c	B
G	h	12–P	a	6–c and e	5–a	C
6–O	g	13–H	h		6–g	A and h A
7–E	e	14–B	e		7–b	E
8–L	i					

Lesson Forty-Nine

Exercise One	*Exercise Two*	*Exercise Three*		
1–D b	1–c	1–E c	8–H a	
2–C a	2–f	2–I d	9–G b	
3–B b	3–h	J b	10–F c	
4–B c	4–b	3–B a	H a	
5–A c	5–e	4–A c		
6–E d	6–g	5–C e		
	7–a	6–D c		
	8–d	B a		
		7–A b		

Lesson Fifty

Exercise One	*Exercise Two*	*Exercise Three*	
1–c	1–f	1–b	7–e
2–f	2–d	2–a	8–c
3–a	3–i	3–b	9–d
4–d	4–a	4–a	10–f
5–g	5–j	5–b	11–g
6–b	6–b	6–a	
7–h	7–h		
8–e	8–c		
	9–g		
	10–e		

Lesson Fifty-One

Exercise One	*Exercise Two*	*Exercise Three*	*Exercise Four*	*Exercise Five*
1–b	1 λυων	1–c	1– λυυας	1–d (perfect
2–d	2–λυοντος	2–e	2– λυσαντος	feminine
3–a	3–λυοντι	3–g	3– λυσαντι	plural)
4–c	4–λυουσα	4–d	4– λυσασα	2–a (future)
	5–λυουσης	5–a	5– λυσασης	3–c (aorist)
	6–λυουση	6–h	6– λυσαση	4–b (perfect
	7–λυσων	7–f	7– λελκως	feminine
	8–λυσοντος	8–b	8– λυλυκοτος	genitive)
	9–λυσοντι		9– λελυκοτι	
			10– λελυκυια	
			11– λελυκυιας	
			12– λελυκυια	

Lesson Fifty-Two

Exercise One	Exercise Two	Exercise Three		Exercise Four	Exercise Five
1–λυθεις	1–d	1–C	a	a–ἔχοντες	a –ἔχητε
2–λυθεντος	2–f	2–G	a	b–ἦν ἔχων	–ἦ
3–λυθεντι	3-a	3–B	a	c–ἕξεις	–εἴπωμεν
4–λυομενος	4–h	4–D	c	d–ἔχεις	–περιπατῶμεν
5–λυομενου	5–e	5–B	b		–ὁμολογῶμεν
6–λυομενω	6–b	6–A	d		–ἀφῇ
7–λυομενη	7–g	7–E	f		–καθαρίσῃ
8–λυομενης	8–c	8–F	g		b –ψευδόμεθα
9–λυομενη		9–D	a		c –ἐθεασάμεθα
		10–B	e		–ἐφανερώθη (passive)
		11–A	g		–ἐψηλάφησαν
		12–E	a		d –ἀκηκόαμεν
		13–H	b		–ἑωράκαμεν
		14–G	c		–ἡμαρτήκαμεν (these
		15–F	d		are irregular in that
		16–C	c		they do not start with
		17–A	g		a reduplication)
					e –πεπληρωμένη (perfect
					participle)

James Found has served as a director of Christian education in the Lutheran Church, Missouri Synod, in the United States and abroad. In 2006 James retired from teaching Outreach and Missions at Concordia University in St. Paul, Minnesota. He and his wife now make their home in Loveland, Colorado.